ANITA IBR

British Government:
The Central Executive Territory

SIGNIFICANT NAMES

Barbara Castle
Hennessey
Thatcher
Lloyd George
Attlee
Wilson
Gordon Walker - partial cabinets
Barnett (believed cabinets not shadowed)

CONTEMPORARY POLITICAL STUDIES SERIES

Series Editor: John Benyon, Director, Centre for the Study of Public Order, *University of Leicester*

A series which provides authoritative, yet concise introductory accounts of key topics in contemporary political studies.

Other titles in the series include:

Elections and Voting Behaviour in Britain
DAVID DENVER, *University of Lancaster*

Pressure Groups, Politics and Democracy in Britain
WYN GRANT, *University of Warwick*

UK Political Parties since 1945
Edited by ANTHONY SELDON, *Institute of Contemporary British History*

Politics and Policy Making in Northern Ireland
MICHAEL CONNOLLY, *University of Ulster*

British Political Ideologies
ROBERT LEACH, *Leeds Polytechnic*

Local Government and Politics in Britain
JOHN KINGDOM, *Sheffield City Polytechnic*

CONTEMPORARY POLITICAL STUDIES

British Government: The Central Executive Territory

PETER MADGWICK
Professor Emeritus
Oxford Polytechnic

Philip Allan
NEW YORK LONDON TORONTO SYDNEY TOKYO SINGAPORE

First published 1991 by
Philip Allan
66 Wood Lane End, Hemel Hempstead
Hertfordshire HP2 4RG
A division of
Simon & Schuster International Group

© P. J. Madgwick, 1991

All rights reserved. No part of this publication may be reproduced, stored in a retrieval system, or transmitted, in any form or by any means, electronic, mechanical, photocopying, recording or otherwise, without prior permission, in writing, from the publisher.

Typeset in 10/12pt Times
by Columns Design and Production Services Ltd., Reading

Printed and bound in Great Britain by
Billing and Sons Ltd., Worcester

British Library Cataloguing in Publication Data

Madgwick, P.J.
British government: The central executive territory. – (Contemporary political series)
I. Title II. Series
320.441

ISBN 0-86003-416-X
ISBN 0-86003-716-9 pbk

2 3 4 5   95 94 93 92

Contents

Preface vii

    1 Introduction   1

PART I   The Nature, Environment and Structure of British Government at the Centre
- 2 The Nature and Environment of British Government at the Centre   9
- 3 The Structure of British Government   19

PART II   The Cabinet
Introduction: The Cabinet as a Principle of Government   37
- 4 The Cabinet as The Colleagues   38
- 5 The Cabinet as Council   53
- 6 The Cabinet as a system of Committees   70

PART III   The Executive Centre
Introduction: The Central Executive Territory and the Executive Centre   89
- 7 The Cabinet Office   95
- 8 The Prime Minister's Office   107

PART IV   The Prime Minister
Introduction: Political Leadership and the Office of Prime Minister   133
- 9 The Office of Prime Minister: Structure and Style   136

	10	The Prime Minister and the Cabinet: Managing the System	152
	11	The Prime Minister and Party, Parliament and People	170
PART V		Cases	
	12	Two Prime Ministers: Harold Wilson and Margaret Thatcher	183
	13	Case Notes	215
PART VI		Conclusion	
	14	The Prime Minister in the Central Executive Territory: Modes of Influence	235
	15	The Central Executive Territory in British Government	258

A select list of introductory reading   266

References   267

Index   270

Preface

This book is concerned with what I call the Central Executive Territory, the collection of politicians, administrators, groups, offices and units at the centre of the executive branch of British government. The book aims to give an account, not to argue a thesis. It assumes that political institutions are significant as well as interesting. It further assumes that British government at the centre cannot be pinned – or penned – down in one simple phrase: prime ministerial, presidential, cabinet-shaped, parliamentary (though these occur in the book); and that political activity is normally diverse, variable and pluralistic. This suits the purposes of an introductory book, since the aim in a reflective subject like this is not to preach the verities, but to stimulate vigorous and careful thinking.

The ground covered is wide and largely hidden from the direct inspection of academics. The writer of a book of this kind must therefore declare very heavy debts to the scholarly journalists and diarists and biographers who have transformed the available account of British government at the centre. Quite simply the book could not have been attempted without the writings of Peter Hennessy, Peter Jenkins, Peter Riddell and Hugo Young, and the diaries of Barbara Castle, Richard Crossman and Tony Benn; among academics, the work of John Mackintosh; among prime ministers, the books of Lord Wilson. It will be evident that many others have contributed substantially to the stock of information and ideas on which I have drawn. I salute them all and trust they will look sympathetically on my attempt to represent in shorter and simpler form the new understanding of government at the centre which we owe to them.

The book was completed in November 1990, during the last days of Margaret Thatcher as prime minister. The account of the office of prime minister offered here was already post-Thatcherist, presenting Mrs Thatcher's historic tenure of office as lying in one segment of the range of prime ministerial modes. Her prime ministership was nevertheless stimulating and illuminating for the understanding of government in the Central Executive Territory, and it raised serious questions about the nature of political leadership.

I am grateful to John Benyon, the editor of the series, for suggesting the topic; to the editors of Simon and Schuster for their assistance and support; to Oxford Polytechnic for a generous contribution to the costs of research; to Diana Woodhouse for indispensable help in the early stages of research; to the Bodleian Library, and in particular the librarians of the PPE Reading Room, for helpful and unobtrusive service; and to my wife, Olive, for dealing on the word-processor with my partial relapse from 'direct input' to the humble ballpoint pen, and coping with the usual abstractedness of an author in travail.

The author acknowledges with thanks permission kindly granted by publishers to reproduce extracts with copyright works: Jonathan Cape: Bernard (Lord) Donoughue, *Prime Minister* (1987); Weidenfeld and Nicolson Ltd. and Michael Joseph Ltd.: *The Governance of Britain*, Harold Wilson, © 1976, Lord Wilson of Rievaulx; Her Majesty's Stationery Office: Falklands Islands Review, Cmnd. 8787 (1983).

Peter Madgwick
Oxford

1

Introduction

There are two major problems in the study of British government: the nature and quality of evidence, and questions of interpretation – the difficulties of vocabulary and underlying concepts involved in the construction of an account.

Evidence

There is a great deal of evidence, but never enough of the right kind. Compared with, say, the medieval historian, the historian of recent and contemporary politics has a mountain of material. It includes:

parliamentary debates and select committee hearings and reports;
government papers: white for more or less agreed policy, green for consultation;
media reports;
memoirs, autobiographies and diaries (including the works of former prime ministers and notably now the Crossman, Castle and Benn diaries);
Cabinet papers (but only after 30 years, and then carefully pruned);
biographies;
commentaries and accounts by participants and close observers;

2   BRITISH GOVERNMENT: CENTRAL EXECUTIVE TERRITORY

government statistics;
surveys of opinion.

Very little of this material is incontrovertible 'fact'. Most of it is produced to persuade. Some of it (especially in the media) is produced under great pressure of time, and with a prime regard for 'news values', visual impact and entertainment. Distortion arises from inevitably partial perception and personal bias. Even when a former prime minister writes about the work of prime ministers, his or her judgement is still a personal judgement though it has to be respected. Government statistics appear to offer us facts, not opinions, but they are notoriously unreliable even when not designed to mislead. The problems of survey evidence are well known.

There is certainly plenty of material for scholars to work on even though its reliability is in question. Indeed there is a problem of overabundance, for it is more than individual scholars can take in, digest, analyse and re-present; and there are only limited possibilities of systematic team research. More worrying to the historian and political scientist is the thinness of evidence about the central and innermost processes of decision making. Some of this is due to the culture of secrecy in British government (see Chapter 2). But even a more open government is unlikely to place on record the detail of processes by which governing goes on, policy is developed and decisions are made. Such a record would be destructive of frank and full discussion, and might in any case miss the informal conversations, the shifts and spurts by which minds are made up and choices affirmed. The exact 'truth' is unknowable.

There is some consolation for the scholar. If the ultimate truth is unattainable, it is the vigorous pursuit that matters. The diarists have demonstrated that truth in an account of a meeting is in the eye of the beholder. Every view is a partial view; and accounts by the Prime Minister or the Cabinet Secretary might be only a little nearer the 'truth'. Complaints about the accuracy of the Cabinet Minutes may confirm this point, while indicating possibly deliberate misrepresentation (or re-presentation) by the Secretariat. So scholars and students in this field settle for illumination rather than truth, getting as near to the truth as they can, near enough to give a credible account, and constantly alert to the elusiveness of the truth.

Interpretation

The problem of 'interpretation' is if anything, more serious than the problem of evidence. First, there is room for doubt about the objective of the exercise. It is assumed that the objective of a study of British government is 'understanding', constructing an account which conveys and illuminates the processes of government. The ultimate purpose is to satisfy curiosity, to inform the citizen of a democracy, to illuminate the nature and workings of society.

Second, it is necessary to 'construct an account'; this is different from simply recording incidents and events, and requires a measure of 'interpretation'. Even the diarists interpret: that is why their accounts differ. The political scientist goes further and has to engage in more and more complex construction. This may seem innocent enough, but of course a 'construct' is not 'what happened' but 'what I think happened'. In a recent re-examination of the Crichel Down case (1954), which was both complex and subject to a simple interpretation, Professor J. A. G. Griffith confessed to a lack of confidence unusual in academics (1987, p. 40). Following his conclusion he wrote: 'At least I think that is what I think'.

A third problem of interpretation is selectivity and partiality (literally partial, hence also biased). An account of this kind is by intention preoccupied with the relations of persons and institutions at the centre of British government. Such an approach is legitimate and enlightening. At the same time it needs to be complemented by other approaches covering other aspects of politics. In particular the people and the life of the Central Executive Territory need to be understood through the study of policy and also through party, in its broadest sense – the collection of assumptions and interests which drive politicians. Nothing in this account of government at the centre should be regarded as asserting the autonomy of persons or institutions. Heroes – and heroines – may sometimes drive history forward, but they are themselves driven, and not always forward.

A fourth problem of interpretation arises from inertia, and the attractions of accepted views. In many cases an interpretation builds up, and becomes 'the conventional wisdom'. This was so in the Crichel Down case: a very complex series of events over a period of at least three to four years ended in a ministerial resignation, which gave rise to a mistakenly simple explanation of the whole episode, relating to bureaucracy and ministerial responsibility. Sometimes the initial thesis is followed by a reaction and a counter-thesis. This can be seen in the waves of interpretation and re-interpretation of Margaret Thatcher as prime minister. Almost as soon as we had accepted that Margaret Thatcher was Queen Boadicea, and had changed the face of Britain, we heard that she was, in fact, a kindly and gentle prime minister, frequently defeated in Cabinet, often compromising in face of political problems and with only a few policy achievements to her credit. The temptation is to choose a clear radical position, or come along later and 'destroy the myths'.

This makes academic study sound cyclic and parasitic, which indeed it is. It may be better to choose a middle way: on the one hand this, on the other hand . . . (always a good tactic for an examinee!). This can lead to a safe self-cancelling conclusion: Mrs Thatcher was not totally different; nor was she essentially the same. The centre, the exact point of balance of opinion, is a safe bet, but unlikely to be very illuminating.

One way to avoid a comfortable adherence to the accepted view, or a facile acceptance of the two-handed approach, is to ask unconventional questions. In the case of prime ministers the measurement of achievement is as illuminating (and as difficult) as the measure of personality – or the structure of the Cabinet.

The conventional wisdom about government includes understandings about government itself. We think we know what this activity or process of governing is. Perhaps we do. But government, like management and education, is always elusive, and government in Britain is particularly so, a culture, a set of assumptions as well as people and institutions. It is tempting to pick up the easily available models – the old-fashioned constitutional myth, a new managerial model or the politics-as-theatre, narrative-plus-prediction of the media. However, British government may differ from all of these: if it is fully comprehended in its culture and context it may well be unique. Two American

INTRODUCTION 5

observers of the early 1970s thought this to be the case. They wrote:

> British government is an idiom; the usages, manners and deportment of British government are much more than a summed set of rules or powers. Contextual knowledge shades into each particular feature . . . The unfortunate observer is likely to be left facing only the grin of the Cheshire cat, or its British government equivalent – abstract concepts of ministerial responsibility, Cabinet government, civil service anonymity and so on.
> (Heclo and Wildavsky 1974, pp. 1–2)

Vocabulary

This study presents an account of government at the centre in Britain. It argues no particular theses except that the centre has changed and developed over the last forty years, and a significant part of the process of high government in Britain now takes place within it. Forty years ago it was reasonable to draw a contrast between British and American government: Britain had neither a president nor any equivalent of the President's Executive Office with its 3,000 employees. Whatever the conclusion about the first contrast, the second is more difficult to sustain, except on grounds of size.

The term 'Central Executive Territory' is used to refer to the complex of Prime Minister, Cabinet, Committees, Cabinet Office, Prime Minister's Office, with attendant ministers, advisers and officials. The Territory is centred on 10 Downing Street but is loosely defined by its active inhabitants, perhaps 300 people altogether, stretching into the upper echelons of the Civil Service. The term 'Territory' is used because this complex is not an institution, nor a set of institutions. It does not operate as a unit or a unity. Nor is it usefully described as a system. Rather, it forms an arena in which bodies contend to carry on the activity of governing.

It is not sensible to abandon the term 'power', but some attempt is made to avoid all its in-built assumptions by use of the term 'force' as a variant. The contenders in the arena are regarded as having variable force, that is, potential resources rather than certain power. Force is intended as a more neutral or passive term than power – a resource for power but with no certainty of availability, use-ability or effectiveness.

Force is like the speed of the wind: its effect is dependent on the countervailing strength and stability of the obstacles in its path. The term has at least the advantage that it divides the concept of power into force and counterforce. The word 'clout' may also be used for personal force. There is of course no implication in either term of violence or physical force.

Power is used mainly to refer to force in operation, and the methods and channels of the application of force. This has the advantage of directing attention to the ways in which the game of governing is played in the Territory.

It is intended that the account presented here should as far as possible break down the rather chunky terms we employ so easily – prime ministerial power, civil service power, cabinet government. We need constantly to remember what kind of activity lies behind the formal terms used to announce it. The wartime communiqués used to say: 'The Eighth Army halted and consolidated its position'. Out there in the Western Desert a corporal and two men fell exhausted into a shell-hole, 'brewed up' and 'kipped down' for the night, unaware that they should conform to the orderly and confident world of the communiqué. So, too, in politics the reality of what is happening on the ground is puffed up by language, and converted into accepted and wholesome rhetoric.

That suggests a final warning. We think and understand by analogy. Battlefields, sport, railways, landscape and the weather figure in our favourite metaphors. Churchill liked the broad uplands, Wilson liked football, Mrs Thatcher (or her speech writers) the simple housewife. The account of the Prime Minister presented here ends with a Beaufort wind scale of prime ministerial force. It has to be said that a meteorological theory of politics may tell us as much about the weather as about politics.

Part I
The Nature, Environment and Structure of British Government at the Centre

2

The Nature and Environment of British Government at the Centre

The Central Executive Territory is not an independent republic. It is part of British government and the British polity or political system. The boundaries of the Territory are fairly clear, though they range in visibility and penetrability from the Berlin Wall to the border between Lancashire and Yorkshire (not very clearly marked, but you soon discover a change in tribal loyalties). The links between the Territory, government and polity are lines or tracks of communication, responsiveness, responsibility and control. While the act of governing always contains elements of illusion there is no doubt that activities within the Territory constitute a large part of the higher direction of the government and polity of Britain. But the influences flow in both directions. What is done in the Territory by way of governing is shaped and constrained by the fundamental character of the British polity.

Concentration

The British polity is highly concentrated. It is a unitary system without a substantial level of sub-central government. Scotland and Wales enjoy only a strictly limited decentralisation of government, and local government has very little financial autonomy and limited administrative independence. There is local government – a general category – but there are no individual Local Governments. Centralisation and concentration of the institutions of government are reinforced by the unity and dominance of the Civil Service, though local government has its own corps of officials. The concentration of the institutions is further strengthened by the normal dominance of the government by a single party, which is itself centralised in structure.

This concentration of government confirms a geographical bias towards London and the South-East. In Britain, economy, polity and society are all dominated from London. The concentration of government in London is part of this metropolitan dominance. Most inhabitants of the Central Executive Territory naturally work and live in the South-East, and a high proportion have never lived anywhere else. This kind of concentration contrasts with the USA, which has no single dominant metropolis; and even France, dominated though it is by Paris, has significant centres of provincial power and a strong tradition of localism. In Britain the Central Executive Territory enjoys a remarkable security from internal challenge by local interests. The Territory's most powerful local interest is its own back garden, the metropolitan area.

The Constitution

The British Constitution is to be discovered in the institutions, procedures and practices derived from 500 years of constitutional legacy, reformed and deformed by the pressures of the mass politics of the last two centuries. The Constitution is based on two principles and one fortunate bit of institution building, plus a party system to obtain, deliver and guard the minimum popular consent necessary to exploit the principles and the institution.

The fundamental principle is the sovereignty or supremacy of Parliament. Parliament has an unfettered power to make laws, to raise and spend money, and to make policy. There are virtually no checks and balances: neither from the Crown, nor the courts, nor other layers or centres of government.

A second, subsidiary principle is the responsibility of the executive to Parliament. This allows the executive to get on with the business of governing, legitimated by its formal answerability to Parliament. These two principles in combination have created the most powerful democratic executive in the world.

The institution is formed by the Cabinet and the Prime Minister, which converted the original royal executive into an executive derived from and answerable to Parliament, thus acquiring a democratic substitute for the Divine Right of Kings, without losing much of the executive power formerly held absolutely.

The necessary support of executive power lay in a party system which developed to gather in, harness, and use the power given to the people by the extension of the franchise in the nineteenth century. Thus the system moved full circle from dominant monarchical executive (the King) to dominant parliamentary executive (the Prime Minister and Cabinet).

The executive is dominant, hence substantial power is located within the Central Executive Territory. However, responsibility to Parliament, though at times weak, is not entirely fictitious. Lines of responsibility run from the Territory to Parliament, and Parliament intrudes on the work of the executive. The role of Parliament is taken up in Chapter 3.

The political culture and political élites

The Central Executive Territory works in a political culture which is conducive to executive power. There is no space here to examine at length this disputed area in British political science. The theory that the British were a deferential people was never defined and never proved. Leaving aside survey evidence, there are elements in British social and political history which indicate the comparative weakness of radical and revolutionary tendencies, and an apparent devotion to monarchy and conservative governments. There has not been a substantial rebellion in Britain since the seventeenth century. The great dates of European revolutionary history, 1789, 1848, 1917 have little resonance in British history. In 1776, in the American colonies, Britain was the oppressor. Britain for the most part continues to adore its monarchy, and there is no widespread contempt for the House of Lords, which is a constitutional anachronism. The

Empire was popular, and it has never been difficult to get the British to go to war. Britain is surely one of the least radical countries in the developed world. The Central Executive Territory is in no danger of subversion and overthrow by the mob.

The deferential or non-radical culture has allowed a political élite to flourish. Here again it is difficult to locate and define with precision, and even harder to demonstrate, influence. But it is clear that there is a layer of persons occupying high positions in finance, commerce, industry, the law and the defence forces, who wield considerable influence by virtue of their position. They are well connected by class and background, as well as by business and professional relations, with the Central Executive Territory. Henry Fairlie used the term 'Establishment' to describe this layer or connection of 'Top People' (see Hennessy 1989, pp. 542ff.). People of the Establishment inhabit the pockets and margins of that Territory or have lines of communication to it.

A more public and extensive version of this 'connection' is the list of 'the Great and the Good' maintained by the Civil Service, and drawn on for appointments to various public bodies. This is not the 'Connection' or 'Establishment', but it indicates establishment attributes – the careful selection of reliable people, male, middle-aged, middle-class, living in the South-East, politically balanced and near to the centre, most unlikely to make trouble or disturb the settled distribution of power. Peter Hennessy gives an account of three of the most distinguished of the Great and the Good in his essay, 'A trio of grandees' (1989, pp. 559–74).

Some examples of the influence of this 'Connection' occur in these pages. For example, Barbara Castle, negotiating as Secretary of State for Health with the medical consultants, was by-passed by Lord Goodman, who talked directly to the Prime Minister. Lord Goodman had previously acted as Wilson's solicitor. At that time he had been reluctant to take Wilson's part in a dispute over a BBC television programme because, he explained, he was a guest in the BBC's box at Ascot (race course). Now there is not much wrong with that, but it is a useful reminder that there do exist exclusive circles in which boxes at Ascot have a familiar and acceptable place.

The report on the outbreak of war in the Falklands was drawn up by a committee presided over by Lord Franks, a former senior

BRITISH GOVERNMENT AT THE CENTRE 13

Civil Servant, and one of Hennessy's trio. The report sets out in some detail the errors made by governments, but in a final section exonerates them from all blame. It is an insider's perspective. Governments in Britain, at least Conservative governments, are never short of friends in high places – and these are influential friends, offering comfort and support on their own terms.

The nature of government

Constitution and culture make life and work in the Central Executive Territory quite comfortable. They are supportive of the dominant executive, and so of the purposes and power of the people of the Territory. But life is not easy in the Territory. Its basic occupation, the business of governing, is by its very nature problematic.

Government is a gigantic industry, gigantic by any measure – numbers employed, expenditure, range of products, extent of market. Gigantism is associated with another problem – the elusiveness of government: how to identify its objectives and define its tasks, how to assure quality, find and secure markets, build public support. There is no firm agreement on what government is for or about, where it is going and how to get there. In commercial terms there are doubts about the nature, quality and demand for its product, about its markets, and public goodwill towards the industry; and whether this industry of government is properly to be nationalised, privatised, regulated, decentralised or sold to the Japanese.

Government is conducted as a public battle with the Opposition. Its style is adversarial: the forensic skills of lawyers (heavily represented in government and Parliament) are joined with the presentational and persuasive skills of the media men. In consequence disagreement with the Opposition and agreement within the Government are both exaggerated. It is as difficult for an Opposition spokesman to agree with the Government, as it is for a minister to disagree publicly with a colleague. The falsity and irrationality of public political discussion infect private debate and diminish the rationality of policy making.

Government is a highly exclusive operation; it is 'winning-side government'. The boundaries of the Central Executive Territory are penetrable in places but not to the Opposition, nor to most members of Parliament. Despite some improvements in policy research and even some pre-election discussion with the Civil Service, an Opposition arrives in office with plans that are not thought through fully and in any detail (for example, Labour had no detailed plans for nationalisation in 1945, nor for the new Department of Economic Affairs in 1964). This is the fault of the system, not of the Opposition parties. It has been argued that Oppositions should avoid detailed plans in opposition – on policy as well as tactical grounds (see Hennessy 1989, pp. 279-82). The trouble is then that broad policies have detailed consequences, which have to be understood and provided for. Nor are there opportunities for Opposition leaders to gain government experience in provincial or regional governments.

Secrecy is another consequence of adversarial politics and an aspect of exclusivity. British government is by reputation the most secretive in the Western world, plainly more so than in the USA, where the media are aggressive, the libel laws as they affect politicians weak, and there is a Freedom of Information Act. In Britain both the culture and the legislation are different. Parliament does not harry the executive, because its majority supports the executive. Television works under fairly narrow guidelines on the centre ground, and is jealously watched by the political parties. Legislation protects 'Official Secrets', not 'Freedom of Information'. An occasional leak discloses not often scandals, but information necessary and unsurprising in a democracy, that for example a minister was fighting desperately against cuts in expenditure, or that he was considering radical and uncomfortable options.

The culture of British government is deliberately and, in its own estimation, virtuously secretive. Secrecy shades into what a Cabinet Secretary famously called 'being economical with the truth', and thus into deception. One striking example of this was the decision not to tell Parliament or the public, or for that matter the Royal Navy, that two major oil companies were circumventing the oil sanctions against Rhodesia (see Ponting 1989, pp. 249–56).

Again, Britain's own nuclear programme was approved in October 1946 by a secret Cabinet committee, and the files now available in the Public Record Office are blank (Morgan 1990, p. 54). The decision was revealed casually to Parliament nearly two years later, and the huge cost was hidden. Yet in the postwar climate of opinion the decision would probably not have caused much controversy – so why hide it? But equally, in a democracy, if it were controversial, why hide it?

Despite the secrecy, ministers feel, indeed are, exposed and vulnerable. They need and want public success and to stand well with their colleagues; they struggle to avoid failure, blame and humiliation. Avoiding blame and seeking credit are major concerns for ministers, more attractive than power itself, which is a means to credit, status and comfort. These concerns, added to department concern for status and territory, are basic forces in British government.

Ministers are visiting amateurs in their departments, unlikely to stay for more than two years, and under strong competing demands for their time and attention – from the Cabinet, Parliament, constituency, and delegations of interest groups and foreigners. This is a familiar theme in ministerial memoirs: 'we were all so tired' – but none the less significant. Denis Healey, a politician of immense capability and stamina, who unusually spent over five years in each of his last senior posts (Defence and the Exchequer) is an impressive witness:

> Re-reading the scanty diaries I kept at the time, I am shocked to find how often each day's record ends with the words 'To bed dog-tired'. The mental fatigue took its physical toll . . . I do not believe I ever took a day off in the whole five years. Nevertheless physical and mental exhaustion is not an ideal condition in which to take difficult decisions.
>
> (Healey 1989, p. 384)

It is a normal condition of British government that ministers have no time to think.

The Central Executive Territory is under constant threat, pressure and attack from the surrounding territories, their inhabitants, groups and tribes. These include:

citizens, as electors and as the governed;
political parties, supporters and opponents;

interest groups seeking favours and resisting disadvantage; the media, seeking news values, balance, commercial advantage; or, in the case of the Conservative tabloid press, beating a drum for their favoured politicians.

The relationship of the Central Executive Territory with the tribes is a wary, bargaining one. Each has something to offer the other – benefits in return for support, support in return for benefits. Unluckily for governments, the relationship is not so simple. The gratitude of those who receive benefits is outweighed by the displeasure and jealousy of those who lose. The media play a different game, and have never believed that it is more blessed to give than to receive.

In these relationships the people of the Central Executive Territory come to realise that politics is a hard game, played ruthlessly, a 'rough old trade'. The nicest people, gentle people, do not get to the top, which is just as well. Some criticism of politicians such as Harold Wilson and Margaret Thatcher seems to assume that politicians ought to be 'nice', as if they were running a church bazaar.

No strong ideological winds blow over the Central Executive Territory. The climate is remarkably free of powerful ideas. The ideological climate is made up of:

> the assumptions and traditions of the high Civil Service;
> the predispositions of senior politicians in high office (as distinct from their party political positions);
> the shifting moods of the people;
> the prejudices of the élites;
> a thin stream of party programme.

Thus there is little steady wind to fill an ideological sail and drive a cargo of policies. On the other hand there is little enough wind to disturb and shift anything at all. The ideological climate of the Territory induces the condition of 'directionless consensus' diagnosed by Richard Rose at the end of the 1960s (Rose 1969, p. 442). The history of Thatcherism in the 1980s showed that there were political forces which could disturb this normal climatic calm.

Constraints on power

The power available to the government of a small country in the late twentieth century is quite limited. Governments have more power than most other institutions, groups or individuals, but this is because most of the others have hardly any power at all. There is an appearance of power. Harold Wilson spoke of the 'levers of power' in Downing Street. Pulling the levers could summon a private secretary or a minister, a limousine or even an aircraft, modernise Britain's nuclear weapons (at great expense) or encourage the reorganisation of secondary schools (at less expense); but it could not defy international bankers, save the pound from devaluation, rescind Rhodesian independence, discipline the trade unions, bring an end to the Vietnam War, or improve the quality of education.

Most domestic problems lie beyond the capacity of governments to resolve to the satisfaction of all concerned, pleasing at once voters, interest groups and the Treasury. The latter is especially important since most problems can be alleviated if not solved by massive public expenditure. To that end improving the efficiency of the economy is essential, but the capacity of governments to revitalise ailing economies is quite limited. The internal constraints – ineffective managers, uncooperative workers, indolent professionals – are compounded by sharp limits on the government's freedom of action imposed by the international framework in which it must work. Some of this is obvious. Britain has yielded part of her autonomy – for reasons which seemed good – to international organisations such as the EEC, EMS, NATO, GATT, IMF, etc. For most of the last fifty years Britain has been bound less publicly to the USA. British governments of both parties have made a virtue of this, boasting of the Anglo-American 'special relationship'. But there have been many occasions when Britain's capacity to act has been subject to American power: Suez in 1956, economic policy in the mid-1960s and mid-1970s, the Wilson Government's policy on the Vietnam War . . . (see Ponting 1989, pp. 48–9, 257–8, 397).

In these circumstances all discussion of power within the Central Executive Territory needs to be qualified by an understanding of the severe limits on the power of British government. It is constrained by the power, capacity or incapacity of industrialists, workers, bankers, teachers; the brute force of the world economy and the military might of the superpowers; and by its own voluntary co-operative engagement with other institutions and groups. Power tends to be shared and bargained for, and there is never enough to go round.

3

The Structure of British Government

Departments in the complex of government

Government in Britain is a federation of departments or ministries.

The Cabinet is a board of the chief executives of these departments.

Neither of these statements is exactly true, but they both state important parts of the truth. Departments are the operating units of British government, in the sense that much of the work of the government is done in some relationship to a department. But that relationship can be thin and remote, for example, in the case of non-central government and non-governmental bodies, such as the Health Service and local government.

The term 'federation' raises other problems: the exact relationship of one department with others, and the nature of the whole. 'Federation' is both complex and imprecise: we could use a more neutral term: a 'basket' (as of currencies), a 'raft', a set, a group, a network or perhaps the most apt term, a government. 'Chief executive' may be misleading too, and raises questions about the different roles of the Minister and Permanent Secretary at the head of the Department.

This problem of the nature of the whole is raised again by the nature of the Cabinet. It is in one important aspect a committee of the chief executives of the departments. But it is more than that: how much more is a major theme of this book.

There are a score of departments headed by ministers (Secretaries of State). The departments are themselves organised into more than 400 sub-divisions (Rose 1987, p. 24). Beyond the ministers are a host of 'semi-detached' organisations, usually referred to as quangos (quasi-autonomous non-governmental organisations), and including local government and the nationalised industries (public corporations). 'Quangos' is the accepted term for a range of bodies of varying status and distance from government, but SDOs (semi-detached organisations) would be less precise and so more accurate.

The departments are formally joined to the government through the minister's membership of the Cabinet, and his formal responsibility to Parliament. These links constitute the 'thing' we call 'British government'. We could construct a diagram and add a picture of Big Ben or Downing Street as a representation of 'government'. But this would be misleading because 'government' is not a 'thing' but a shifting set of variable relationships. If this were not so the study of politics would be an easier subject.

Some indication of the part of the ministries in the complex of government can be briefly indicated:

1. Over half of government expenditure (in the sense of disbursement, not control of funds) is not carried out by ministries (though it is subject to control by them).
2. The Department of the Environment sponsored eleven quangos with annual expenditure of more than £10m each in 1983–4: Audit Commission; Countryside Commission; Development Commission; Historic Buildings and Monuments Commission; Housing Corporation; New Towns, including Letchworth Garden City and Commission for New Towns; London Docklands Development Corporation; Merseyside Development Corporation; National Heritage Memorial Fund; Nature Conservancy Council; Sports Council (Hennessy 1989, p. 439).

Departments: function, size, spending

Departments vary in function and size; some are massive and most are big spenders. The Department of Health and Social Security was the biggest spender by far, the Department of Defence the biggest employer. The Treasury and the Home Office make the biggest demands on legislation (Rose 1987, pp. 59–60). Education manages to be a high spender, but with only approximately 2,000 civil servants – about the same as the Welsh Office (the reason for this may be evident).

The Department of Health and Social Security offered the best example of the massiveness of government activity. It was, says Hennessy, 'the institutional embodiment of the explosion of the welfare state'. Each year it spent over £60bn, processed nearly 7 million claims for benefits, answered nearly 100,000 letters from the public (one third through MPs), and took over 6,000 Parliamentary Questions (Hennessy 1989, pp. 422–3). It is the best example of government elephantiasis and, for mainly this reason, the DHSS was divided into two departments in 1988.

Departments obviously vary in function and include the Treasury (management of the economy, taxation and public expenditure); the Home Office (law and order, immigration, broadcasting); the Foreign Office; the Ministries of Defence, Health, Social Security, and Education; the economic ministries (Trade and Industry, Employment); and the territorial ministries (Scotland, Wales, Northern Ireland).

The social, economic and territorial ministries all have programmes of resources and services to deliver, and are concerned with high expenditure for clients who may be individuals, localities, industries or countries. Defence is also a high-spending ministry. Hence the Cabinet is divided between spending and non-spending ministers, and between different kinds of expenditure.

The departmental ministers sitting around the Cabinet table represent very different interests. Many of the policy disagreements contained within the Cabinet are focused in the continuing struggle over public expenditure. Strange alliances are formed as ministers barter support for each other's programmes.

In the competition between departments the Cabinet Office and the Prime Minister's Office may be seen as non-spending central departments normally allied with the Treasury against the big spenders.

The role of the minister

Much of the work of a ministry is routine and uncontroversial. The work is overseen by officials and the minister can know little about it, except for what is drawn to his attention by officials or by public complaint, or by the diligent and sharp-eyed reading of reports or occasional visits to 'see the work for themselves'.

The minister's role is thus semi-detached, at the top but not in touch, on a cloud rather than a mountain. This is not so strange or surprising: most peak jobs – managing directors, field marshals, college principals – are like that (and this may be justified in management theory). If the minister cannot oversee the detailed work of his ministry, he or she can operate in other modes:

1. By policy initiation – arising from previous commitment by the party, or general political leaning.
2. By policy selection – choosing from a range of proposals offered by officials and clients and interest groups.
3. By support of the department in its annual struggle for a share of funds and legislative time.
4. As manager of the department, ensuring that it is conducted efficiently, and gives value for money.
5. By being responsible to Parliament for the department.
6. By representing the department in public.

Of these roles, (5) is compulsory, (3) and (6) are normally pursued. Policy initiation and selection depend on the nature of the department's work, its profile and political sensitivity, and the drive of the minister. Ministers are not trained for the management role as understood in the 1990s, though some have picked this up. It is not an essential role for a minister. His proper role is political: relating to the Cabinet and Parliament, and to the development and presentation of policies in the context of his party's principles and programme.

That formulation is an ideal, and it fits easily in the context of Cabinet and Prime Minister with which this book is concerned. But the other and more passive roles of the minister are also represented in the Cabinet. The context and the substance of Cabinet discussion range from the political and strategic to the detail of the refitting of DHSS offices in the West Midlands, or the closure of a railway line in mid-Wales.

Departments: defending the territory

Departments are jealous of their departmental territory. This kind of professional jealousy is normal, a middle-class equivalent of the worker's demarcation dispute, seen at its worst in the legal professions. The Civil Service regards itself as different, and even morally superior, because the civil servant defending his department's traditional zones of work is defending a territory and an ethos rather than a pay packet. (Sceptical critics believe the Civil Service has contrived – like most other professionals – to adduce the highest motives for the extension of its own rewards and privileges). This is a second kind of adversarial politics, a Whitehall mode to match the Westminster mode, and quite significant for policy and the allocation of resources.

Territorial jealousy is enhanced by the natural blurring of boundaries. There are no clear lines between functions, departments and SDOs (quangos), and there is nagging anxiety that what you do might be done as well by someone else, especially now that privatisation is in fashion; or, worse, might not need doing at all.

There are many illustrations of a department's defence of its territory:

1. The Treasury's 'seeing-off' of the upstart Department of Economic Affairs, established by the Labour Government in 1964, to take over some of the Treasury's economic management functions.
2. The Foreign Office's successful resistance to numerous attempts to break its privileged monopoly of overseas representation.
3. The destruction by the Ministry of Housing and Local

Government of the Labour Government's new Ministry of Land and Natural Resources. This was, as recorded by Crossman, a classic triumph by Whitehall over the elected government.

> Last Saturday, when I was appointed, she [Dame Evelyn Sharp, the Permanent Secretary] drove back from her country cottage at Lavenham and told me the moment she got to London that, largely owing to me, the Department had been sold down the river by Harold Wilson's decision that Fred Willey should be in charge of planning and that I should do housing. . . . The Dame explained to me that what I had unconsciously done was to demolish the whole basis of her Department, because in her view – which I now suspect is correct – it's quite impossible to give physical planning, the land policy to a new Ministry without giving it all control of housing. . . . As soon as she realized this Dame Evelyn got down to a Whitehall battle to save her Department from my stupidity and ignorance. . . . I had imagined that the final decision had been taken after a personal talk I had with Harold on Sunday morning by telephone, when I explained what Dame Evelyn had told me. . . . On Monday morning I talked to him again and he again assured me all was O.K. On both occasions he rebuked me and Dame Evelyn for the way she had been waging her Whitehall war; and he said, 'You don't know what she is like, going behind my back to the civil servants.' I knew quite well what she was like and I knew she had gone to the head of the Civil Service, Helsby, and to Eric Roll, head of George Brown's new D.E.A. Regardless of anything that Harold had said, she continued the war, capturing Fred Willey and putting him in a room by himself in our Ministry while she got hold of his new Permanent Secretary, Mr Bishop, and lectured him. Yes, she fought and fought. When on Wednesday afternoon at a meeting I turned to her and said, 'Well, Dame Evelyn, you've won,' she replied, 'It's been the worst two days of my whole life.' 'Yes,' I said, 'but you have saved physical planning for us,' And she said, 'Of course, I always win. But it was exhausting.'
>
> (Crossman 1975, pp. 24–5, 22 Oct. 1964)

The following year Crossman was again in trouble, and was again defeated by his officials, when he tried to 'give away' sport to the Ministry of Education (Bruce-Gardyne 1986, p. 65).

Most ministers acquire the territorial jealousies of their departments. The officials are difficult to resist, indeed frequently quite convincing; and the minister's own interests, and his ministerial responsibility to Parliament, dispose him to seek the defence and, if possible, the enhancement of his department's concerns. 'The normal way [for a Minister] to gain respect and advance himself is to enhance some of the great purposes of his department' (Heclo and Wildavsky 1974, p. 135). 'Great purposes', they add, 'usually cost money, so the Minister has work to do'.

Few ministers can resist the attraction of winning public funds. It is like runs on the board at cricket, as Macmillan said of his massive programme of building 300,000 houses a year. The Education Minister in the Heath Government offered a typical minister's boast to a conference of educationists in November 1971. 'I have done everything possible to show my confidence in the future of higher education. In my monthly battles with the Treasury, I managed to get another £76m for student grants and last week announced the biggest ever development programme for further education and polytechnics' (quoted in Heclo and Wildavsky 1974, p. 135). The minister, Mrs M. Thatcher, later, as prime minister, repented of this enthusiasm for public expenditure in general, and higher education in particular.

Public expenditure issues raise in acute form the difficulty for all departmental ministers of choosing between the concerns, interests and priorities of the department and of the government as a whole. It may be argued that it is the prior duty of the minister to 'fight his corner'. This was Churchill's advice to a new minister, endorsed by Lord Boyle (1980, pp. 1–12). The minister fights his corner because no-one else will; the departmental interest ought not to go by default, and needs to be fitted into the ongoing consideration of a moving pattern of public expenditure. But a wise minister, who wishes to carry conviction, should learn when to press hard, and when simply to 'put down a marker' and withdraw.

The Treasury

The Treasury is a superdepartment, and the Chancellor of the Exchequer is a superminister. The potential of the Treasury is comparatively high for several reasons:

1. For its functions, which include the management of the economy and the control of public expenditure, two overriding policy areas, which in other countries are dealt with by two ministers.
2. Following from the importance of these functions, for the extent and quality of its information (Callaghan complained about his lack of information after he moved from the Treasury to the Home Office).
3. For the quality of its officials: it aims to recruit 'the best and the brightest'.
4. For the penetration or colonisation of Whitehall and Downing Street by former Treasury officials.
5. For the political weight of the Treasury through the seniority and standing of Chancellors of the Exchequer, and its representation in Cabinet by two ministers.
6. For the interest of the Prime Minister in the affairs of the Treasury. It is generally conceded that the Chancellor needs the Prime Minister's backing, and in dual alliance they are difficult to beat.

However, the Treasury is subject to severe constraints, and its potential is not always realised in practice. Its fundamental weakness is that anything like close control of the economy is beyond the power of government. Even the figures it deals with are often wrong, and economic theories uncertain. So even if the Treasury were all-powerful in Whitehall, it would still be weak. But it is not now all-powerful. The making of economic policy is more pluralistic, shared with other departments. The Treasury has lost power to the Cabinet Office, and its former responsibility for the Civil Service is shared. It has been subjected to continuous and deliberate challenge by countervailing institutions (DEA, CSD, CPRS), though significantly all these have disappeared. Countervailing individuals, especially special advisers, have also had a hard time but others (including Wilson's roving minister Harold Lever, and Mrs Thatcher's adviser, Sir Alan Walters) seem to have had some success in evading Treasury opposition.

Prime ministers regularly intervene in Treasury business, because of their political responsibilities and in conformity with their title of First Lord of the Treasury. The tide of managerial reform which swept over Whitehall in the 1980s disturbed it a little. Its relations with the Bank of England are uneasy: Denis Healey, Chancellor from 1974 to 1979, wrote of the Bank as 'seeing itself as the guardian of mysteries which no ordinary mortal should be allowed to understand' (Healey 1989, p. 374). The Treasury's Victorian reputation for saving candle-ends remains, but the actual impact of the Treasury on the level of public spending has done no more than slow the rate of growth. The Treasury's acceptance of optimistic rates of growth in the economy as a justification for higher spending indicates its failure to persuade politicians of its own Spartan principles.

The quality and reputation of Chancellors of the Exchequer reflect the ambivalent power of the Treasury. Chancellors are at once powerful, harassed and unpopular with their colleagues – so the power can rarely be exercised fully and decisively.

There is much evidence of the uneasy relationship of chancellors with colleagues. The Chancellor's claim to substantial power is resented and resisted. This is particularly true in the process of preparing the Budget. Roy Jenkins 'hit the roof', Barbara Castle wrote, at what he thought was 'an intolerable pre-emption of budgetary policy and no Chancellor could be expected to stand for it' (Castle 1984, p. 725, 4 November 1969). Similarly, Healey angrily rejected a suggestion that he should consult fully about his Budget proposals in 1975. 'I am not prepared to accept the inhibitions and constraints on my Budget responsibilities that this might imply' (Castle 1980, pp. 402–3, 31 May 1975). Mrs Castle referred at other times to the 'Chancellor's dictatorial power in matters greatly affecting other Departments' (1984, p. 121, 28 April 1966), the 'ingrowing arrogance to which all Chancellors . . . are prone' (1984, p. 241), and the 'God-complex' which chancellors, like foreign secretaries, soon acquired.

Against this must be set the evidence that chancellors carry heavy burdens, attending all major ministerial meetings, usually with a case to defend or defeat. Jenkins compared the Treasury with the Home Office. In the latter there were sudden tropical storms, fading away; by contrast the Treasury was 'a long dark arctic winter'. He complained of the 'endemic nature of the Treasury crisis; the size of the stakes if things go wrong; and the amount of time which has to be devoted to dealing with one's colleagues . . . (*Sunday Times*, 17 January 1971, quoted in Campbell 1983, p. 115). The Chancellor finds few friends among the spending ministers, and the non-spending ministers, fearful of making enemies, are reluctant allies of the Chancellor.

'If the Prime Minister is not on the Chancellor's side, nobody's on his side', said Enoch Powell, once a Treasury minister, who resigned. The relations of prime ministers and chancellors have often been difficult. Macmillan always believed the Treasury was 'Up to No Good' (Bruce-Gardyne 1986, p. 69). Wilson established the Department of Economic Affairs to compete with the Treasury, but economic crisis tamed this bid for independence. Heath tried to be his own Chancellor. Prime Minister Callaghan had served as chancellor and, wrote Bruce-Gardyne, 'knew which side his bread was buttered' (1986, p. 70). Mrs Thatcher was suitably heartless about public expenditure, but was much too independent-minded and lost one of her chancellors, Nigel Lawson, by resignation. Indeed, the comparative frequency of resignations and threats of resignation by chancellors confirms the difficulties of the relationship of prime minister and chancellor, and the fragility of the chancellor's power.

If prime minister and chancellor are able to get their act together, they are virtually unbeatable. They can dominate their colleagues and achieve their policies. Their political power is thus substantial: whether that power enables them to dominate the economy too is another matter.

Thus the Chancellor and the Treasury have great potential but heavy responsibilities, and only the appearance rather than the substance of power. The Chancellor has political force or clout, but never enough to guarantee the consistent delivery of the policy objectives arising from his responsibilities. Hence he often lacks power.

The higher Civil Service

The higher ranks of the Civil Service in the departments and the Treasury and Cabinet Office constitute a community of policy managers, sometimes called a 'mandarinate' (to imply a narrow caste of privileged rulers), and described by the American observers, Heclo and Wildavsky, as a village community, sustained by personal relationships within a shared framework of values. 'The civil service is run by a small group of people who grew up together' (Heclo and Wildavsky 1974, p. 76, quoting a Treasury official). The culture derives from similar backgrounds, the Oxbridge classical scholar being the older model, heavily reinforced by years of service in the lower ranks. Department officials constitute an invisible presence at the Cabinet table, and an evident force in the Central Executive Territory. The mandarin's policy community is built into the structure of the Territory through the official committees and in the Cabinet and Prime Minister's Offices.

The higher Civil Service in Britain has bureaucratic rather than political aspirations. The aim is to keep itself and the minister out of trouble, more positively to support the minister, and to send him 'into battle without a policy hair out of place' (Castle 1980, pp. 528–9, 20 October 1975), and to provide a polished administrative service under the system of ministerial responsibility to Parliament.

The Civil Service is non-partisan, and expects to serve ministers of any party with equal loyalty. A number of able and forthright politicians of strong views have testified that this is the case, though there are voices on the other side. In practice the Civil Service has a political position of a kind. It is against radical change and in favour of continuity and the departmental view, and good government as they see it based on an understanding of reality, 'the facts'. This is not a party political position; but it is a political position, a central ground, dependent on bureaucracy, but under Parliament.

All of this adds up to a position of considerable force for the civil servant as the permanent expert professional serving the temporary visiting amateur. So the question is not whether the civil servant is powerful, but how he fits into a pattern of interlocking functions and related patterns of force, checks and balances.

Something of the concern of a top civil servant for persuading ministers gently away from their wilder schemes was conveyed in an interview on Channel 4 News given in 1987 by Lord Bancroft, a former head of the Home Civil Service (quoted in Hennessy 1989, pp. 509–10). Bancroft had referred to party conferences as 'vexatious affairs in which normally sensible people temporarily lose their marbles', and leading to policy commitments, some of which might be, in Bancroft's term, 'garbage'. Given such policy commitments 'the permanent secretary might have to tread very delicately perhaps suggesting modifications of a relatively minor nature in the priority given to those policies . . . because the permanent secretary must steer a course in which he retains or gains the trust of the new Minister but, at the same time, carries out his responsibilities of bringing to the attention of the new Minister . . . the difficulties of implementing some of the policies which are in the manifesto . . . .It's not that the permanent secretary wants to get in the way of the wishes of the electorate, but he has got, in the words of one of my predecessors, to be "faithful to the facts"' (Hennessy 1989, p. 509). Bancroft's views, expressed thus freely in retirement, confirm the force of the bureaucracy in the Central Executive Territory – a potent force, certainly a necessary force, and often, given the sheer difficulty of governing, a force for good.

Parliament

Parliament is notoriously weak in relation to government. Parliamentary sovereignty is not a constitutional fiction, but the immense power derived from it is delivered through a disciplined party system to the political executive. The main function of Parliament is to provide the personnel of government and to support them in office; the making of policy is a function of government. Thus a system based on parliamentary supremacy becomes a system of executive dominance. Parliament provides the formal processes of law making which register and legitimate law. It also has subsidiary functions of scrutinising government administration and representing the people (mainly dealing with constituents' grievances).

However, this does not mean that Parliament is of no account in government. The functions listed are substantial and fundamental. There are possibilities of influence along the way. Parliament is in fact an essential element in the structure and environment of government at the centre. It is joined to the Central Executive Territory in three ways:

THE STRUCTURE OF BRITISH GOVERNMENT 31

1. Party is the organising mechanism of British government. Parliament is the structure by which party is bolted on to government. Party discipline, though intense, ubiquitous and even ferocious, cannot entirely drain mind and humanity from the mechanism. For all the crudity of the Whips Office, the relationship of government to members of parliament via party is a little more subtle than simple control. Relations are managed. There is a sense in which the Government knows that in Parliament it comes face to face with its Maker.

    Of course, it is demeaning to Parliament that its residual power is effectively the power of the majority party. The Opposition counts for very little. But the majority derives its standing and influence from Parliament.

2. Ministerial responsibility is the organising principle of British government. A minister may take that responsibility quite lightly. At the minimum, all he must do is to stand up in the House of Commons and say 'I take responsibility'. Even major errors can be accounted for in this way. But in a forum and a culture devoted to talk and debate a minister's retreat into 'the less said the better' can be damaging to reputation. The party saves the minister once, but remembers the offence.

    However, it is misleading to see ministerial responsibility operating solely in the context of ministerial error and the occasional incidence of resignation. The principle of ministerial responsibility determines the pattern of government in Britain. Legislation and questions and statements in Parliament are dominant considerations in the making of policy and in the administration of departments. The party majority is 'taken for granted', but on a full repairing lease. The loyal assume that their loyalty will continue to be earned; the government knows it is not in danger but chooses prudently to comfort and reward the faithful.

    Apart from these considerations of majority support, the massive weight of the procedures of British government are predicated upon ministerial responsibility. It is the job of the Civil Service to see that policy is constructed and administration carried out under the responsibility of the minister to Parliament. In this way the official serves the

Constitution, but he also serves himself; for ministerial responibility provides a more or less comprehensive cover for the official. The Civil Service needs Parliament, even if the minister sometimes wishes he could do without it.
3. Parliament is still one of the major arenas for political theatre. This is not a trivial point, for the public, popular and representational elements of politics are essential to the building of consent. Parliament is much less significant than television as a theatre of politics, but it is highly significant for the chief players in the game of politics. Political standing at Westminster is essential for ministers (thus giving some reality to ministerial responsibility) and necessary to any aspiring politician and to leading opposition members. Egos are always at stake. Standing in the House is not the same as standing with the public, but in Westminster it is regarded as such, and so acquires significance. In any case, the televising of the proceedings of Parliament has narrowed the gap between popular and Westminster reputations.

'It is essential to remain a House of Commans man. Remember you belong to this place'. Such was the advice of a Conservative minister quoted by Headey (1974, p. 67). Parliament is, in the words of Heclo and Wildavsky, 'the ever-present outsider . . . the permanent and proper stranger whose very presence indirectly helps nurture the sense of community within the Executive' (1974, pp. 244–5).

In territorial terms Parliament is the surrounding territory, a commuter-land, somewhere between Inner and Outer Circle. The boundaries are well-defined, and most of the time the inhabitants of this Inner–Outer Circle know their place.

The British Constitution provides a kind of 'shape-memory' for British government. Like some metals, government works in many shapes and patterns which are modifications and falsifications of the original form. But there is a tendency under pressure to return to a pristine shape. So the British Constitution tends to re-assert itself; a shape is remembered. This is true for Parliament as it is for the Cabinet.

International institutions

British government is a member of numerous international institutions, notably the European Community, and the North Atlantic Treaty Organisation. Strictly, these are not part of the permanent structure of government. They are arrangements freely entered into by government, and from which it may withdraw. But in practice withdrawal is difficult. Membership of such organisations is more than a constraint on government, it also changes the structures of policy making. The most obvious example of this is the procession of ministers and officials to Brussels to take part in the decision making of the European Community. It is no longer possible to leave 'foreign' policy to the Foreign Office, since economic policy and many other aspects of domestic policy have a foreign or transnational character.

This is a useful reminder that the Central Executive Territory, though predominant over all other territories in Britain, is itself locked into, and to some extent subordinated to, an international economy and political system. Territorial power is not sovereign power.

Part II
The Cabinet

Introduction: The Cabinet as a Principle of Government

The Prime Minister lives in and with and by the Cabinet. The Cabinet is a constitutional principle (or a principle of government) as well as an institution. It represents the Cabinet as Council, the Cabinet system (of committees and sub-committees and meetings) and the Cabinet as 'The Colleagues' (Cabinet ministers mainly). Cabinet also represents the constitutional principle of collectivity and the mode of working, collegiality. It is the working framework and moral code of British government, honoured often in the evasion, but acknowledged, even respected. (The strength of the British Constitution is measured by the respectful language used in its evasion.)

The Cabinet is not based on a constitution, or a set of rules, but on precedent and practice firmed into custom and convention; but the working rules of Cabinet government are set out in a confidential document handed to new ministers, Questions of Procedure for Ministers. This, Hennessy says, is 'the nearest thing we have to a written constitution for British Cabinet government' (1986, p. 7). 'Questions' has grown over the years from four pages in 1945 to twenty-seven in the mid-1970s. It deals with simple procedures for a Cabinet Minister, but also sets out rules on committees, collective responsibility and confidentiality. The latter is heavily emphasised. The Cabinet procedures of British government are not public procedures. Hennessy prints the 1952 version, much of which remains unchanged (Hennessy 1986, pp. 8–13).

4

The Cabinet as The Colleagues

Selection

Selection: who are The Colleagues?

Fifty years ago the Government included only about 60 ministers, one third of them in the Cabinet. By contrast, a modern government includes about 110 ministers, ranging from the Prime Minister and 20 or so members of the Cabinet through Ministers of State to the humblest Parliamentary Private Secretaries (unpaid posts of assistant to a minister, much increased in numbers since the 1960s). Thus about one third of the majority party in the House of Commons constitutes the Government, but only one in seventeen or so ministers is in the Cabinet. Every minister is bound by loyalty ('the payroll vote'), ambition and the convention of 'collective responsibility', which enjoins silence or support. Within this large group of ministers are 'The Colleagues', the Prime Minister and senior ministers, most of them members of the Cabinet, and amounting to about one-fifth of the total ministerial complement.

The Colleagues who make up a British government have emerged as colleagues in parliamentary and party politics, sometimes over years in opposition. The team (or 'squad' in sporting terms – the select group from which the team is chosen) emerges from a selection process based on performance in the

House, acceptability to the party's members of Parliament and ideological position or leaning. In the Labour Party in opposition, election to the Shadow Cabinet and even to the party's National Executive Committee may ensure selection to the group of colleagues in government; though a leader of the Labour Party enjoys some freedom of action, especially as Prime Minister. Conservative prime ministers face no formal restraints but, like all prime ministers, must construct a Cabinet which is related to sections and support within the party.

Selection: political friends and enemies

In the composition of the Cabinet, some colleagues impose themselves by party status and/or following, regardless of their empathy, or lack of it, with the leader; in particular those whom the leader 'vanquished to achieve the Crown' (Bruce-Gardyne 1986, p. 20). The Prime Minister must take some advice (from Chief Whip or elder statesmen, say) without consulting widely on what must in the end be a personal and sometimes painful choice. Apart from personal and political considerations that choice is constrained by the need for lawyers, a Lord and a lady, and an approximation at least to a Scotsman and a Welshman. One final constraint is that posts and persons must match up. 'The process of Government-making is a jigsaw, in which all the pieces must somehow be made to fit' (ibid., p. 21). It is evident that prime ministers use some jobs to park particular people, friends, enemies – the Overseas Development Ministry has been used in this way, sometimes in, sometimes out, of Cabinet.

Thus the Colleagues are selected initially by self and party and finally by the Prime Minister, and even the most dominant Prime Minister must live and work perforce with enemies as well as friends, or in one formulation, with enemies and functionaries as well as sycophants. For example, Wilson's first Cabinet included few political friends, only two or three who had voted for him in 1963. Wilson manoeuvred against Callaghan but dared not dismiss him, and left Brown to destroy himself. It was only after Brown's resignation that Wilson began to feel some trust in his Cabinet.

The record of Wilson's cabinets is of constant grouping and regrouping: there was always an inner circle, but its membership changed, as Wilson included or excluded his enemies on tactical grounds. Wilson did not trust many of his colleagues. Crossman records his anxiety in 1967 about dismissing from the Cabinet (then 23) two inadequate ministers. 'It's not easy. I can't trust the rest of the Cabinet and those two provide me with two important votes' (Crossman 1976, p. 410, 5 July 1967). The accounts suggest both that Wilson had paranoid tendencies, and that he had a lot to be paranoid about.

In her first two administrations at least, a negative response to Mrs Thatcher's famous question, 'Is he one of us?' did not mean exclusion from her counsels. Mrs Thatcher seems to have had some capacity to convert or silence those who were not by inclination One of Hers. Nevertheless, her early cabinets included many political opponents: she was at first in a minority in her own Cabinet. Some she dismissed and two, Heseltine and Lawson, were driven towards resignation, but still died by their own hand.

Lloyd George said, 'There can be no friendship between the top five men in a Cabinet' (quoted in T. Jones 1954, p. 52). 'The Colleagues' are not, then, a group of friends (no more than the board of a company is) nor a mix of friends and enemies. They are united by parliamentary experience, the pursuit of party goals, and the love of power; and divided by disagreements on goals, timing, methods – and personal chemistry. No one who has experienced the tensions, continuous personal rivalries and occasional malice of a board room, a committee, a common room, would expect the Colleagues to be solidly united by mutual respect or personal affection.

This is an observation not simply on human nature in general, or on the special tensions arising from personal ambition, competition and vulnerability, though these play their part. Political activity adds its own pressures and tensions arising from the heavy and unending workload of ministers, the public vulnerability of elected politicians, and the potential of faith and commitment to generate bitterness and schism, the conversion of doubt into moral betrayal. The Labour Party, a secular church for some, is especially capable of long-running schism, as in the 'betrayal' by MacDonald in 1931, and the Gaitskell-Bevan split in the 1950s, which had a significance for Harold Wilson. 'After 1960 the one identifying feature of a true Gaitskellite was a dislike of Harold Wilson' (Ponting 1989, p. 9). The 1970s governments produced another gallery of alleged traitors. Such rivalries and resentments had an impact on policy making.

Personal and political rivalries among 'The Colleagues' are inevitable, and may not be disabling or even harmful. There is plainly something to be said for 'creative tension', the stimulation of disagreement rather than comfortable compatibility. But distrust and rivalry do not make a helpful context for developing and agreeing policy.

Distrust among The Colleagues was also evident at times under Mrs Thatcher, as a series of resignations showed. Both European and financial policy making was damaged by Mrs Thatcher's long-running feud with the Chancellor of the Exchequer, Nigel Lawson, and the Foreign Secretary, Geoffrey Howe.

Selection: departmental ministers

The Colleagues are in the main departmental ministers and in the Cabinet itself (the 'Cabinet Council') they outnumber non-departmental ministers. The balance within cabinets has changed.

The contemporary cabinet, by contrast with 1902, excludes the Commonwealth, Colonial and India Offices; separate Admiralty, War and Air Offices; and the Post Office. It includes a massive Defence Ministry; various economic ministries (Trade and Industry, Employment, Energy, Transport, Agriculture); a massive Environment Ministry, including Housing; the Health and Social Security Ministries; and a Welsh as well as a Scottish Office. Thus, (i) external and defence representation has declined (from 7 in 1945 to 2 by the 1970s); (ii) spending and programme ministries have increased; (iii) there are new ministries to manage economic affairs.

De-selection and reshuffles

The Prime Minister has the right to dismiss as well as appoint. As late as the 1870s the right was not firmly established, and Gladstone experienced some difficulty with ministers who, he told the Queen, showed 'a tenacity of attachment to office certainly greater than is usual' (quoted in Gordon Walker 1972, p. 82). This is an interesting indication of the status of the

Cabinet. But by the end of the century the Prime Minister was clearly edging ahead of the Cabinet; it was beginning to be his Cabinet rather than the Cabinet. A prime minister still needed to be prudent in his dismissals, but the right was his, as Macmillan demonstrated in 1962 when he dismissed seven of his Cabinet colleagues. That turned out to be imprudent, for Macmillan's Government never recovered its confidence; the same was true for Mrs Thatcher's brutal reshuffle in July 1989.

Ministers are more often 'reshuffled' than dismissed, and some reshuffling takes place in most years. This is intended to replace the one or two ministers who leave office for any reason each year, to encourage and hold the loyalty of back benchers and junior ministers by promotion, to fit persons to jobs more closely and to 'freshen' the look of the Government. However, frequent movement and short stays in particular departments have a damaging effect on ministerial effectiveness. It is unusual for a minister to stay more than two years in one department, and some manage only a year or less.

These simple facts explain a good deal about government in Britain. The balance of the Colleagues and Cabinet is weighted towards programmes and expenditure. Insofar as modern government is about the management and control of public expenditure, this system sets up 'The Colleagues' to fight one another, and more significantly to fight the Chancellor of the Exchequer for money. The non-department, non-spending ministers, including the Prime Minister and the Chancellor of the Exchequer, are numerically and to some extent politically in a weak position. Some ministers stay for two years or more in one office, learn fast and master enough of their subject to be reasonably effective. Others can be no more than visiting amateurs, reading a brief on the way to a meeting, hoping not to be found in error in public.

Standing

The Cabinet has a certain exclusivity derived from its place in government, and all Cabinet Colleagues share in that exclusivity. They are separated by their position both from Parliament and from their ministerial colleagues outside the Cabinet. They are comparatively a little better informed about (and in theory carry responsibility for) the whole range of government policy. Non-cabinet ministers are by comparison bound to their departments, prone to tunnel vision, and cut off from the irresponsible camaraderie of the House of Commons. The British system of government produces a 'winning side' and permanent losers. The Cabinet Colleagues are, then, players on the winning side; the rest are reserves, and ground staff, with backbench fans; the Opposition are hooligans without tickets, excluded from the game.

If all Cabinet Colleagues enjoy exclusivity, some are more exclusive, have a higher standing, than others. The Prime Minister without doubt enjoys the highest standing, though the relative height of prime ministerial standing is both variable and obscure. The Chancellor of the Exchequer enjoys high standing derived from his office, and the influence it gives him over much of government policy. Moreover some part of this influence is exercised in secrecy, in negotiation with other countries, the IMF, international bankers, or in the peculiar confidentiality which attaches to the preparation of the 'Budget' (that is, taxation proposals). If, in addition, the Chancellor is of a sharp intellect and forceful personality, he may exercise significant personal influence. Denis Healey notably wielded such influence in the Labour Cabinets of 1974–9. He was 'a major Cabinet figure . . . Neither of his Prime Ministers found it easy to impose upon him changes of economic policy. They had to convince him intellectually and politically and to do that they needed firm conviction and a well-argued case' (Donoughue 1987, p. 33).

However, the Chancellor's responsibilities are too important for him to be left alone. The Prime Minister, as Prime Minister, First Lord of the Treasury, and next-door neighbour of the Chancellor, looks over the Chancellor's shoulder. In effect, major financial policy is agreed with the Prime Minister. When serious disagreement arises, it is the Chancellor who gives way – or resigns. 'It has always been the Chancellor's prerogative to call it a day' (Heclo and Wildavsky 1974, p. 168). 'Defeat is almost unthinkable for a Chancellor' (Healey 1989, p. 164). This means that defeat is infrequent but very damaging. Thorneycroft resigned in 1958; and Lawson in 1989.

Such resignations indicate the fundamental importance of the Chancellor's policy field, rather than the inevitable high influence of chancellors. In the beginning economic policy has to be in the hands of a senior and high-calibre politician; in the end economic policy is much too important to be left outside the sphere of the Prime Minister and even the influence of The Colleagues.

In the first Wilson Government, Prime Minister and Chancellor fought devaluation together, but in the end Callaghan was left isolated with a failed policy and, following devaluation, he moved to another post. Other offices may confer differences in standing, though much still depends on the office holder. For example, a weak Foreign Secretary may find his policies shaped by the Prime Minister in Cabinet or in summit meetings. An undistinguished minister in a department of moderate significance may acquire standing by his connections with an influential interest group or a current of opinion (Barnett 1982, p. 51).

Differences in standing arise from political position and prestige ('clout'). Departmental responsibilities confer standing and position, but only a few departments are continuously at the centre of a government's concern. Thus Crossman complained to Mrs Castle in 1966, 'I'm not really a Cabinet Minister, any more than you are; I'm a Departmental one' (Castle 1984, p. 117, 25 April 1966). However, Crossman's view of his role fluctuated. A few months later Crossman noted in his diary, 'I'm going to be a Cabinet Minister' and Castle recorded that Crossman 'went into the attack again today' (at Cabinet) 'full of his new-found enthusiasm for behaving like a Cabinet Minister' (1984, p. 158).

In the Labour Cabinet of 1974–9 Michael Foot's vote counted as more than one according to Joel Barnett – and since he lost on the big issues, the Prime Minister gave way on smaller matters. Evident ability counts too. In the same Cabinet Crosland gained influence by the clarity and force of his contributions to discussion, though not everyone thought they were helpful. He still lost his general argument in favour of public expenditure, but may have gained freedom of choice about the targets of his own cuts. Bluster generally does not improve a minister's standing. Barbara Castle had the courage to fight, but her fate was often to go down fighting.

In some administrations, 'The Colleagues' are similar in standing and ability, an undifferentiated team under a comparatively dominant prime minister. This was the case in the Heath Government, 1970–4. At other times 'The Colleagues' include two or three political notabilities of prime ministerial calibre. This was certainly true in Attlee's Government (1945–51) – Morrison, Bevin, Cripps, were all experienced ministers of heavy 'clout' with claims to the prime ministership. Again, even after thirteen years in opposition, Wilson's Cabinet (1964–70) included men of the highest intellectual calibre, and one or two claimants to the prime ministerial throne. The abundance of talent ought to be helpful to prime ministers, but they do not appreciate competition from ambitious colleagues. Nor is there a high correlation between intellectual quality and political achievement. Among colleagues, intellectual quality may be valued lower than trustworthiness and reliability. There may even be a sympathetic hearing for a respected but inarticulate colleague; but the support of relatively passive ministers is taken for granted, and their occasional intrusion forced down by a tough chairman.

Most Cabinets include a minister who is in effect the Number Two in seniority, the Prime Minister's right-hand man. He may or may not be called 'Deputy Prime Minister' – for example, George Brown under Wilson, and Whitelaw and Howe under Mrs Thatcher. The Prime Minister may prefer that the Deputy is not the heir apparent.

Apart from these comparative heavyweights, there is a scattering of ministers of high personal influence: for example, Lords Carrington and Hailsham under Mrs Thatcher. It is said that Hailsham single-handedly defeated an early proposal for student loans, but of course, other factors, including backbench opinion, were involved.

Solidarity

The Colleagues are held together in solidarity, but also driven apart by disagreements and competition. Politics is thus two-faced – loyalty and disagreement – and the solidarity of the Colleagues is a punctured solidarity.

Solidarity is derived from a number of sources:

1. Parliamentary experience: the development of the team of leaders over years of service in Parliament.

2. Social origins: Conservative colleagues still reflect some homogeneity of background. In the late 1980s the major private schools were still better represented than state schools (though the last three Conservative prime ministers were educated at state grammar schools), and most Cabinet members are graduates of Oxford or Cambridge (the latter unusually well represented recently). Labour Cabinets have also drawn a majority of their members from Oxbridge (Wilson had thirteen in 1976, Callaghan twelve), but the Celtic universities are now well represented on the Labour front benches. Very few senior politicians of any party can now claim a genuine working-class background, though John Major seems to have come from a lower level in the lower middle class than his two predecessors.
3. Political values and party loyalty.
4. The normal group loyalties of executives publicly committed to objectives and achievements, anxious for reputation and concerned to do well.

These sources are reinforced by:

5. The rules and conventions of the Cabinet, notably collective responsibility (see Case Note, Chapter 13).
6. The public distrust (encouraged by the media) of apparent disunity – 'Cabinet splits'.

Solidarity is not total: it is punctured by leaks and broken by dissent and occasional disloyalty. It could hardly be expected that twenty or so senior politicians carrying heavy responsibilities would always agree or, in the constant chatter of Westminster, would be able to, or would wish to, keep their disagreements hidden. 'Leaking' by informal briefing of the media happens frequently, indeed it is now a routine procedure, in which the Prime Minister's Press Office takes a leading role. For example, Wilson often briefed the media, sometimes giving an account of Cabinet discussions. The Cabinet meetings during the IMF crisis in 1976 were fully reported in *The Guardian*, written up and performed in a television documentary, and recounted in the published diaries of participants. In the Westland affair an item of policy making was effectively transferred from the Cabinet agenda to the public platform and the media.

The tendency to leaks reinforces the endless exhortation to, and attempted imposition of, secrecy. On one occasion, at the height of an economic crisis, George Brown told the Cabinet: 'Naturally you won't want to be told, for fear of the information leaking, how serious the situation is' (Crossman 1975, p. 26, 22 October 1965).

From time to time solidarity breaks down completely. Normal or acceptable dissent in one of the Colleagues becomes persistent and acute. In one notable case, Tony Benn was described as a member but not supporter of the Labour Government of 1974–9 (Donoughue 1987, p. 50). Occasionally one of the Colleagues resigns. There are a few resignations of this kind, on policy grounds and in conformity with the convention of collective responsibility: Thorneycroft and other Treasury ministers in 1958, Heseltine in 1986, Lawson in 1989, Howe in 1990. Motives are often more complex than simple disagreement. An exhaustive list would not be very long – about 26 resignations since 1945; but there are enough to indicate that the solidarity of the Cabinet can be fragile (see Case Note, 'Collective responsibilty', Chapter 13).

The fragility is emphasised by the frequency of the threat of resignation. This is the iceberg of which actual resignation is the tip. Resignation itself has the serious disadvantage that it removes the minister from the scene, and usually from all possibility of further influence. A threat of resignation may be more effective, though a prime minister may judge that the threat is not serious, and that the departure of the minister may do little damage (this is usually the case). The accounts and diaries of Cabinet life suggest that Colleagues often feel they are pushed beyond endurance (as we all are among family and friends, and in business and work life) and frequently say they would find this or that policy unacceptable. Mostly, they, like the rest of us, swallow the unacceptable.

There are a few examples of the successful use of the threat of resignation, though it is in the interests of both sides to minimise the element of threat. For example, Roy Jenkins as Home Secretary in 1967 threatened resignation rather than impose restrictions on satire in the live theatre. Jenkins, as a liberal Home Secretary, felt strongly about this matter, stood his ground and won. This was nicely calculated – not a central policy issue, and the Minister took a conscientiously strong position. In the 1976 financial crisis, Anthony Crosland held an articulate and apparently strong position on public expenditure cuts (he was against them); but he did not threaten resignation and, having argued his case, he accepted the overall Cabinet position. In the summer of 1989 the Chancellor and the Foreign Secretary are said to have threatened resignation in order to secure concessions from the Prime Minister in the 'Madrid conditions' for entry to the Exchange Rate Mechanism.

Resignation is quite rare, and the really serious threat of resignation not much more frequent. Some Cabinet ministers openly disagreed with British accession to the EEC, as they were allowed to under the dispensation, but continued to serve after the decision had gone against them. Tony Benn seems to have disagreed more or less openly with much of the policy of the 1974–9 Labour Government, but he remained a minister nevertheless. Some of Mrs Thatcher's colleagues disagreed with her approach to government; but very few resigned, though many were dismissed.

Altogether, then, the Colleagues normally play as a team because this is in their joint and several interests, it is comfortable and clubbable, and satisfying. Those occasional group photographs of the Cabinet never look very friendly or relaxed: there is rivalry and malice, some cruelty, but little hatred. They stand united in the love of power and contempt for the Opposition (see Chapter 9 for further discussion of resignations from the point of view of the Prime Minister).

Job satisfaction

Being a Cabinet Minister is a job not at all like any other, but nevertheless a professional occupation conferring high status and a modest income, interesting work, and a marvellous support staff. As in most executive-type jobs, there is some satisfaction for burning ambition or the desire to prove oneself. Most senior politicians admit to some kind of exhilaration at problems solved, crises managed, policies implemented. There is the possibility of service in a just cause, and real achievement. In a moment of exhilaration Barbara Castle wrote, 'Life is rather fun. And oddly enough I don't worry about my burdens half as much as I used to' (Castle 1980, p. 332, 5 March 1975). However, there is also the probability of frustration and failure, and the near-certainty of a heavy burden of work in a condition of continuous publicity and vulnerability – your words, appearance, dress and personal life under constant critical scrutiny.

Days and nights in the life of a cabinet minister

Work

'How does one solve the problem of finding the time to equip oneself to be a fully effective member of Cabinet? I work sixteen to seventeen hours a day non-stop and there is still not enough time' (Castle 1980, p. 314, 20 Feb 1975; see also Castle 1980, pp. 49–50, 25 March 1974; pp. 208–10, 4 November 1974).

Barbara Castle's evidence is substantial, detailed and vivid, but she represents only one ministerial and executive type – working with enormous energy and total commitment near to the point of exhaustion. Such people seem to have inner resources of drive and doggedness ('doggedness is my only virtue', she wrote – 1984, p. 525) and exhaust their colleagues before they exhaust themselves.

Joel Barnett worked a seven-day week, including evenings and nights, and wrote that good health and the ability to manage on little sleep were invaluable assets for a minister (1982, p. 16). But Anthony Crosland rarely took home more than one box of papers; Lord Hailsham, when Secretary of State for Education, refused to take any boxes home. Roy Jenkins took a relaxed approach and was said to work a 4-day week: 'One of Roy's failings will be never to kill himself with work' (Castle 1984, p. 358). Jenkins himself claimed he worked a 9-hour day; as Chancellor of the Exchequer, this went up to 12 hours a day, plus 6 hours on Saturday and Sunday (Campbell 1983, p. 116). He still believed writing was harder work. Denis Healey found the work heavy, but much worse in Opposition, when it was both heavy and frustrating, since it was largely without influence (1989, pp. 569–70).

Reputation, ambition, food, drink, and gossip

These are the fuels of ministerial life – to stand well with your colleagues, to advance your career beyond theirs; and, so the evidence of the diaries suggests, to measure out your life with food and drink, laced with endless talk about politics and gossip about colleagues. Quite a good life really, and not at all unfamiliar in executive dining suites and senior common rooms.

Diary of a cabinet minister: Barbara Castle, 25 March 1974

> Diary of a typical day, after a weekend spent with my nose in red boxes. Left [home] at 8.45 am for London, reading briefs all the way. Mass meeting with officials at the House at 10.30 am to discuss my statement. . . . Frantic last-minute negotiations with Treasury, who want to take out every word that might seem to commit us to anything (despite the fact that the Prime Minister has cleared the statement). Over to No. 10 at 11.30 for Budget Cabinet. . . . Straight back to office for sandwiches and an urgent official meeting on our Uprating Bill. Back to the House at 3 pm to be in good time for my statement. . . . Up to my room to do a few constituency letters, then back to the Department for another mass meeting of officials . . . Then a quick change [a visit to the dying Dick Crossman] . . . dashed to Lancaster House where I had to receive, and dine with, doctors from America and Canada. Left at 9.30 pm for the rate support grant vote in the House . . . Worked on my boxes in my room. Home at midnight . . . got to bed at 1 am. Another box has arrived, but to hell with it. I have two major speeches, two major statements and Parliamentary Questions to do this week, and the burden is oppressive. I do not sleep well.
>
> (1980, pp. 49–50)

A similarly hard-pressed day in November is recorded in a more positive way. Mrs Castle was engaged in a struggle with the powerful medical profession, in particular the consultants who, she believed with some justification, were 'not totally committed to the National Health Service'. This is the combative Minister, exercising her considerable forensic and political skills, leading her ministerial colleagues and dominating both top civil servants and overmighty pressure groups. Some of her colleagues had counselled her to be 'overwhelmingly non-provocative' but she relished a row. Preparing for two television broadcasts she 'felt almost frivolous. Who are these people to dictate that nothing shall be changed, even by a duly elected government?' (1980, pp. 208–10, 4 November 1974).

These two diary entries present the up and the down of ministerial life – a day of grinding burden, and a contrasting day of equally hard work, but satisfying because something was achieved.

Media attention

Barbara Castle is again a good but not entirely representative witness. She felt she must always take care with her dress and appearance, and noted with admiration the care taken by the then new Leader of the Opposition, Mrs Thatcher ('two dresses in the course of an afternoon', even in 1975). Both Castle and Thatcher were correct in their approach: colleagues on the Labour side (Shirley Williams, Michael Foot) lost political points through carelessness in appearance.

At times Barbara Castle felt harried and persecuted by the media, for example, at a TUC conference – 'They had got me covered all right and I was afraid to yawn, sneeze or even smile. Such are the hazards of public life' (1984, p. 507, 4 September 1968). Mrs Castle had particular problems – as do all Labour ministers – in avoiding accusations of privilege when seeking medical treatment in a hospital; and was even afraid to wear spectacles in public because the frames were 'private'. Labour politicians are particularly at risk if they make any use of private facilities. This is a special example of the normal risks run by Labour politicians in face of an aggressive and politically-biased tabloid press. However, it should be added that Conservative ministers can be taunted for not themselves using the 'state' institutions for which they are responsible.

Rewards

Hard work in the public eye has its own rewards. Barbara Castle referred to the 'vitamin of power' sustaining her through six hours of reading on a Sunday evening; and she notes Mrs Thatcher's blooming appearance due, she felt, to the same sustaining vitamin. There is some awareness of the rewards of a public reputation, coupled with some anxiety that a place in history is elusive. She felt she would be remembered for some of her work as Minister of Transport (speed limits, the breathalyser, the outlawing of 'bald' tyres).

Alas, the achievement of individual ministers is normally soon lost, and success and failure are ascribed indiscriminately to the Prime Minister. (The best-remembered Minister of Transport ever was Hore-Belisha, who cleverly gave part of his name to a pedestrian crossing beacon.) The best-remembered Ministers for Education were Butler for the 1944 Education Act (the 'Butler Act'). Mrs Thatcher, known rather unfairly as 'the milk-snatcher', and Kenneth Baker, whose schemes of in-service training gave school children 'Baker day' holidays.

In practice, most ministers live in a present which stretches out to the next election. In that shorter time-span most would choose some recognition and encouragement from the manager (the Prime Minister) and the shareholders (the voters) and a steadily sympathetic press. The British mode of adversarial politics ensures routine vilification and ridicule, mainly but not exclusively from the Opposition and in the overwhelmingly Conservative tabloid press. Nor is the job secure. A minister may be dismissed at what may seem the whim of the Prime Minister, and cast out of power entirely by what may seem the perversity of the electors.

However, not all is lost. Ministers may retire to fight another day, or to write their lucrative memoirs; or to take up well-rewarded jobs in private or public industry or commerce. It is now evident that few Conservative ministers lose financially when they quit office, and some may gain so much, earning three or four times their ministerial salaries, that they can hardly afford to stay in office. Resignation or dismissal thus become a positive pleasure, sometimes disguised as 'wanting to spend more time with my family'. This development is of some constitutional significance because Conservative ministers are no longer tied by the demands of the mortgage and the family and a pension to stay in office, come what may.

5

The Cabinet as Council

The full Cabinet, called here the Cabinet Council, meets for two hours or so once a week – sometimes less under Mrs Thatcher, and occasionally longer and more frequently under Mr Wilson. Harold Wilson in his farewell statement said he had presided over 472 Cabinets in about eight years in office; Mrs Thatcher notched up 394 in over eleven years.

The Cabinet Council is by convention at the centre or apex of the cabinet system since by convention the Cabinet has the final authority to ratify and legitimate decisions. But this authority must be understood as informing, shaping and capping the cabinet system, rather than as a supreme authority wielded daily over the development of policy and the taking of decisions. The Cabinet is formally but not operationally at the top of a hierarchical structure.

The working of the Cabinet Council is determined by five uneven factors:

1. Its composition, both personal and political (The Colleagues).
2. The nature of the political agenda: both party programme and externally imposed problems.
3. Time and pressure of work.
4. The pressures, restraints and supports arising from the work of officials and the departments.
5. Management by the Prime Minister, including management of the committee system.

Composition

The Cabinet, like most groups working in close combination towards common objectives (like a football team, for example) develops a character of its own, derived from the mysteries of personal chemistry. Such factors as political position and standing are part of this interaction, but do not alone explain the characteristic quality of a Cabinet.

The individual characters of a Cabinet fall into recognisable types:

- silent, relatively docile;
- articulate and reasoned but not necessarily decisive (Anthony Crosland perhaps);
- voluble and enthusiastic (Benn on Concorde, or the Harrier VTO jet, or electric cars, or giving 'one of his extraordinarily fluent tirades on democracy' (Castle 1980, p. 342);
- ideologues and keepers of the party conscience or manifesto, sometimes confused (Barbara Castle);
- departmentalists;
- optimists, known to themselves as realists;
- pessimists, known to themselves as realists (Jim Callaghan playing Jeremiah);
- leaders, usually including Prime Minister and Chancellor of the Exchequer; also some regarded less favourably as bullies (Denis Healey);
- peacemakers, creators of compromise, fixers, purveyors of common sense, the safe pair of hands (Whitelaw, Howe);
- the self-conscious role players, usually also diarists or memoir writers (Crossman, Castle, Wilson).

This list gives some indication of the working of the Cabinet: the quality of speakers; sources of ideas; approach. The composition of the Cabinet is related to its work and function. It is more than a collection of departmental ministers, but less than a superstrategic council; it is more than a collection of party politicians, but less than a group of statesmen and philosophers.

The nature of the political agenda

The political agenda has a substantial impact on the Cabinet, but it is not an agenda over which the Cabinet or the Prime Minister have much control. Most of it comes from the past or from the condition of national and international affairs. Some problems are worrying, time-consuming and insoluble (Northern Ireland is an obvious case). Other problems erupt into crises, requiring sudden, unplanned action. Even a prime minister who is said to have enlarged or renewed the agenda is for the most part tackling old problems with new policies (or new rhetoric).

Some part of this unplanned and unattractive agenda is inaccessible to most members of the Cabinet. Foreign affairs are left to the Prime Minister and the Foreign Secretary, except at times of crisis, when it may be too late to formulate or reformulate policy. Benn recorded for 16 December 1976: 'At Cabinet, Foreign Affairs, the first time Crosland had admitted there were Foreign Affairs for a long time', (1989, p. 688). Barbara Castle noted her discovery of the Government's Rhodesian policy while watching television (1984, p. 114, 8–17 April 1966). Defence matters are also likely to be beyond the Cabinet's reach: too technical, too secret or simply too important to national security to be submitted to collective decision. (The defence budget was as invulnerable as the agriculture support budget, whatever the government.)

Similarly, economic affairs are mostly dealt with by the Prime Minister, the Chancellor of the Exchequer, the Treasury and the Governor of the Bank of England, in an international context which is beyond national control. Decisions on public expenditure have to be negotiated with departmental ministers, but the decision process is normally now removed from the agenda of the Cabinet Council itself. Cabinet ministers lament the power of the Chancellor in effect to make policy for their departments. Barbara Castle complained: 'It really is ridiculous that the Chancellor should have the absolute power to interfere in the policies of other Ministers without consulting them'. She referred to the 'ingrowing arrogance to which all Chancellors after a certain time are prone' (1984, p. 241, 11 April 1967). Chancellors do not agree: for example, Butler was totally complacent about the independent power of Chancellors; Healey reacted angrily to interference.

This largely imposed and inaccessible agenda acquires a momentum from the urgency of the problems and the dynamics of the decision system. The effect of momentum could be seen in 1990 in the promotion of entry to the Exchange Rate Mechanism of the European Monetary System through summitry, the media and adversarial politics from an option requiring careful discussion to an inevitable act. This is a familiar technique by which a decision in principle is deferred, while making small practical decisions which anticipate and pre-determine the larger question of principle. Momentum is natural but it can also be enhanced by careful stage management. The whole business of British accession to the European Economic Community was managed in this way under Wilson (see Ponting 1989, p. 210). By contrast, Mrs Thatcher's vigorous stand against further and precipitate monetary integration with Europe, notably in the Autumn of 1990, showed a prime minister struggling to halt momentum – and finally swept away by it.

Time and pressure of work

Leaving aside the territorial claims and prerogatives of senior ministers, some policy questions are simply too difficult for the Cabinet. For example, on a discussion of Selective Employment Tax, Crossman reported, 'Nobody could quite follow what [the Chancellor] was saying, and he had the easiest time in the world' (Crossman 1975, p. 510, 2 May 1966).

Of course, ministers are not stupid, but some questions are highly technical (consider the European Monetary System or nuclear power issues), and time for briefing is short. Only three or four Cabinet Ministers will be adequately informed. In any case there is little time for serious attention to the huge amount of business facing a government. The 'Cabinet Council' has to be highly selective or hasty and superficial, or both, with selectivity somewhat erratic. Great issues may be decided in haste just before lunch (with the Prime Minister anxious to prepare for Question Time). Sometimes trivial issues may be debated at unjustified length (Barnett 1982, p. 103).

The work of the officials and departments

The Civil Service likes to send its ministers into battle perfectly briefed and fully armoured. This meticulous preparation and briefing of each member of the Cabinet by department officials, and of the Prime Minister by the Cabinet Office, reinforced by interdepartmental communication and negotiation, represents an unseen influence which shapes Cabinet discussion and decision. It is a conspiracy in the cause of good government. The provision of assistance and support to ministers confers on officials a substantial, but not determining, influence.

Management by the Prime Minister

Prime ministers control the Cabinet system, and within it, the Cabinet Council. This has been the case since the later nineteenth century when Gladstone and Disraeli established the sole right of the Prime Minister to summon a meeting of Cabinet. 'Within the confines of Cabinet tradition and subject to the advice of the Secretary to the Cabinet, it is the prime minister, and not the other members of the Cabinet, who controls the composition, structure and procedures of Cabinet (Burch 1988, p. 22). This is a central condition of government in Britain. The cabinet system is both the framework in which the Prime Minister must work, and an instrument of prime ministerial force. This question is taken up again after a fuller account has been given of the role of the Prime Minister.

The conduct of business

Room and seating

The Cabinet Room is a long, narrow room with windows overlooking Horse Guards Parade. It is dominated by a boat- or coffin-shaped table, designed to make it easy for every member of a Cabinet of about twenty to see and hear each other. The Prime Minister sits at the centre, looking out, with the Secretary of the Cabinet to his left. Ministers are arranged around the table according to seniority and standing, as assessed by the importance of the office and the favour of the Prime Minister. Despite the design of the table, ministers at the far ends may experience some difficulty in hearing all that is said, and more particularly in catching the eye of the Chairman. When the Cabinet meets at the House of Commons, as it does infrequently, the room used is too small for all members to sit at the table.

Agenda and papers

Meetings of the Cabinet are held once or twice a week on Tuesday and Thursday mornings in the two or three hours before lunch. The House meets at 2.30 pm and the Prime Minister, supported by members of the Cabinet, must be in his place for Prime Minister's Questions on those days. Under Mrs Thatcher the Cabinet met on Thursdays only. Callaghan made more frequent use of the full Cabinet for special purposes – in July 1976 to agree a package of measures to present to the IMF and in January 1979 to deal with the winter crisis.

The agenda of a Cabinet meeting is normally prepared two weeks in advance by the Prime Minister and the Cabinet Secretary with the help of the Leader of the House of Commons or another senior minister. The agenda includes foreign affairs and parliamentary business as a matter of routine, and this allows some scope for the raising by ministers of relevant matters not specified in the agenda.

The Prime Minister controls the agenda and may exclude matters from discussion; for example, Wilson excluded devaluation until 1967 (when it was forced on him) and Mrs Thatcher has at various times excluded matters on which, as she saw it, no alternative policy was acceptable. On the other hand, a minister may choose not to bring matters to Cabinet, though this may be risky. For example, Lord Carrington chose to deal with the Falklands without reference to Cabinet or Parliament. He recognised that debate would not have helped the Foreign Office policy of slow disinvolvement, but responsibility for what turned out to be a disaster could have been shared (see Case Note, Chapter 13).

Control of the agenda of Cabinet is without doubt a weapon in the hands of the Prime Minister, as it is of any chairman. For a minister on his own and without political clout there is difficulty in securing consideration of his concerns by Cabinet; and even Michael Heseltine, having both clout and supporters, was effectively blocked by the Prime Minister over Westland. A prime minister learns to gauge at what point opposition in Cabinet becomes unmanageable and requires concessions. For most cabinets and most prime ministers the threshold of unmanageability is quite high. In any case the Prime Minister can always deal with the matter elsewhere in the system, so that confrontation in the full Cabinet is infrequent.

Papers for a meeting of the Cabinet are normally sent out at least 48 hours beforehand. In emergencies this is not always possible. But these are not the only occasions when hard-pressed ministers take decisions without the benefit of reading the papers. Here is one good reason for not taking the simple view: Cabinet discussion, good, bilateral decision, bad!

Chairing

Harold Wilson wrote a good short guide to the proper chairing of the Cabinet:

> The normal procedure is for the Prime Minister to ask the minister tabling a paper to speak to it, and to be immediately followed by any other minister who has himself submitted a paper disagreeing with, qualifying or supplementing the first.
> The Prime Minister may then wish to indicate how the discussion should be handled and decisions taken. He may, for example, say that the question raises, say, three issues, and it might be helpful to discuss each separately, without prejudice to the decisions to be taken at the end. Or interim decisions on each of the three may be taken, and the viability of the package as a whole considered at the end, when it will be necessary to deal also with a fourth question, handling and presentation. Alternatively, particularly on a major or new issue, he might suggest that Cabinet begins with a 'second reading' debate (on the general principles), which enables members to make their set-piece contributions, which must be short, possibly raising fundamental and long-term issues. . . . Even with such cases, a great deal of preparatory work will have been done in clearing the ground and identifying points for decision at high-level Cabinet committee meetings, usually with the Prime Minister in the chair.
> It would be usual for the Prime Minister to open such a

discussion. On other issues, where papers had been submitted by departmental ministers, he would be unlikely to speak first, but would be ready to steer and guide the discussion to the point of taking the required decision.

... The Prime Minister must be ever-alert to issues which raise fundamental, doctrinal or almost theological passions on the part of one or more ministers, and do all he can to avert an unnecessary clash without sacrificing principle, and without fudging an issue on which a clear decision has to be reached, binding the Cabinet. ...
Above all, the Prime Minister must be ever-watchful of the political implications and dangers of a given course of action.

Summing-up is vital: it is the fine art of Cabinet government. The great improvement over the past thirty years is due not only to the style of Clement Attlee: the consistent improvement in the service provided by the Cabinet Secretariat is itself a guarantee of clarity.

(Wilson 1976, pp. 49–50, 55)

Wilson's guide offers sensible advice for the conduct of meetings. Those who exercise or suffer chairmanship will recognise that it is not always easy to put such advice into practice. In particular chairmen may be distracted or tired or bored, or over-committed to one point of view or one project or one member. Consistently effective chairing of meetings is not so easy, and the diarists of Wilson's Cabinet (and what a trial to the Chairman and other members they must have been) have testified that he occasionally fell below his own high standards.

The first rule of cabinet procedure is that the Prime Minister as Chairman directs the work, deliberations and conclusions of the Cabinet; procedurally he or she is in control. Ministers normally speak only by invitation of the Chair, but of course lively discussions generate spontaneity, hence interruptions and cross-talk. In any case, interruptions are difficult to stop, except in a very tightly controlled debate, and some ministers with political clout find it hard to keep silent in face of (what they see as) ill-informed and unreasonable remarks by their colleagues. Mrs Castle mentions Denis Healey as one who 'could never contain himself'.

The discussion, so far as may be judged, is as rational in content and tone as any other committee facing serious business and heavy responsibilities – no less and no more. Simple assertions of fact or faith are not very productive, but are made nevertheless. Argument backed by reason and evidence is respected. Clear, sharp, short speeches have a greater impact than rambles around the complexities of a subject; hence, Crosland's reputation, at least with Joel Barnett, as the minister who had 'the greatest impact on Cabinet decisions on most issues'. (Crosland, who had taught economics at Oxford, was good at exposition, and made his children prepare their requests to him in reasoned 'points'.) However, intellectual force alone may enhance Cabinet discussion but cannot ensure high-quality Cabinet decisions. The seven holders of Oxford Firsts in Wilson's 1964 Cabinet did not ensure good government. In the face of problems which are not open to intellectual solutions political weight and 'nous' still count.

Votes in Cabinet are unusual. The Prime Minister 'takes the voices' informally (making a judgement about the balance of opinion) or formally by going round the table. The latter procedure has the disadvantage for the Prime Minister that it shifts the decision to the members of the Cabinet, depriving the Chair of room for manoeuvre. Brown and Crossman complained to Wilson about open voting. 'Take the voices, then make up your own mind', George Brown said, with a generosity he might later have regretted (Crossman 1976, p. 80, 20 Oct. 1966). However, when a Cabinet is seriously divided and resolution is not urgent, the Prime Minister is likely to defer a decision rather than attempt to force one through a divided Cabinet.

Cabinet minutes are conclusions rather than a full record of discussion. For a major item, the conclusions will take the following form:

1. The Minister's proposal: the problem, how serious, options for dealing with it, the recommendation (based on the Minister's paper and his introductory remarks).
2. Main response from, say, the Chancellor, or a Minister responsible for an adjacent policy area, arguing for or against (again, a summary taken from the Minister's papers).
3. The debate: points made for and against, usually without attribution.
4. The Prime Minister's summing up: the balance of arguments, and the balance of opinion in the Cabinet, leading towards a recommendation.

5. The decision: a precise formulation of the Prime Minister's summing up.

Notes are taken by senior officials from the Cabinet Office, though the Cabinet Secretary is of course present. It is also usual for the Prime Minister's PPS to sit in the Cabinet room. These are normally the only officials present, and they are there for service, not advice; though clearly the Cabinet Secretary, sitting at the Prime Minister's side, is able to offer advice on procedure, in effect on the processing of the agenda. If the Cabinet's discussion moves into purely political matters, the Secretary ceases to take notes, and may indeed withdraw.

Hennessy records that Sir Burke Trend, as Cabinet Secretary, 'had an acute sense of the dividing line between the administrative and the purely political. If he judged that Cabinet discussion was moving from one to the other he would put down his pen, shut his notebook, put both his hands on the Cabinet table and make sure that the two other note-takers did likewise. Occasionally he would nod and all three would slip out of the room' (1989, pp. 216–7). The withdrawal of officials might occur, for example, if the Cabinet started to discuss the timing or tactics for the next election; or, as happened in November 1990, whether the Prime Minister should resign.

The minutes are written up by the Secretariat as an impersonal record of decisions, not of debate and division. The Cabinet Secretary, Sir John Hunt, told a select committee in 1977: 'The Cabinet Secretariat does not set out to angle the minutes, and, if we did, we would not get away with it . . . the job of the minutes and, above all, of the conclusions, is to reflect as much agreement as is there' (11th Report of Expenditure Committee, 1976–7, *Minutes*, Vol. II, pp. 75–7, 14 February 1977).

The Prime Minister does not participate in the drafting of the minutes (Wilson 1976, p. 56). In the strictest sense this is plausible. It is unlikely that the Prime Minister checks and corrects the draft of the minutes. But it is equally unlikely that the draft does not accurately represent what the Prime Minister had clearly indicated in his summing up (Wilson stresses the importance of this), or what he should have said if he had summed up correctly; and if the agenda has been properly prepared before the meeting, both Prime Minister and Secretaries will know roughly what kind of Minutes should emerge. It is good practice, not cynicism, for a chairman to have a draft of the desired conclusion in advance, in his head at least.

Some very sensitive matters (including national security and some economic and financial issues) are 'recorded elsewhere' (Castle 1984, p. 555). The formal recording of dissent is unusual, though ministers have sometimes complained that the minutes may give a misleading impression of agreement. The Cabinet is recorded as 'noting with approval' the Prime Minister's summing up, when in fact some members noted with heavy hearts and through clenched teeth . . . (see, for example, Benn 1989, p. 678). In January 1976 a Cabinet Committee was minuted as having agreed to the signing of the 'Radcliffe Declaration' (on ministerial memoirs) by all ministers. But this was not in fact agreed, and no minister ever signed the Declaration (Donoughue 1987, pp. 123–4).

'It is almost impossible to get the minutes changed, especially', wrote Barbara Castle, 'if the Prime Minister has an interest in the official version' (Castle 1980, p. 252). The Chairman says, the minutes are accurate, you are wasting time, let's get on with the agenda, the matter is in any case still open, or else it is closed. During the Westland crisis, Michael Heseltine succeeded in obtaining an apology and correction, but too late to help his cause. The Castle diaries indicate occasional attempts to re-open a question and reverse a previous decision – for example, by Callaghan in March 1967 (Castle 1984, p. 234). But note that Callaghan was a minister with clout, he may have threatened to resign, and expenditure decisions tend to be serial, that is, never quite concluded, always with scope for a little more or a little less – unless the Prime Minister insists as she did in the 1980s on firmer discipline.

The atmosphere of Cabinet, once it is called to order by the Chairman, is for the most part quite formal, in the sense of business-like rather than 'starchy'. Relaxation would be fun, and might help build consensus, but is time-consuming and inefficient. Ministers are usually addressed by office, not by name. Speeches are expected to be short, a few minutes only since the main points are set out in a paper. Mrs Thatcher favoured three to four minutes maximum, Lloyd George said a man making a five-minute speech is 'voted a bore straightway'; Wilson more expansively at a Chequers meeting allowed ten minutes, overrun by Mrs Castle to eighteen (Castle 1980, p. 484, 4 August 1975). Three or four ministers once ran a sweepstake on the length of a speech by Mrs Castle (Gordon Walker 1972, p. 108). Speeches indicating or celebrating agreement, adding nothing to the debate, are discouraged. (In Attlee's Cabinet a junior minister was exceptionally invited to attend to support a paper from his department. Attlee did not invite him to speak; he asked if any member had any question, there was none, and the minister was ushered out again, his first appearance in the Cabinet being entirely silent.)

A substantial part of the business of Cabinet is by its nature uncontroversial, or no longer controversial, since it has been 'pre-processed' within the system. As in most such bodies the choices are made in the end by a kind of half-prepared hunch. The evidence and arguments for alternative courses cannot be accurately weighed. But weightings come to be accepted, and 'a bias builds up for and against this programme and that'. A tide begins to flow. Ministers without strong views spot and ride the flowing tide. 'Rational argument has little to do with it' (Castle 1980, p. 481, 3 August 1975).

Mrs Castle found the atmosphere of Cabinet 'hypnotic' and 'paralyzingly anodyne' (1984, p. 301, 28 September 1967). 'Nobody who has not been in Cabinet can realize how difficult it is to use the sort of brusque arguments that are used regularly in the rough and tumble of politics outside' (ibid., p. 220). 'The whole procedure is designed to dull the political edge of argument. Politics seems particularly indecent in that almost disembodied atmosphere' (ibid., p. 119). Later she commented on a long speech by Wilson on devaluation: 'As he droned on no-one would have guessed that a major political drama was being played out – one never does at Cabinet' (ibid. p. 149). She particularly disliked 'those ghastly long Albert Hall-type meetings at which every member of the Cabinet speaks in turn and it takes three-quarters of an hour to get one item ventilated round the whole room' (Castle 1984, p. 417, 2 April 1968).

These comments are a little unfair. If Cabinets were as dull as that, her 1,500 pages of diary would be very boring indeed. In fact, Mrs Castle records some lively meetings of Cabinet, in which formality had to make way for vigorous argument based on strong political commitments and in some cases equally strong personal antipathies. Wilson's Cabinets were particularly heated at times, a consequence of able and 'heavy-weight' ministers facing acute and insoluble problems under inadequate control by the Prime Minister.

Barbara Castle recorded a scene at the end of a Cabinet in March 1968: 'the most unrestrained attack I have ever heard' by Callaghan. In recording an exchange between Callaghan and Roy Jenkins, the diarist uses such words as 'nastily', 'offensively', 'viciously', 'steely hate'; after which Roy and Jim 'outstared each other across the table'. This does not sound at all formal or anodyne. The Chairman, who had been making familiar complaints about leaks, had lost control of his meeting, but he had nothing to fear, for as Mrs Castle notes, 'there is going to be no united front there to oust Harold' (Castle 1984, p. 414, 29 March 1968; also see pp. 350-1 and, for example, Crossman 1977, p. 480, and Benn 1988, pp. 6-7). In the last stages of abandoning the 'In Place of Strife' proposals on industrial relations, Wilson is reported to have lost control of himself to the embarrassment of colleagues, threatening ministers 'in a hysterical way' (Crosland 1982, p. 204).

Mrs Thatcher's later Cabinets were probably less prone to open squabbling, and she kept a tighter control (at least after the first two years). But anger lurked there too. When Heseltine continued to criticise the proposal to abolish the GLC, Mrs Thatcher was provoked 'to deliver him one of the most violent rebukes I have ever witnessed in Cabinet' (Prior 1986, p. 150).

Apart from outbreaks of anger, formality also breaks down in the face of boredom or indifference. Ministers, not concerned with the item under discussion, get on quietly with other work, hoping not to be addressed by the Chair when not paying attention. The passing of notes, or polo mints, seems to be a favourite activity for relieving tedium, and even the Prime Minister and the Cabinet Secretary have been known to do this (Castle 1984, p. 314). The notes may contain serious or more likely malicious comment; or doggerel verse. Sir Geoffrey Howe is reported to have worked out in Cabinet, and passed to nearby colleagues, an anagram of the name of the African leader

Mugabe – E ba Gum (Prior 1986, p. 117). Cabinets do not normally enjoy coffee breaks; it may be that their introduction would be a most productive reform.

The Cabinet process: the conciliar mode

Most ministers have a strong departmental focus. They judge themselves, and believe they are judged by others, by their success in promoting the aspirations and policies of their department. This often means increasing the expenditure of their department. The department officials are strongly inclined to this view, confusing the public interest, or the interest of the Government as a whole, with the private interests of the department. Mrs Thatcher, when Secretary of State for Education, boasted of her success in acquiring and spending funds. Sir Keith Joseph was quite unusual, and regarded as odd, when he argued, as Secretary of State for Education, that higher expenditure on education was not required. Ministers who move from one department to another argue with conviction against a case they had previously supported. Denis Healey, moving from Defence to the Exchequer, instantly lost his enthusiasm for a defence role 'East of Suez'.

The departmental focus of about half of the Cabinet weakens its effectiveness in collective decision making. Departmental ministers 'fight their corner' against all comers, but also form alliances and make deals, usually in the pursuit of public spending. The Chancellor, always in the business of resisting expenditure, has to move in to make his own deals, and the department minister must consider how far he dare antagonise the Chancellor. Anthony Crosland, a steady proponent of public expenditure in theory, was checked by the prudent consideration that he might become Chancellor himself one day.

The Cabinet is in politics, not business. It is party political: in a 'good' sense concerned for political values and the building of consensus; and in a 'bad' sense given to partisanship, narrow sectarianism and an excessive concern for vote winning. There is no escape from this position in a democracy, nor should there be – though one may hope to minimise the damage.

The Cabinet as Council does not deal exclusively with major

policy, grand strategy and the making of history. The party's election manifesto gives a new government a substantial policy agenda, but one lacking in legislative and administrative detail. This will run out or be abandoned after a couple of years. Normally, policy development is a long-term matter, working slowly through the system and arriving at Cabinet only when already processed and requiring formal authorisation or clearance for legislation. A good deal of policy is necessarily made 'on the hoof', in response to events and the moves of others – crisis management rather than policy development. The Cabinet agenda is reactive rather than creative.

The Cabinet agenda may be divided into five overlapping categories:

1. Major policy: resolution of disagreements, and final authorisation.
2. External affairs: reporting of conferences, summits, negotiations.
3. Crisis-management, e.g. of a small war, a major strike, an oil spillage, a collapsing policy.
4. Matters of immediate political controversy or actual or expected political sensitivity. (In the Labour Cabinet of 1977 the question of direct elections to the EEC generated more heat than the fundamental issues of public expenditure.)
5. Comparatively trivial matters of keen interest to a member: the price of milk per gallon to producers (of some interest to farmer Callaghan), or the multi-fibre agreement (which affected a constituency interest in Lancashire). There may be some differences in the sensitivity of Cabinet. But Scotland, Wales and Northern Ireland are represented in the Cabinet, and a Labour Cabinet is likely to include representatives of the Midlands and Northern England.

There is an important distinction to be made between items on the agenda for report or registration and legitimation, and items for open discussion and decision. Thus Cabinet's dealings with foreign affairs are often at one remove, receiving reports 'ex post facto', too late to affect the course of negotiations and denied full information because of confidentiality. Similarly, economic policy may be discussed in general, but decisions on the Budget, and on exchange and interest rates, will be reported rather than submitted to Cabinet. On budget and currency matters Cabinet is notoriously consulted very late or not at all.

The proportions of these items in the Cabinet agenda are not known, and in any case the categories are imprecise and overlapping. However, it is clear that the Cabinet Council works unevenly; its agenda is carefully structured, but is easily disturbed and 'blown off course'.

Wilson's Cabinet spent a good deal of time on Rhodesia, and Wilson himself on Rhodesia and Vietnam. Heath's Cabinet spent more time on public-sector wage claims than any other issue. The 1974–9 Government was locked into internal battles over public expenditure, and external struggle with the trade unions. The problems of governing Northern Ireland, while never central to the national agenda, pressed on the Cabinet agenda at critical times.

The Prime Minister, as Chairman, can control the discussion to a rigid timetable, but at the cost of destroying all spontaneity and damaging consent. Harold Wilson's Cabinets appear from the published accounts to have been quite often open, free and spontaneous, but also shaped by the 'top-of-the-head' enthusiasm and anxieties of leading members including the Prime Minister himself. Attlee's Cabinets were by contrast well-disciplined, and not given to unnecessary talk. Mrs Thatcher's reputation as a dominant Prime Minister does not mean that her Cabinet meetings were always tightly controlled.

Anyone with experience of committee meetings (including academic ones) will recognise the difficulty of formal control. Major items notoriously are nodded through, especially at lunchtime; trivial matters unexpectedly generate lengthy argument; tensions and tempers flare unpredictably; opinion fluctuates and changes in ways which baffle explanation. Difficult business will routinely be passed to committees. Much of this mild chaos of committees is not discreditable in face of irreconcilable interests and insoluble problems. The Chairman's task is not always to stifle discussion and make rapid progress, but to 'ride' the tides and currents of opinion, building agreement and only sparingly imposing a decision before it is talked through.

If the Cabinet Council works in this way, then it is only in a formal sense the apex of the decision-making system and the highest court of policy-making appeal. For most of its work it operates as a net. The Cabinet 'net' is for receiving, halting and bouncing issues – imposing a stop or pause and sending them back into the system in another direction, at a different pace. The net may be loose or taut, gently catching or bouncing around and back. The objective of the Cabinet game is to get your policy 'into the net'. But of course the receptivity of the net is frequently changed, with the Prime Minister handling the crank which tightens the net.

6

The Cabinet as a System of Committees

The development of the committee system

The Cabinet is a system of committees and meetings, tied into the Cabinet itself (the Cabinet Council). The function and status of the Cabinet Council are a matter for debate – dominance, supervision, co-ordination, court of appeal and final authority? or just another rather large unwieldy committee? Older accounts emphasised the final authority of the Cabinet without saying much about the processing of decisions up to final authorisation. Recent accounts are less certain of the primacy of the Cabinet, both because the traditional view was misleading and because the role of the Cabinet has changed. The Cabinet Council has become one part of the Cabinet system – no less and no more – or so it may be argued. The Cabinet Council might be seen as the control tower of a large airport used by independent airlines. But the traveller hopes that the control tower sees and arranges all aircraft movement: in the case of the Cabinet this is not so!

The total Cabinet committee system includes both formal (or regular) and informal (or non-regular) meetings. Where two or three ministers are gathered together to discuss government business, that may be seen as a kind of informal Cabinet committee. But for a meeting to carry such status, two further conditions apply: the Prime Minister should know about it, and the Cabinet Secretariat should service and report it. Hence a

CABINET AS A SYSTEM OF COMMITTEES

meeting of ministers not to forward Cabinet business but to discuss the Prime Minister's defects (and perhaps to move to overthrow her) would not be an informal Cabinet committee. There is one case of a minister asking that a chance meeting on a train (in which he had made commitments he later regretted) be not regarded as a meeting at all. It is not sensible to regard completely informal and even chance meetings in the corridor or on the stairs as any kind of Cabinet committee – while accepting that such encounters can be helpful and conducive to advancing government business.

The distinction is important. The Cabinet committee system needs boundaries, so that meetings within the boundaries have some authority. The distinction arose in controversial form at the beginning of the Westland affair when Michael Heseltine protested that a particular meeting did not carry the authority of a Cabinet committee, and did not therefore bind him to its decisions.

Michael Heseltine's sense of grievance was understandable in the circumstances, and perhaps justified. In matters of keen dispute, sticking to correct procedures may be seen as fair to both sides; though it may also be seen on one side as delaying decision and action, and on the other as a useful tactic for protest. However, the distinction between formal and informal committees should not be used to degrade the informal further. Informal meetings are not part of the fully legitimated decision process, subject to collective responsibility. But they are nevertheless a necessary and useful part of decision making. No government has managed or is likely to manage its affairs without them. They are not an invention of Mrs Thatcher.

If we make no distinction between formal and informal, we can find Cabinet committees in the early eighteenth century when ministers, not always including the new-fangled 'prime minister', met together to discuss government business. In the formal sense, Cabinet committees originated in the mid-nineteenth century as *ad hoc* committees reporting to Cabinet, or responsible for legislation. The first permanent Cabinet committee was the Committee of Imperial Defence, established in 1903. Thus the informal had been transformed into the formal and regular.

The two world wars in the twentieth century had a major impact on central government. In 1914–18, particularly after

Lloyd George became Prime Minister in 1916, many more committees were set up including the small 'War Cabinet' itself. The Cabinet Office dates from this time too. Most committees were abolished at the end of the war, but between the wars there were standing committees on Imperial Defence, Home Affairs and Finance, and on average about twenty *ad hoc* committees. With the advent of war in 1939–45 the system was much expanded. This was part of what Hennessy calls 'Hitler's Reform'. In 1945 the Prime Minister, Attlee, established a system of Cabinet committees served by the Cabinet Office. Attlee had been Deputy Prime Minister during the war, and ranks with Lloyd George as a considerable reformer of central government.

The Cabinet committee system is more or less hidden from view, though recent ministerial memoirs have revealed the existence and working of committees, and Mrs Thatcher has on one occasion formally admitted to the existence of some committees. This secrecy is characteristic of British central government, but has some justification, in that it reinforces the responsibility of the whole (the Government or the Cabinet) rather than the part (the committee). Hence, in theory, it is not possible for the Prime Minister or other senior ministers to say: 'the X committee thought up this policy, it's nothing to do with us!' In practice, senior ministers, including the Prime Minister, do seem to say (in briefings to the press) something very like that. This points to a problem at the heart of British government: is the Government to be presented as a solid unit, or as fragmented, a coalition of people whose agreement is not total? The latter is (of course) true, but is regarded as politically damaging, so the committee system, along with much else that is part of the reality of government, is largely secret.

Despite the secrecy, we know a little about the committees. There are Standing Committees, including major committees concerned with Economic Strategy, Overseas and Defence Policy, Home and Social Affairs and Legislation. Mrs Thatcher admitted to the existence of these committees in a written reply in the House of Commons (4 July 1983). The first two were chaired by the Prime Minister, Home Affairs by the Deputy Prime Minister, and Legislation by the Leader of the House. A government may have 20 or so such Standing Committees. In addition there are likely to be 60–80 *ad hoc* committees. These are curiously code-named MISC or GEN for alternative governments. Some of these are sub-committees of the Overseas and Defence Policy Committee. The higher policy committees are for cabinet ministers only; others include non-cabinet ministers. Committees range in membership from about ten down to three or four.

Almost all of these committees are 'shadowed' by official committees, that is, committees of officials, which are often 'interdepartmental'. A few committees are 'mixed' (including officials and ministers), mainly in the fields of intelligence and emergency planning. Heath, when Prime Minister, deliberately made much use of such committees. However, the advantage of direct official advice and expertise is offset by the reluctance of officials to disagree with their own minister in his presence.

Such modesty notwithstanding, official committees are regarded by most observers as exercising substantial influence. Officials possess all the usual advantages of professional expertise and experience. They can also exploit their connections to establish the basis of an interdepartmental deal which blocks the aspirations of individual ministers. Both Crossman and Castle have complained of this official 'frameworking' of decision (to coin an apt term). Mrs Castle said she had believed that ministers considered their priorities in the light of their political programme, made decisions and 'refer[red] these decisions to an official committee to work out the administrative implications . . . But 'I was soon disabused of that. . . . The official net is terrific, the political net is non-existent . . . I was never allowed to take anything to cabinet unless it had been processed by the official committee. In the official committee the departments had all their interdepartmental battles . . . and having struck their bargains they then briefed their Ministers on it, and so at Cabinet meetings I suddenly found I wasn't in a political caucus at all. I was faced by departmental enemies' (*The Sunday Times*, 10 June 1973, quoted in Headey 1974, p. 120).

The Cabinet committee system has flourished since 1945. Attlee appointed altogether 461 committees (313 *ad hoc*) in six and a quarter years; Churchill, 246 in three and a half years (109 *ad hoc*). Wilson in his second administration set up 120 *ad hoc* groups in two years, Callaghan 160 *ad hoc* groups in three years.

It looks, then, as if an average post-war government established about 50 *ad hoc* committees a year. By contrast, Mrs Thatcher in the 1980s thinned out the committees, just as she slimmed down meetings of the Cabinet itself. In 1985 Peter Hennessy counted 150 committees over six and a half years – a sharp change from Attlee. 'Without doubt', Hennessy concludes, 'Mrs Thatcher is running the slimmest Cabinet machine since before the Second World War' (Hennessy 1989, p. 311). This fits Mrs Thatcher's general approach to her office: firm conviction, rapid 'knockdown argument', leading to decision and action. However, it must be emphasised that Mrs Thatcher developed a system which was already in place.

Mrs Thatcher went further than her predecessors, but all modern prime ministers have transacted a substantial amount of business in committee (and no prime minister has dispensed entirely with the full Cabinet). Barbara Castle provides one of many illustrations. In July 1974 she complained that Harold Wilson's 'Cabinet – and particularly Harold – is in the mood these days to settle everything in committee, so Cabinets get shorter and shorter and the discussions on major policy items more perfunctory'. Rebutting criticism of a procedure which required ministers to brief themselves fully, the Prime Minister had interrupted to say she should not assume colleagues had not read their papers (1980, p. 158).

Cabinet committees play in the following four modes:

1. As sub-committees, subordinate to Cabinet and reporting to it.
2. As substantially autonomous, developing a policy or a decision which they may expect will be legitimised by Cabinet.
3. As an instrument of the Prime Minister.
4. As a channel for official advice and influence.

The diarists of Harold Wilson's Cabinets show that Cabinet committees play in all four modes, depending on the issue, the personalities and the political situation. Cabinet committee meetings are more relaxed than those of the full Cabinet. One Cabinet Secretary said it was like playing on your own club ground rather that at Twickenham (Hennessy 1989, p. 214); but the presence of civil servants (unless specifically excluded) imposes some discipline. Many of the cabinet committee meetings recorded by Barbara Castle and Richard Crossman included open, sometimes lively and heated discussions, often chaired by the Prime Minister, but not dominated by him. Such meetings seemed to occur most naturally and frequently when the Government faced a critical problem, not open to easy or agreed solutions – economic policy, prices and incomes, trade union reform, Rhodesia. But Wilson's Cabinets were notable for including five or six senior ministers who carried substantial political 'clout'. It was not politically possible for Wilson constantly to exclude them or deny them a voice in policy making.

The Prime Minister and the committee system

Even so, the Cabinet committee system is for most of the time an instrument in the hands of the Prime Minister, and a major element in the development of prime ministerial control. First, the committee system is by its nature exclusive. The major committees are the preserve of senior ministers, an inner circle of heavies and (to some extent) trusties. Hennessy records two instances of the distress of the excluded:

1. Seasoned Cabinet minister walks into the Commons tea room late on a Thursday morning. 'What are you doing here?' asks a Tory backbencher. 'I thought you'd still be in Cabinet.' 'Cabinet?' replied the Minister. 'Oh, we don't have those any more. We have a lecture by Madam. It's government-by-Cabinet-committee now. Half the decisions I read about in the newspapers.'

   (Hennessy 1986, p. 99)

2. One Cabinet minister, a member of the Economic Strategy Committee but not of this most secret inner group, which was meeting straight afterwards, was a bit slow to gather his papers. As he was about to leave, Sir Geoffrey Howe, then Chancellor of the Exchequer, launched into his paper on the plan to abolish exchange controls. 'Oh', says the laggardly minister, 'are we going to do that? How very interesting.'

Embarrassed silence. Then Sir Geoffrey says, 'X, I'm afraid you should not be here.' X departs Cabinet door left.

(Hennessy 1986, pp. 101–2)

Second, the system requires a manager – to appoint, select chairmen, determine agenda and arrange the reporting and progressing of outcomes. Such responsibilities, and their related power of control, fall most easily and naturally to the Prime Minister. The powers of the chairman, appointed by the Prime Minister when not the Prime Minister himself, are formidable. Barbara Castle noted with dismay an episode in which the chairman of a sub-committee on devolution brushed aside a revolt by members, saying simply that the matter would go to the Prime Minister's committee 'without comments' (Castle 1980, p. 693, 17 March 1976).

Third, the system is productive, and most decisions taken by the committee will not be undone in tbe Cabinet Council itself – either because it is freely recognised that the conclusions of the committee are soundly based and broadly acceptable, and/or because there is no time, and it is too late, to re-open the matter, and/or because it is regarded as procedurally improper to appeal to the full Cabinet. Indeed it would be absurd, a denial of the whole purpose of the system, if decisions were frequently appealed to Cabinet. The Cabinet itself guards its authority, but still has a concern for an effective committee system, and no wish to act as a court of appeal, where its interests and sympathies are not engaged.

On this matter Wilson wrote: 'On the question of "appeals" to Cabinet, a tendency developed in the 1960s for a defeated minister almost automatically to seek for a rerun at Cabinet, even if he was in a minority of one. This threatened to congest the work of Cabinet, and to weaken the authority of the committees and their chairmen. I had to direct – and make public – that no appeal to Cabinet could hope to succeed unless it had the backing of the chairman of the committee. Under any government, committee chairmen are experienced ministers who have enough nous to know when, for administrative or political reasons, the matter should be taken higher, irrespective of their own views on the decision reached' (Wilson 1976, pp. 65–6).

Fourth, the system is supported most of the time by senior

ministers since they are more often included than excluded, since they win sometimes and may hope to win more often, and since they are relieved of participation across the whole range of government business. Of course, ministers are not consistent in their support of the committee system. For example, Mrs Castle can be found on one occasion delighted that a unanimous committee decision affecting her department would not be taken to Cabinet by the Prime Minister; and on another occasion complaining that the Chancellor of the Exchequer was introducing orally (without a paper) proposals for £250 million of public expenditure approved by a Cabinet committee (Castle 1980, p. 361).

Gordon Walker, writing both as an academic student of government and as a former Cabinet minister, argued that there was in Wilson's first administration what he called a 'partial Cabinet', in effect part of the Cabinet which 'acted for a time as if they were the Cabinet' and carried its full authority.

> Typically a partial Cabinet is different from an inner Cabinet in that it is an organized part of the Cabinet system. Typically a partial Cabinet is a standing or ad hoc committee presided over by the Prime Minister, which may – in matters of great moment and secrecy – prepare policies in detail and sometimes take decisions without prior consultation with the Cabinet as a whole. The Cabinet is in due course informed and consulted. The partial Cabinet depends upon a distinction among members of the Cabinet that is analogous to the arrangements for the distribution of Foreign Office telegrams.
>
> (Gordon Walker 1972, p. 88)

Gordon Walker's 'partial Cabinet' reflects his general view of the standing of Cabinet committees. He refers to a new principle in the Cabinet system: namely that a Cabinet committee was parallel to and equal with the Cabinet. Within its jurisdiction and subject to possible reference to the Cabinet, a committee's conclusions had the same force and authority as those of the Cabinet itself (1972, p. 41). He argues that partial Cabinets, but not prime ministerial government, 'have become an accepted and established part of the Cabinet system' (1972, p. 91).

The examples of partial cabinets given by Gordon Walker relate only to issues of national security and the conduct of war.

It is unlikely that in the long term the authority of Cabinet can be regularly delegated to one committee (and Gordon Walker seems in his longer definition to agree). The idea of a partial Cabinet does not appeal to excluded ministers, and it is not surprising that such a marked constitutional change has not been accepted, except in special circumstances (most recently by the Falklands War Cabinet).

The committee system is in the hands of the Prime Minister, but it also strengthens the Cabinet as a collective instrument of government. The Prime Minister can use this instrument to secure his or her own ends, but cannot totally escape from the collective embrace of the system. This is why Gordon Walker sees the partial Cabinet as a denial of prime ministerial government. Similarly, Wilson was not a 'prime ministerialist' in his understanding of the office. He argues strongly against what he calls the 'facile' views of the Crossman 'confrontation' school, that the committee system strengthens the Cabinet as a whole. The argument is persuasive. Wilson was an experienced prime minister who had thought more than most senior politicians about what he calls 'governance', and his judgement is set in the context of an account of how the system actually works. He wrote:

> ... it is fanciful to suggest that by these means [the use of committees] the Prime Minister's power is enhanced at the expense of that of the Cabinet. For one thing, it would be extremely difficult for even a megalomaniac prime minister (who would not last long) to plan to set aside an agreed, or substantially agreed, decision of a powerful committee consisting of seven or eight of his Cabinet colleagues. His role is to see that the committee system, as an indispensable part of the Cabinet machine, works satisfactorily – by delegating enough to the committee and giving them authority, but also by being sufficiently politically and administratively sensitive to know when to respond to an appeal by a dissatisfied minority, or to spot the case that ought to go straight to Cabinet. But when this is what he decides he must make this clear in advance, not weaken counsel and the standing of his ministerial colleagues by invoking Cabinet to reverse a decision they have taken.
>
> (Wilson 1976, p. 65)

Thus for Wilson the committee system itself is broadly neutral in relation to the distribution of power; it all depends on how the system is used. But in practice it is a powerful instrument available to the Prime Minister for the management of policy making. *paradoxical argument to previous.*

An account of a committee meeting

NB: DEFINING POLITICS!

Politics is a disputatious business. Politicians (mostly) hold strong views, struggle to advance them, and are skilled (or experienced anyway) in the arts of competitive advocacy. It is neither surprising nor discreditable that politicians fight among themselves. So there is some sense in the conflict and conspiracy model of Prime Minister and Cabinet relations: there is no friendship at the top, as Lloyd George said. Nevertheless, a fair amount of Cabinet business is not highly controversial, and is simply work to be shifted. Joel Barnett's account of Cabinet committees (mainly on public expenditure) shows meetings dominated by entrenched departmental positions and official briefs. He recalls an instance of a minister reading out 'I agree with the Chief Secretary', unaware that the Chief Secretary had reversed his position overnight. On other occasions, he reports, ministers sided with their political allies, without much regard for the specific issues. Barnett does concede that sometimes a case might be decided on its merits, or on the quality of the arguments.

Such accounts of Cabinet committees are of course much influenced by the objectives of the reporter. Barbara Castle was a departmental minister with a concern both for her department and the broad political objectives of the Labour Party, and with a proper regard for her own place in the Government. Barnett, as Chief Secretary, was responsible for the control of public expenditure, and naturally expressed little confidence in a system which seemed to give him little support against marauding and extravagant departmental ministers.

Here is an extract from his account of a Cabinet committee:

> When all the preliminary lobbying has been done, the Cabinet Committee discussion itself rarely changes Ministers' minds. Often, the senior Cabinet Minister cannot attend personally, and sends a

junior Minister who is not able to move from his Department's view. Even when senior Ministers attend themselves, as they normally do on major issues, it is not often possible to make them change their position. . . . On complex issues, Cabinet Committees are just about the worst possible way of arriving at sensible decisions. Ministers would come to the meetings with long briefs prepared by officials who had been members of the appropriate Official Committee which 'shadowed' the Ministerial Committee. In fact, 'shadowed' is an inappropriate term, for the Official Committee, after carrying out the detailed analytical work intended only to set out the options for Ministers, usually left their Ministers in no doubt whatsoever as to which was the best option – the one they recommended.

(Barnett 1982, p. 27)

In most cases, the Ministers most directly involved had either read the brief late the previous night, or started to do so as the argument proceeded. More often than not . . . they would follow the line of the brief.

(Barnett 1982, pp. 40–1)

Informal committees

Aside from the standing and *ad hoc* groups which make up the formal Cabinet system, beyond the code-named MISC and GEN Committees, are the informal groups put together by the Prime Minister for particular purposes. They are for the most part task-oriented groups working directly for the Prime Minister. These groups are doubly secret in that their existence is not usually made known, even to other ministers, though normally Private Secretaries at least will be present to take a note. This is not part of the official record of Cabinet proceedings. Three of the more substantial kinds of informal committee are discussed below.

Inner Cabinets *Sometimes used by PMs*

Inner Cabinets have no clear constitutional standing and are difficult to define. Typically, an Inner Cabinet is a group of Cabinet ministers called on by the Prime Minister with some regularity (not always in a meeting of the whole group) to advise on policy and conduct the business of government. Most prime ministers use something like an Inner Cabinet from time to time.

Wilson used what he called a Parliamentary Committee and then a Management Committee (1968–70) to tie in some (not all) of his senior ministers. It was intended that the meetings of the Management Committee be attended by the Cabinet Secretary but not reported to Cabinet. Ministers who were members liked such Inner Cabinets, but it does seem that there was uncertainty about their proper role and function.

In certain circumstances, notably war and the threat of war, the Inner Cabinet may act as a surrogate or partial Cabinet, in Gordon Walker's meaning. But otherwise the Inner Cabinet is defined by its complement of heavies and trusties, and shades by membership into a kitchen Cabinet, or by specificity of task into a series of *ad hoc* Cabinet committees. Inner Cabinets tend to break down because excluded ministers resent the privileges of the members, and re-assert those of the Cabinet as a whole.

The Inner Cabinet found favour with some Cabinet reformers before the full development of the committee system was recognised. There are several justifications offered:

1. It is suitable by its size and concentration of selected senior ministers to review and decide on major strategy, meeting more frequently, or at greater length, or less formally.
2. It can more easily rise above the pressures of the spending departments (but major spenders may be members, and if they are not, and know about it, they will not be content).
3. The membership can be arranged to strengthen the Prime Minister's position, notably by excluding his enemies. The inner Cabinet is more collective than fragmented bilaterals, and so may serve both Prime Minister and Cabinet better.
4. It is likely to be more leakproof than the full Cabinet (fewer members equals fewer potential leakers). Leaks are disliked because they may discredit the Prime Minister, alert opposition within the Government, and abort the policy.

The true inner Cabinet is distinct from a kitchen Cabinet because it is ministerial, but Wilson mixed them occasionally. Tony Benn records a meeting on 22 July 1967 at Chequers attended by five ministers, plus Wilson's Political Secretary (Marcia Williams), Press Officer (G. Kaufman) and Special

Adviser (T. Balogh). The meeting discussed devaluation, which at that time was not on the agenda of the full Cabinet. Benn commented tolerantly 'I think every prime minister probably has to operate like that' (1987, p. 508). The status of such a meeting is of course quite different from Gordon Walker's more formal 'partial cabinet'.

None of Wilson's arrangements seemed to work satisfactorily or for long, since excluded members of the full Cabinet insisted on knowing what was going on, and wanted to take part. But in a more extended and fragmented system of *ad hoc* committees and informal meetings, partial and inner cabinets fade into the background. No-one – except the prime minister presumably – can keep track of the system.

Economic committee or seminar

Both James Callaghan and Mrs Thatcher have used a special group to deal with the more sensitive aspects of economic policy, including exchange and interest rates. This group was not a normal Cabinet committee (hence the seminar label). The membership was wider, but carefully selected. Under Callaghan, this group included, as well as the Prime Minister, the Chancellor and Harold Lever (Chancellor of the Duchy of Lancaster), representatives of the Bank of England, the Treasury, the Cabinet Office, the No. 10 Policy Unit and Private Office, and the Head of the CPRS.

Hennessy comments: 'The Cabinet's salad days as the key economic forum were past. But the Treasury's did not return.' He quotes Callaghan: 'I liked to hear what they all had to say . . . and try to weigh up what were the different views they had. All very helpful to me. . . .' (from a broadcast interview, 1986). Hennessy concludes: 'Callaghan made it all sound matey and almost routine. But it was more than that – it was a skilful manifestation of an old pro bringing ancient satrapies to heel. It was also highly secret (Hennessy 1989, p. 260). The existence of the group was probably unknown outside its membership. The seminar, by whatever label, was an instrument of prime ministerial dominance at the very centre of economic policy making.

Healey, the Chancellor, saw the group naturally from a

different point of view. 'It proved useful at least in keeping No. 10 informed on what I was doing.' He adds: 'We never had the sort of public argument between prime minister and Chancellor which proved so damaging to market confidence during the Thatcher Government' (Healey 1989, p. 450).

Under Mrs Thatcher the economic seminar continued, eventually dropping the name. It dealt with similar subjects, with a shifting membership – 'an amoeba-like group' says Hennessy, and quotes 'an insider' saying, 'It's a habit of working, not an approach' (Hennessy 1989, p. 313). It is clear at this point that the informal groups may be better perceived as part of a shifting decision-making process than as solid institutions of government.

Most ministers would accept that such secret inner councils are necessary, even though they derogate from Cabinet government. David Howell, a minister dismissed by Mrs Thatcher and no admirer of her prime ministerial style, seemed in this exchange with Hennessy to concede the value of such groups: '. . . the nexus of any government in this country is No. 10 and the Treasury and with the Bank of England as the Treasury's appendage. . . . Cabinet government is only a layer of government and there is a kind of inner Cabinet government, whether it's called that or not, under different prime ministers, it always tends to develop. On top of that there must be an even more inner kind of government concerned with very very sensitive issues of which exchange control is one. It would have been inconceivable for exchange control to be tossed around and knocked around in Cabinet' (Hennessy 1989, pp. 315–16).

Prime ministerial decision groups

These are groups called together by the Prime Minister to resolve a problem, develop a policy, or come to a decision. For example, Barbara Castle reported that Harold Wilson wanted to make progress on her White Paper on Industrial Relations (1969) but was afraid of leaks, which would certainly arouse opposition. 'He is therefore scrapping the ministerial committee set up and intends to call just three or four Ministers together as soon as possible under his chairmanship to discuss my White Paper. From there it will go straight to Cabinet' (1984, p. 566, 4 December 1968).

We know that a similar procedure was used to consider and reject Michael Heseltine's proposals for a vigorous (and expensive) programme for the Inner Cities in 1981. Following Heseltine's work in Merseyside, he had prepared a minute under the title 'It Took a Riot' advocating such a programme and he actively campaigned for it. The Prime Minister's group rejected the proposal. Heseltine could have taken the issue to Cabinet, but knew he would lose there too. This is an interesting demonstration that the procedures of Cabinet, and its collectivity, are determined in the end by the political balance within the Cabinet and the determination of the Colleagues, as well as by the choice of the Prime Minister.

Hennessy calls this group 'a loaded ministerial group', and that may indeed indicate a strategy implicit in some such meetings. He describes the normal pattern under Mrs Thatcher in this way. 'The Prime Minister asks a minister to prepare a paper just for her, not for the Cabinet or a Cabinet Committee. . . . The minister is summoned to No. 10 with his back-up team. He sits across the table from Mrs Thatcher and her team which can be a blend of people from Downing Street Private Office, the Policy Unit, the Cabinet Office and one or two personal advisers. She then, in the words of one insider, proceeds to "act as judge and jury in her own cause"' (Hennessy 1989, p. 314).

Mrs Thatcher was concerned with the product rather than the process of decision making, and not much interested in the institutional structure. In consequence she was not interested in meetings for their own sake. (By contrast, Harold Wilson liked meetings for their own sake, but believed, correctly, that they were very leaky). Nor did Mrs Thatcher appreciate paper work, though she was good at it. Mrs Thatcher differed from some of her predecessors in her approach to the office of prime minister. But for all prime ministers the business of government is pushed forward for the most part outside Cabinet – by minute, bilateral conversation and by telephone. 'A great deal of business is . . . carried out by inter-Ministerial correspondence; [almost always] copied to, say, half-a-dozen other Ministers, or to the rather larger number of Ministers who make up a Cabinet committee, or to all the members of the Cabinet. The photo-copier is nowadays both literally and figuratively an essential element in the machinery of government' (Pliatzky 1982, pp. 36–7). All that

CABINET AS A SYSTEM OF COMMITTEES 85

activity is tied into, even underpinned by, Cabinet as a structure of institutions and procedures. But that structure should not be confused with the business of government.

The most significant and most continuous prime ministerial decision group is the immediate entourage of the Prime Minister, whether or not organised as partial, inner or kitchen Cabinet, the inner group of 'heavies and trusties' plus some officials and advisers closest to the Prime Minister, with whom major issues are discussed (and even agreed). This closet entourage may support or usurp the Cabinet committees, and exert a heavy influence on the Cabinet Council itself. It will be further discussed when considering the Prime Minister.

Part III
The Executive Centre

Introduction: The Central Executive Territory and the Executive Centre

Prime minister and Cabinet do not exist as isolated pinnacles of British government. They exist in the Central Executive Territory of British government. The two sets of officials and advisers making up the Prime Minister's Office and the Cabinet Office might best be referred to as the Executive Centre.

Number 10 includes about 30 senior officials and advisers, the Cabinet Office about 35. There are just over 100 ministers of all ranks. Senior officials in the departments number 200 or so, with another 200 to 300 involved in high policy making (these figures are necessarily approximate). So altogether there are between 400 and 600 politicians and officials concerned at the highest level with government policy making. In the USA the Executive Office of the President includes in total about 3,000; and in France, 700.

The inhabitants of the Central Executive Territory may be ordered into a diagram but the simplicities of the diagram do not represent the complexities of the relationships. For example, it seems reasonable to place the Prime Minister in the centre, but it is less clear whether the Prime Minister should be seen as enclosed by, or apart from, and superior to, the Cabinet. Similarly, the place of officials (civil servants) is problematic, though there is no doubt that they belong in the Centre, and exercise significant influence.

GOVERNMENT: CENTRAL EXECUTIVE TERRITORY

The Executive Centre in Britain does not have the formal identity of the Executive Office in the USA. There is no door marked Executive Centre, though the new iron gates at the entrance to Downing Street might plausibly carry such a nameplate. The famous door of 10 Downing Street, apparently the entrance to a private, gentleman's residence, gives access to a substantial part of the Executive Centre. This charming deception – an exercise in the domestication of power – might be regarded as characteristic of the British Constitution. If the Executive Centre inhabited a clearly identifiable building (like Parliament) it could more easily be perceived as an institution. Without a concrete embodiment, the Executive Centre survives, indeed prospers, as a concept and a working arrangement.

In institutional terms the Territory comprises:

1. A structure, with qualities of order and even rigidity, and a capacity to restrain and shape.
2. A network, of interrelating parts, with good internal lines of communication, and its own codes.
3. An arena or territory, in which groups struggle for occupation and advantage, construct trenches and fortifications and dig last ditches. A fog of battle hangs over the scene, and there is some uncertainty about the identity of the enemy.

The battlefield metaphor is attractive but misleading. The Central Executive Territory has serious governmental functions which are more complex than the imperatives of war, despite similarities of language. At the same time the Territory cannot be understood without recognising that its comparative informality opens its professional relationships to all the pressures inherent in human relationships, notably pride, envy, jealousy, ambition – and a few more.

The work of the Central Executive Territory comprises:

1. Policy development, especially in the areas of national security, management of the economy, and public expenditure.
2. Decision taking, and crisis management.

3. The resolution of conflict within the Centre and the Government.
4. Co-ordination of policy and oversight of its implementation.
5. The building of consent in Parliament and among the people.

These functions reflect the highest responsibilities of the Government for the security and welfare of the nation, to be served with strategic vision and purpose. But they also reflect the everyday and brutal realities of the pressures on government – to manage the immediate crisis, resolve overt conflict, and serve the overriding goal of winning the next election.

The Downing Street complex

At the heart of the Central Executive Territory is a small collection of units and offices centred on No. 10 Downing Street and the Cabinet Office. It comprises the Cabinet Office (including the Cabinet Secretariat, but also scientific, statistical and historical sections), and the Prime Minister's Office (including the Secretariat, but also the Policy Unit, the Efficiency Unit, the Press and Political Offices). This complex fills a gap which existed in the nineteenth century. Before Lloyd George, prime ministers enjoyed very little assistance beyond two or three Private Secretaries. In particular the work of the Cabinet was badly serviced, and its decisions notoriously ill-recorded. (After a meeting of Gladstone's Cabinet in 1882 two ministers agreed they did not know what had been decided, but thought there must have been some decision, as John Bright had resigned!)

The Downing Street complex dates back to 1916, when Lloyd George established a Cabinet Secretariat (for 'servicing' the Cabinet) and a 'Garden Suburb' of huts housing support staff and advisers for the Prime Minister. Between the wars the Secretariat survived, but the Garden Suburb was replaced by civil servants. In 1940 Churchill brought back a personal staff of advisers headed by Professor Lindemann and specialising in statistics and charts (though offering general advice too). This arrangement ended in 1945. An Economic Planning Staff began to develop under Attlee, but Cripps took it to the Treasury. All prime ministers, except Attlee, also had a circle of confidants, or 'friends'.

Both Wilson and Heath approached high office with deliberation. Planning came into fashion. Heath, as Leader of the Opposition, established a group of retired civil servants to examine the problems of support for the Prime Minister. Out of this initiative and Wilson's reformist drive there grew the Civil Service Department, the Prime Minister's Policy Unit and the Central Policy Review Staff. Of these only the Policy Unit has survived, and that seems to be the one substantial gain. Indeed, a characteristic of the Downing Street complex has been that it is subject to frequent change in structure, personnel and, to some extent, function. Thus it shares in the famed flexibility of the British Constitution. The flexibility is largely at the choice of the Prime Minister, and is an element in prime ministerial power.

The main changes in the Central Executive Territory over the last three decades include the following:

1. The Macmillan reforms following the Plowden Report: the functions which had been carried out by one, and then two, Permanent Secretaries were divided between three Permanent Secretaries, heading the Cabinet Office, Treasury and Civil Service (Cabinet Office and Civil Service responsibilities were later re-united, but the crucial separation was between Treasury and Cabinet Office).
2. The establishment of the prime ministerial Policy Unit (1974).
3. The establishment and later abolition of the CPRS (1970 and 1983).
4. The establishment and later abolition of the Civil Service Department (1968 and 1981).
5. The establishment of an Efficiency Unit (1979).
6. An increase in the number of special advisers to ministers.
7. Considerable movement in and out by prime ministerial advisers and friends.

These changes in the Central Executive Territory, and in particular the rapid development of the Downing Street complex, reflect the concern of two Prime Ministers, Wilson and Heath. Both were former civil servants, fascinated by the structure and procedures of government. Wilson had established the Fulton Committee on the Civil Service, and claimed the authority of its report for his appointment of policy advisers and, later, formation of the Policy Unit (Wilson 1976, p. 98) as well as the establishment of the Civil Service Department. Heath was concerned that Cabinet should be able to take strategic decisions. He issued his own statement on 'The Reorganisation of Central Government', reorganised some departments into 'giant departments', and established the CPRS. Thus there was some deliberation and purpose in the development of the core executive. It was not based on passing whim or fancy, but in detail it was 'made up as we went along'. One factor which drove its early development was technological – the need for the Prime Minister to have continuing access to a secure system of global communication. Wilson claimed Number 10 had the best telephone switchboard in London (1976, p. 81) – an interesting case of technology influencing structure.

There is more certainty about the location of the core executive: in the area between 10 Downing Street, Whitehall and Horse Guards Parade. Number 10 itself is justly celebrated as the gentleman's town house which is the historic residential office of the British chief executive. It is in fact a large house and a mansion behind it, knocked together and making altogether 160 rooms on five floors. This 10 Downing Street complex communicates with the neighbouring residence of the Chancellor of the Exchequer (No. 11), the Chief Whip (No. 12) and with the Cabinet Office, which has its main entrance in Whitehall. Number 10 has a fine staircase and some magnificent state rooms, as well as a flat, offices and bedrooms. It is equipped as a major government communication centre. Staff work whatever hours are required, and there are facilities for sleeping and modest eating on the premises. About a hundred people, mostly secretaries, policemen and messengers earn their living behind the famous door. It remains in size, style and atmosphere a house. This is significant for the working of the Prime Minister's side of the core executive – facilitating, though not guaranteeing, close working relations between advisers, civil servants and prime minister.

At the same time, the house sets a physical limit to the expansion of the Prime Minister's entourage. The Number 10 complex is significantly smaller than the space available to most chief executives. Leo Pliatzky comments: 'the time to worry about our going over to a Presidential system will be when a British prime minister decides to build a White House or an Elysée Palace' (Pliatzky 1989, p. 11).

7
The Cabinet Office

Development and structure

Number 10 Downing Street connects by a broad passage and a locked green baize door to the Cabinet Office. The locked door (to which the Cabinet Secretary and the Prime Minister's Principal Private Secretary have keys) emphasises the distinctiveness and integrity of the position of the Prime Minister. The Cabinet Office, with a total staff of 750 or so, overflows into the Old Treasury Building. It is in all but name a Department of State.

The Cabinet Office is at the very centre of the Executive Territory. It is the engine room of British government; the motive power is mainly political, but the officials of the Cabinet Office tend the engines. They also provide and service the Chart room, where the course of the ship can be chosen and mapped. The metaphor is attractive, for it allows that there is a captain on the bridge crying 'full steam ahead!' and down below the engineers and navigators can only complain about the oil pressure and the icebergs.

The maritime metaphor is helpful to understanding, but not very precise. It is tempting to stress the new importance (and that is not a precise word either) of the Cabinet Office by some adaptation of Richard Crossman's well-known statement on prime ministerial government: 'The post-war epoch has seen the final transformation of Cabinet and prime ministerial Government into Cabinet Office Government. Under this system prime minister follows Cabinet into the "dignified" part of the Constitution . . .' (Essay writers in a hurry, please read on!) (Crossman 1963, p. 51, and adapted by the author).

This is not the case. The search for a single location of power in British government is vain. But it does seem reasonable to say that since the 1970s the Cabinet Office has developed as a major department for central policy capability, to some extent diminishing, but not displacing, the Treasury. It is not a prime minister's department, but it provides the support for a more strongly prime minister-driven government.

The Cabinet Office includes the Office of the Government's Chief Scientist and a historical and a statistical section, but the main part of the Cabinet Office, which is engaged in policy-support functions, is the Cabinet Secretariat. This includes about 35 senior staff (Assistant Secretary and above). The pace and scale of change can be appreciated by reference to the number of postings to the office from the departments. This ran between 1945 and 1964 at about 8–10 each year on average, but rose in the 1970s to an average of about 30 each year. (Lee 1990, pp. 238–9). These officials are 'high-fliers' for whom the Cabinet Office is now an alternative to the Treasury as a training ground and launch pad. They are 'on loan' to the Cabinet Office; secondment is preferred because it is not intended that the Cabinet Office should have policies of its own. They claim to acquire a loyalty to the Cabinet Office, but clearly their function and value depend on their contribution to the 'Network', knowing the issues, and the people.

The recent development of the Cabinet Office has been apparently haphazard, yet remarkably rapid and pointed:

1. The Office acquired a defence and overseas section and an economic section in the 1960s. This reflected changes in the Ministry of Defence and the establishment of the Department of Economic Affairs and related to the debate then going on about large departments and Cabinet structure. The growth of diplomacy by 'summit' conferences has also increased the need for briefing and support for the Prime Minister as international statesman.
2. The establishment of the Civil Service Department 'provided an opportunity to give the Cabinet Office its own vote

in the supply estimates. It sprang forth as an institution in its own right, not under the general sway of the Treasury' (Lee 1990, pp. 236–7).
3. The abolition of the CSD was equally helpful to the Cabinet Office. The Office took over recruitment, training and personnel functions. The Cabinet Secretary became Head of the Home Civil Service (initially this was a joint appointment with the Permanent Secretary to the Treasury). Sir Robert Armstrong, the Cabinet Secretary, was uneasy about the range of his responsibilities but accepted them, built them into procedures, and coped with the work by devolving committee and policy briefing work to his Deputy Secretaries (Seldon 1990). The abolition of the CPRS led to the creation of another section in the Cabinet Office.
4. The Cabinet Office also serves as a roof or parking place for special units and initiatives. A few are substantial but temporary – devolution was dealt with in the 1970s by a Cabinet Office Unit. One or two, notably the Efficiency Unit, became permanent. In this way the Cabinet Office serves usefully and significantly as prime ministerial territory.
5. The Cabinet Secretary co-ordinates and advises on security matters. This is an area of some diplomatic and constitutional significance, given to scandal and even farce. The Cabinet Secretary handles these matters for the Prime Minister – to his relief.

The Cabinet Office developed the following structure of secretariats, headed by deputy secretaries and corresponding to major areas of Cabinet business and related permanent Cabinet committees:

- Economic
- Home (including legislation)
- European
- Science and Technology
- Security and Intelligence

These committees are the operational units of the Cabinet Office. Their heads, the deputy secretaries, engage in a constant round of official committees and meetings, chairing, attending, preparing, recording and following up. The process is meticulous, but the pace is fast.

The deputy secretaries meet regularly under the chair of the Cabinet Secretary, in a committee including the Prime Minister's PPS. This is the steering committee for Cabinet business, just a few steps away from being the Steering Committee of British government. The Cabinet Office and Cabinet Secretary always had high prestige. In 1945–6 Bridges had been Cabinet Secretary, Head of the Home Civil Service and Permanent Secretary to the Treasury. In 1990 Sir Robin Butler was Cabinet Secretary and Head of the Home Civil Service. The post of Cabinet Secretary has serious and substantial functions, and potentially high influence.

The work of the Cabinet Office

The work of the Cabinet Office may be presented as routine: the servicing of the Cabinet machine – timely, concise but fully consulted papers, nicely focused on the issues, clearly setting out the options, pointing towards decisions – and afterwards progressing those decisions to implementation; and co-ordinating the whole pattern of government policy. The Cabinet Secretary told the Expenditure Committee in 1977 that the Cabinet Office prepared a chairman's handling brief about background papers, points likely to come up, issues to be settled. 'It is not primarily a brief about political advice; it is a chairman's brief' (11th Report of Expenditure Committee, 1976–7, Minutes, Vol. II, pp. 752–3, 14 Feb. 1977).

'Handling brief' is a useful term of art, indicating that the Cabinet Office manages the process but does not determine the outcome. This is 'policy management', but not, please, policy determination. But preparing the brief may involve 'clearing' with departments, reconciling points of view, indicating the scope and limits of agreement. The ambiguous nature of the Cabinet Office operation is well conveyed by Heclo and Wildavsky in this extract:

> Let us suppose that the Treasury and Cabinet Office prepared

briefs for the Prime Minister on a disputed policy. The Treasury will be concerned largely with expenditure implications and, if these do not appear to be major, it might do little. The Cabinet Office will try to balance evenly the pros and cons, extracting the main points from the mass of papers provided by the rival departments. All committee members in the Cabinet Office network are encouraged to bring out the broader issues. . . . The wider the considerations, the more difficult is agreement. Though the official committee will probably have a chairman and/or secretary from the Cabinet Office, they must deal essentially with what the protagonists put before them. The content of the brief to the minister who is chairman of the Cabinet committee will depend a great deal on the reservoir of experience and quickness of thought that the man who writes it brings with him to the Cabinet Office.

Sometimes the Cabinet Office man can draw on prior departmental experience to write an expanded brief, but if so, it is sheer coincidence. Mostly he is a talented layman trying to relate the issues to a wider context. . . . Faced with the need for expediting business, the Cabinet Office can only occasionally say that a matter a department wishes to have decided immediately should be subjected to further analysis. For the most part the Cabinet Office has been (and must be) preoccupied with day-to-day pedestrian work – writing briefs, keeping minutes, checking up on progress, getting papers from departments, arranging for legislative proposals to come forward, clearing everything with the main participants. At its base, any man with experience will tell you, 'The Cabinet Office is a high-grade machine'. Only in rare periods . . . may the Cabinet Office become a seed-bed of change.

(Heclo and Wildavsky 1974, pp. 314–15)

Harold Wilson referred to an improved process of Cabinet Office clearance of major papers with departments, thus expediting Cabinet discussion and approval (Wilson 1976, p. 53). He also paid tribute to the contribution of the Cabinet Office to the preparation by clarification of Cabinet decisions, thus facilitating summing up by the Prime Minister. 'Summing up is vital; it is the fine art of Cabinet government' (ibid., p. 55.). But anyone familiar with committee work will see that the steady, consistent, long-run and skilful performance of work of that kind has a massive impact on the shaping and determination of business. Bernard Donoughue has described this 'influence through process', instancing the role of the Policy Unit in the formulation of pay policy in 1975 (see Case Note, Chapter 13).

This is one way in which the Cabinet Office becomes the official power house of British government at the centre. There is another. The Permanent Secretary who heads the Cabinet Office is the senior civil servant, the Secretary of the Cabinet and sometimes also the Head of the Civil Service. He becomes, by the accumulation of authority and proximity to the Prime Minister, effectively the Prime Minister's Permanent Secretary. He is literally at the Prime Minister's right hand, or face-to-face in meetings, often alone for the Cabinet minister meetings are less frequent and the relationship less close.

This seems to have been accepted by Harold Wilson. Wilson served in the Cabinet Office in his early years: hence 'his respect for the hierarchy, with the Cabinet Secretary sitting at the peak, was established for life' (Donoughue 1987, p. 10). Wilson wrote in his own account, 'The Secretary of the Cabinet is, in a sense, the "prime minister's permanent secretary", to use a phrase of [Burke Trend's] on handing me my first brief in 1964; but his loyalty is, no less, to Cabinet and the doctrine of Cabinet government. . . . Within that clear setting, the Secretary of the Cabinet . . . does brief the prime minister for meetings of the Cabinet and Cabinet committees. . . . (Wilson 1976, p. 96). Wilson stresses that there is in effect a constitutional structure determining these matters, and that structure is Cabinet-shaped, not Prime Minister-shaped. There is also the view of Sir Robert Armstrong: 'the Cabinet Office has seen itself and has been seen as the servant of the Cabinet and Government collectively. . . . It is not a "prime minister's Department"' (in *The Daily Telegraph*, 8 December 1986, quoted in Hennessy 1989, p. 388).

The Cabinet Secretary, then, has a defined role in this Cabinet model of British government, and indeed has particular responsibilities for that model of government, notably for the maintenance of records, the protection of confidentiality and the sustaining of the central convention of collective responsibility. The Cabinet Secretary is as near as one can get in Britain to an Office of Keeper of the Constitution (comparable to the Clerk of Paliaments).

Ambiguities

Nevertheless – and not surprisingly in the British system – there are ambiguities about the office. Donoughue lists three:

First was the uncertainty [referred to above] as to whether the Cabinet Office should be concerned simply with administration – with making the wheels of Whitehall turn smoothly – or whether it had an independent policy role. . . . A similar ambiguity arose concerning whether the Cabinet Secretary's prime responsibility lay to the Cabinet as a collective whole or personally to the Prime Minister, on whose right hand he always sits in Cabinet. . . . This leads naturally into the third ambiguity concerning the Cabinet Secretary, which is whether he, or the Principal Private Secretary who runs the Downing Street Private Office, is actually the Prime Minister's primary official adviser.

(Donoughue 1987, pp. 28–9)

The substance of the first ambiguity is caught and confirmed in the Heclo extract above (pp. 98–9). This demonstrated how routine preparation for a meeting is driven towards policy advice by the complexities of the subject and the attention to detail of the secretariat. Hennessy notes the burden and complexity of the making and distribution of records of Cabinet business, conveyed in the traditional green vans three times a day (Hennessy 1989, p. 391).

The second ambiguity – serving the Prime Minister or Cabinet – is not wholly eliminated by Wilson's emphasis on the proper constitutional position. In practice Cabinet Secretaries have come to be very closely associated with the Prime Minister. Castle reports Wilson as 'clearly pretty matey with Burke Trend'; later she describes Trend as Wilson's 'personal henchman' (Castle 1984, pp. 55, 306, and 115). This is confirmed by Crossman (e.g. Crossman 1976, pp. 159–60). Mrs Thatcher was very close to Sir Robert Armstrong. Leo Pliatzky, formerly Second Permanent Secretary to the Treasury, and a perceptive and shrewd observer, sums up the position: '. . . the Secretary of the Cabinet himself, while in one of his aspects the servant of the Cabinet as a whole, also has a special position in relation to the prime minister (1982, p. 101). Cabinet Secretaries have even advised on ministerial appointments, from an official point of view, of course. At the same time the PPS and the Head of the Policy Unit attend the weekly meetings of Cabinet Office officials to plan Cabinet business. This central ambiguity of British government has probably come about inadvertently. Lloyd George set up the Cabinet Office as part of a general strengthening of the Prime

Minister's interventionist capability. However, the Cabinet Office itself, by its force and functions, constrained the free development of a prime ministerial department. Whatever Lloyd George intended, it can be argued that the ambiguity is inherent in Cabinet government.

The third ambiguity – competition with the Prime Minister's PPS – can be extended. It is not without significance that Macmillan and later prime ministers liked to have the PPS or a PS sitting in the Cabinet room during meetings of the Cabinet – a transgression of the boundary between the Cabinet Office and the Prime Minister's Office. In the broader sweep of government business the Cabinet Secretary has a rival or partner in the Permanent Secretary to the Treasury – this is a fourth ambiguity. These two Permanent Secretaries are the Civil Service princes of the Central Executive Territory. (One of the great princes, Sir William Armstrong, reputed in the early 1970s to be Edward Heath's Deputy Prime Minister, was a former Permanent Secretary to the Treasury, but at the time of his high influence he was Head of the new Civil Service Department. The abolition in 1981 of the CSD left the field clear for the two 'senior' Permanent Secretaries.) There is no reason to expect that these two great officers of state will not work closely together; normally they have similar backgrounds, which may include service in the Treasury, the Cabinet Office and the Prime Minister's Office. If they do work closely together, then they are indeed princes. This was the case in the 1940s and 1950s (Bridges and Brook) and in the 1960s and early 1970s (Trend and Armstrong). They were the dominant duos of their generation, according to Hennessy, who quotes Lord Rothschild arriving to run the CPRS: 'Until this week I never realised the country was run by two men whom I'd never heard of' (Hennessy 1989, p. 213).

Portrait of a Cabinet Secretary, Sir Robert Armstrong

Sir Robert Armstrong served as Cabinet Secretary and Head of the Home Civil Service from 1979 to 1987. His career is significant in two ways. First, his philosophy and approach to the office were characteristic of the ethos of the higher Civil Service in Britain. Second, his career was marked by a series of events which most untypically revealed the stress in the non-political roles assumed by the higher Civil Service, and breached the curtain of secrecy which normally hides that stress.

Sir Robert was in many ways a typical 'mandarin'. Educated at Eton, Oxford and the Treasury, he joined the Civil Service at the age of 23 and, as Hennessy wrote, 'glided up the hierarchy as if on motorised castors' (1989, p. 665). He served as Principal Private Secretary to two prime ministers, Wilson and Heath, and to Roy Jenkins as Home Secretary. He became Cabinet Secretary in 1979 and head of the Home Civil Service from 1981 (jointly 1981–3), a remarkable concentration of power (which appears to be permanent, but may not be!).

He was not a 'Thatcherite', but he did see the role of the official as serving the government of the day in a completely professional but non-political way, making the system work, and achieving the highest quality of government within the political direction of the elected government. Characteristically he favoured 'open government' only in a limited and practical sense; he believed that the processes of taking decisions must be confidential, and that an extensive Freedom of Information Act would simply drive decision taking 'underground'. Armstrong would, perhaps, in the light of his experience, acknowledge that there was a necessary tension between service to the public and service to the government of the day. He would not dispute that his kind of official wields immense influence, but subject to the iron constraints of the highest professional standards of integrity and public service.

Sir Robert Armstrong's career was marked, even marred, by a series of happenings in the 1980s which drove him onto the public stage. Thus an essentially private and non-political servant of the government was seen defending in public controversial political decisions. These 'happenings' included the following:

1. The banning of trade unions at GCHQ, a decision which turned out to be legally imperfect.
2. The Ponting case, in which a middle-ranking civil servant leaked confidential information to Parliament, and was acquitted when prosecuted under the Official Secrets Act.
3. The Westland affair (see Case Note, Chapter 13) in which

Armstrong was put up by the Government to explain the leaking of a confidential document before a Select Committee of the House of Commons, thus defending the Prime Minister as well as the Civil Service.
4. The 'Spycatcher' affair, in which Armstrong was put up by the Government to support its attempt to secure the banning of a book by a former agent.

In all these cases Sir Robert performed as a good professional. He disagreed with the Government over GCHQ, but (of course) defended the decision. Over Ponting, he took a firm Civil Service line: 'leaking' was unprofessional. In Westland he defended a difficult position with great skill, converting the alleged faults of politicians into reprehensible but forgivable official misconduct. Only in the alien and disrespectful environment of the Australian courts did he give a less than polished performance, which included his famous admission that he had been 'economical with the truth'.

Sir Robert had been propelled by these events into quite untypical public performances. But a recent predecessor, Sir William Armstrong, had also been propelled by events in 1973–4 into a public and political role. Yet the full weight of the professional ethic should be a barrier to the intrusion of the Cabinet Secretary into public political roles. It does seem that the job of the Cabinet Secretary is so near to the heart of the central executive government, that there is no clear boundary between the political and the administrative roles.

Cabinet Office: influence on policy

The Cabinet Office clearly has an influence on policy making. This arises initially from the Cabinet-shaped structure of government, and from the pressures of administrative processing. In this way clerks become administrators, become policy makers. 'The machine can actually influence and limit policies while nominally going through the merely administrative function of processing' (Donoughue 1987, p. 5). Cabinet Office influence arises further from the complexity of government policy making. Pliatzky gives one illustration of this process. He notes that the issues of 'fully fledged industrial policy . . . would have to be resolved through the Cabinet Office machinery (rather than bilaterally between the Treasury and the Department of Industry) and in the last analysis, under the Prime Minister's aegis' (1982, p. 125). He adds, 'the committee arrangements were adapted accordingly'.

The passage economically indicates the sources of Cabinet Office influence: the policy is too complex for bilateral agreement, and the Prime Minister wishes to be involved. The Cabinet Office thus has a handle on the issue and moves in to provide the framework for resolution. This is not to say that procedures determine policy, but that policy can only be developed within narrowly drawn procedures, which bring significant areas of official advice to bear.

Prime ministerial use of the Cabinet Office

The Cabinet Office is a natural location to which some policy issues flow. In some cases the flow can be directed. For example, in the case of the exploitation of revenues from North Sea Oil, in 1977, the Prime Minister 'pulled' the issue back to the Cabinet Office and Policy Unit in order to avoid the disagreements of two ministers (Healey, Benn) and the Treasury. In 1978 the emerging problem of unemployment was studied by a Cabinet Office Committee, with the Cabinet Secretary 'acting as a very positive Chairman' (Donoughue 1987, p. 146). This was in face of disarray among the relevant departments, each of which 'adapted varied attitudes to unemployment according to their departmental traditions' (ibid., p. 147).

Thus the Cabinet Office provides the Prime Minister, as manager of policy making, with an alternative arena. The extent of its influence is impossible to measure. It is in a position to exercise influence and it is known to have exercised influence on particular issues and events. But it is necessary to take into account: (1) its relatively small size (about 35 senior officials); (2) the burden of its routine business; (3) its overriding responsibility to preserve a measure of neutrality – its 'honest broker' role (Hunt 1987, p. 70). Departments are naturally jealous of their 'own' territories and do not warm to Cabinet

Office talk about the need to knock departmental heads together.

These reservations suggest that Britain does not have Cabinet Office government; but the Cabinet Office does have a significant part in the control mechanisms of British government (governing in the engineering sense). The motive power of British government lies elsewhere, in Number 10 and in the departments. Policy is initiated elsewhere, but developed and managed in and by the Cabinet Office. However, since the policy process is confused and circular, it is difficult in practice to distinguish precisely its functions. Policy is rarely as indentifiable as the destination of a ship, or the plan of an architect.

8

The Prime Minister's Office

The Prime Minister's Office

Through the green baize door of the Cabinet Office is Number 10, the territory of the Prime Minister. This is now (since the mid-1970s) usually referred to as the Prime Minister's Office. Altogether over 100 people work there, of whom about 30 are senior officials and advisers. The sections of the Prime Minister's Office (c. 1990) are set out below:

1. Private Office (Secretariat)
   Principal Private Secretary and five Private Secretaries (Home, Foreign, Economic, Parliamentary, and one dealing with diary, engagements, correspondence with public, etc.).
2. Policy Unit
   Consists of about seven to eight members, including civil servants, academics and businessmen.
3. Press Office
   Headed under Mrs Thatcher by Bernard Ingham.
4. Political Office (which may include a 'Chief of Staff')
   Concerned with party and electoral matters, parliamentary relations (Parliamentary Private Secretary), and the Prime Minister's constituency work as a member of Parliament (Political Secretary).
5. Special Advisers
   About seven to eight specialists from outside government.
6. Efficiency Unit

Located in the Cabinet Office, but working with prime ministerial encouragement.
7. Kitchen Cabinet, or 'Friends'
Personal advisers and counsellors.

The Prime Minister's Office is of the highest significance in the operation of the Central Executive Territory, but it is quite remarkably small in relation to its functions and by international comparisons.

The Prime Minister's Office has a history. All prime ministers have had secretaries (in the sense of supporting officials and personal assistants) as well as advisers, friends and cronies. In the nineteenth century, prime ministers had two or three Private Secretaries. The PPS emerged in the 1900s as a personal and political appointee heading the office as 'a team to help the prime minister, sharing often in the prime minister's social life, playing bridge and dining with Asquith, and in Bonham-Carter's case, even marrying his daughter' (Jones 1987, p. 42).

Personal advisers, confidants and 'kitchen Cabinets' have continued, but the Prime Minister's Office has been developed and formalised since 1900 as a support structure for Britain's chief executive. The history of its development is complicated, because the building of this institution was almost haphazard, a reaction to the pressure of events rather than deliberately planned; and prime ministers have wisely avoided the complete formalisation of their office.

1. Four factors stand out in the evolution of the Prime Minister's Office:

1. Defence provided an important pressure for change in this as in other areas of the Central Executive Territory – from the Imperial Defence Committee in 1902 to arrangements for Intelligence Assessment in the 1980s.
2. Lloyd George's organisation of Number 10 in 1916 for the effective prosecution of the war is the single most deliberate act of modernisation of British government at the centre.
3. After 1945, and particularly after 1970, the pressures of the economy and the European issue forced prime ministers into greater responsibilities for policy and more continuous intervention.

4. Two prime ministers, Wilson and Heath, were both institutional constructors and modernisers, perhaps less original than Lloyd George because they developed what was already there; and their predecessors, notably Attlee and Macmillan, had not neglected the effective working of Number 10.

The process of development has produced a Prime Minister's Office which in the early 1990s has a clear but variable structure and function. The sections of the Prime Minister's Office can be analysed by structure (units or individuals), mode of appointment (political, official or personal), and function (advice, administrative servicing, personal support). We can sum up in this way:

- The Private Office is a mainly official unit, mainly concerned with administrative servicing.
- The Policy Unit is mixed official and political, with mainly advisory functions.
- The 'Kitchen Cabinet' includes personal and political appointees, offering whatever support the Prime Minister wants, and probably not often working as a unit, kitchen or other.

The Private Office

The Private Office is the main official support for the Prime Minister. It includes about six senior officials, headed by a Principal Private Secretary (PPS), a Deputy Secretary in Whitehall ranking. The PPS has special access to Permanent Secretaries, but his rank clearly gives the Cabinet Office and the Cabinet Secretary seniority in the crucial 'pecking order'. The five Private Secretaries are of a lower rank, but still high-powered, and senior by Civil Service standards.

The Prime Minister does not have a personal secretary or PA to do his or her typing, or buy flowers for his wife, or bacon for her husband (as Mrs Thatcher did once). For this kind of work the Prime Minister can call on a pool of typists, who will if necessary produce a 20-page speech in under an hour while the Prime Minister is at dinner.

The Private Secretaries serve on secondment from their own departments for up to three years. This is considered long enough for effective work, and short enough to ensure that the Private Secretaries do not become a remote super-mandarinate. Plainly the arrangement strengthens the official network, which is the basic shadow structure of British government. An official may occasionally encounter a conflict between the interests of his parent department and those of his work in the Private Office. Donoughue notes that Foreign Office officials occasionally came under pressure, and Treasury officials 'showed courage' (Donoughue 1987, p. 31).

The Private Secretaries are crowded into two rooms, with the connecting door left open. They work closely together perforce but, making a virtue of necessity, they are encouraged to look at each others' work, and must all serve their turn in the round-the-clock operation of the Office.

Most prime ministers develop close relations with one or two Private Secretaries. James Callaghan remembered his Private Secretaries with respect and affection. He claimed when he was Prime Minister that four future Permanent Secretaries and two Ambassadors had served as his Private Secretary at some time in his 30-year ministerial career. Here is Callaghan on the Prime Minister's Private Secretaries:

> The Private Office, whose room is the only one that opens directly into the Cabinet Room, is in every sense closer to the Prime Minister than the Think Tank, the Policy Unit or even the Secretary to the Cabinet. It is small in numbers, staffed on secondment by civil servants drawn from a number of Departments, with the Treasury and the Foreign office always supplying at least one apiece. . . . Their tasks are limitless, bounded only by the number of hours in the day and the curiosity and energy of the Prime Minister. But a prime task is to sort out essential items for him to consider from the flood of reading matter that reaches the office in the form of Cabinet memoranda, correspondence from colleagues, resolutions from the Party, letters from the public, pleas from industrialists, seekers of honours, foreign telegrams and so on, in a never-ending forest of paper.
>
> The Private Secretaries are the focal point for the Prime Minister's activities: they coordinate his engagements; take responsibility for assembling material for his speeches and usually have an important hand in drafting them; ensure he is properly briefed before Cabinet and other meetings at home and when paying

THE PRIME MINISTER'S OFFICE

official visits overseas; act as eyes and ears by maintaining a close liaison with other Ministers' Private Offices; act as the link with the Queen's Private Secretary; and act as a filter through which those who wish to see the Prime Minister must pass. . . .

The Private Secretaries are among the few who may walk into the Prime Minister's room at any time, and if he is wise enough to strike up a trusting relationship with these young men and women, he will benefit greatly by being offered the frank opinions of three or four of the best and most intelligent members of their generation. They understand the mysterious ways of the Whitehall machine and how to make it respond, and are almost certainly destined to rise to the top of their profession. They act as though they share your successes and care about your failures, and as you all face the music together a corporate spirit develops.

(Callaghan 1987, pp. 405–6)

The main functions of the Private Office are as follows:

1. Gate-keeping

   All papers directed to the Prime Minister pass through its hands, and are forwarded with appropriate comment. This includes papers from the departments, but also from the Cabinet Office. The latter are more likely to be passed on with little comment, because the Cabinet Office commands direct communication with the Prime Minister, and the Prime Minister's Office knows about the matter anyway (see Figure 8.1).

2. Shadowing/minding the Prime Minister

   The Private Secretaries watch the Prime Minister, literally watching, listening, eavesdropping (including noting telephone conversations), unless specifically excluded. They are normally in attendance at all meetings with ministers, and one usually attends Cabinet committee meetings. Ministers are usually unattended when they meet the Prime Minister –

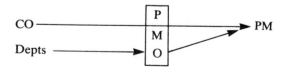

Figure 8.1

a significant illustration that the Prime Minister is not just another minister.

Pursuing these two functions, the Private Office can support the Prime Minister in any way he or she needs – with advice, information, the drafting of a letter, speech or paper, shaping an agenda, or informal discussion of issues. These functions are largely 'servicing' – smoothing pathways, expediting; but they can be pursued positively, 'pro-actively'. The support is so good, so comfortable, that a prime minister can relax into it, forsaking initiative and taking his agenda and cues from his faithful Private Secretary. But the Private Office does not set out to capture the Prime Minister, and is indeed not well adapted to function as a surrogate chief executive. Nor will the Cabinet Office and Cabinet itself easily accept that position. The Private Office is essentially a support, not a substitute for the Prime Minister.

The Prime Minister's Policy Unit

The Policy Unit was established by Harold Wilson in 1974 to strengthen and systematise the previous rather loose arrangements for advice and support on policy. It has remained under succeeding prime ministers, though its precise role has changed with different prime ministers, and as a consequence of shifts and changes in the central executive. These include abolition of the CSD and CPRS, the establishment of the Efficiency Unit, the coming and going of advisers and the general increase in the number of political advisers in the departments. In the 1970s the Unit had nine or ten members; under Mrs Thatcher it was rather smaller, but settling at seven to eight. Its basic nature and purpose are described below.

1. The Policy Unit is very close to the Prime Minister. Its head is a personal appointment, usually someone already known to the Prime Minister. The Unit then, forms a distinct prime ministerial entity, but with working relations with other units in Number 10 – good and cordial relations some of the time. Number 10 is a 'place of distinct entities but not rigid demarcations' (Jones 1987, p. 59).

2. It requires and generally has received privileged access. The head and members of the Unit must learn to work with department officials and ministers; if not, the unit is marginalised. Donoughue records his 'strenuous' but successful negotiations with the Cabinet Secretary on this matter. 'He was able to attend official committees, all Cabinet Committees with the prime minister in the Chair, and many others besides; and the weekly meetings of the Deputy Secretaries in the Cabinet Office, which considered the Government's future program. He was not, however, allowed to attend the weekly meeting of all the Permanent Secretaries' (Donoughue 1987, p. 23).
3. It is mixed in membership, including specialists (e.g. economists, accountants), businessmen, academics and civil servants, all notable for high intellectual power.
4. It is 'light on its feet', carrying no burden of departmental duties, and able to roam, intervene, stay clear.
5. It has, and is intended to have, a political cutting edge. In 1974 Bernard Donoughue, its first head, emphasised this in a memo to staff:

> The Unit must ensure that the Prime Minister is aware of what is coming up from departments to Cabinet. It must scrutinise papers, contact departments, know the background to policy decisions, disputes and compromises, and act as an early warning system. The Unit may feed into the system ideas on policy which are not currently covered, or are inadequately covered. . . . The Unit should feed in 'minority reforms' which departments may overlook, or which fall between departmental boundaries, or which are the subject of worthy but unsuccessful Private Members' Bills. This is especially the case with issues which concern ordinary people (and of which Whitehall may be unaware). [The political dimension in its work was underlined:] The Prime Minister has assumed responsibility as custodian of the Labour manifesto. The Unit will clearly be aware of the political dimension in Government. It must maintain good relations with the party organisation. The individual Ministries must not become isolated from the Government as a whole and lapse into traditional 'departmental views'.
> (Donoughue 1987, pp. 21–2)

Under Mrs Thatcher the Unit became slightly more partisan in personnel and thrust and included members from the

Conservative Research Department and the 'right-wing' Centre for Policy Studies. All heads of the Policy Unit have had a known political commitment. Some have been university intellectuals, and there is a difference, in substance as well as style, between a don of the left and a businessman of the right.
6. It does not deal with foreign policy, because foreign policy is in the hands of the Foreign Office and requires specialist professional advice – or so the Foreign office insists.

These are the major characteristics of the Policy Unit. It has also concerned itself with:

- commenting on departmental proposals;
- acting as a Think Tank, looking out for, creating, and bringing forward new ideas and identifying issues which are important but neglected;
- following up the course of policy proposals, including implementation;
- in particular, bringing to the Prime Minister's attention the ideas and issues which are easily hidden or suppressed, including politically difficult ideas, and intra-departmental matters which are not opened up by inter-departmental conflict.

The Think Tank function of the Policy Unit conflicted with the work of the Think Tank known as the CPRS. A distinction was made between the long-term concerns of the CPRS, and the short- to medium-term perspective of the Policy Unit. The conflict vanished with the abolition of CPRS in 1981, but the Policy Unit, in its early days at least, concentrated on immediate and practical issues. The Unit was heavily involved in pay policy under the Callaghan government. For example, the Treasury invited the Unit to participate in the drafting of a White Paper in 1977, and the Prime Minister took over a detailed proposal from the head of the Unit in January 1979 (Donoughue 1987, pp. 139 and 173). This proposal, it has to be said, collapsed; and the indication of these examples may only be that 'desperation' dissolves normal relationships and hierarchies – the Admirable Crichton theory of politics. (In J. M. Barrie's play, the butler,

Crichton, took over the headship of the family he served when they were shipwrecked; this arrangement ceased as soon as they were rescued.)

The Policy Unit has been remarkably successful (notably compared with CPRS) in surviving, securing acceptability, building good relations, having an input into policy, and achieving its main objective of offering policy advice and support to the Prime Minister. It has been particularly effective where the Prime Minister is weakest, in commenting on departmental policies.

The Unit was initially successful in winning the confidence of civil servants. David Willetts, one of its members in the 1980s, wrote:

> Any person trying to break into the world of Whitehall policy advice wants to get into the virtuous circle of being recognised as influential, and therefore worth providing with information, which in turn increases one's ability to provide influential advice. . . . To get into the virtuous circle it is important to have good relations with knowledgeable, conscientious, and intellectually honest Whitehall officials. . . . Over the past few years the Policy Unit has successfully got into this virtuous circle without surrendering its prime loyalty to the prime minister and its commitment to this Government's strategic objectives.
>
> (Willetts 1987, p. 454)

The Unit was weaker under Hoskyns, 1979–83, partly because of changes in membership, partly because of a deterioration in relations between the Policy Unit and the Civil Service. Generally, ministers have co-operated with the Unit because it is a necessary channel to the Prime Minister. But a Policy Unit brief to the Prime Minister is not negotiated or cleared with the department. The Policy Unit is there to help the Prime Minister in relation to the departments. Ministers, some at least, have other routes to the Prime Minister's ear, but the Policy Unit route is a main line and express service.

The Press Office

The Prime Minister's relations with the media largely determine his or her reception by the people and the party, and thus have a substantial impact on the standing of the Prime Minister. The post of Press Officer at Number 10 developed during the 1930s. Only one post-war Prime Minister, Clement Attlee, neglected this aspect of the work – probably to his cost in the elections of 1950 and 1951. It is more usual for prime ministers to take great, even obsessive, care in the presentation of themselves and their policies and achievements. To this end the Prime Minister's Press Office has played a significant part in the Central Executive Territory, the more significant because there is no Cabinet Press Office.

In the case of Joe Haines, under Harold Wilson, and Bernard Ingham, under Margaret Thatcher, the Press Office seems to have influenced the making of policy as well as its presentation. Joe Haines, himself a distinguished journalist, acted for most of the period 1974–6 as Wilson's 'main political adviser', and wrote most of his public (not parliamentary) speeches (Donoughue 1987, p. 25). Haines's own lively account of those years (Haines 1977) demonstrates his close involvement with the Prime Minister, and his distrust (on behalf of the Prime Minister) of the Treasury and Foreign Office.

Mrs Thatcher's Chief Press Officer, Bernard Ingham, attained an extraordinary notoriety, not only as a 'vigorous exponent of the prime minister's views with the media' (Jones 1985, p. 91), but as an influential adviser to the Prime Minister. Both Haines and Ingham were, of course, paid from public funds, but Ingham was a career civil servant. Hence a question is raised about the close and public involvement of a civil servant with work which might be regarded as of a party political nature. Most officials serve a government which is by its nature party political, but do not defend or promote it in public (except perhaps under pressure before Select Committees). But it is clearly a main part of the duties of a Press Officer to defend and promote the Government. Perhaps the British political culture, for all its dependence on party conflict, is excessively sensitive about this separation of good (officials) and evil (party politics).

There are three tendencies evident in the development of the Number 10 Press Office:

1. The heightened significance of presentation for the Prime

Minister at a time of saturation television reporting of politics.
2. The heightened professional standing of press and public relation officers arising from (1) and leading to a close association of the messenger (the Press Office) with the message (press briefings, media strategy).
3. The Prime Minister's need for personal advisers, supporters, confidants – in short, friends.

The Political Office

Number 10 includes a small Political Office, which supports the work of the Prime Minister as a party politician and a member of Parliament. It has been recognised in the Civil Service Yearbook since 1983, but it is staffed by temporary outsiders. The Political Office is concerned with the Prime Minister's relations with his or her constituency, back-bench members of the parliamentary party, the national party organisation, and all other supporters and correspondents.

Again, the significance of the communicator grows with the significance of the communication. In 1979 Mrs Thatcher appointed a distinguished businessman as a political 'chief of staff', acting 'as a general-purpose political adviser, an emissary and a discreet aide with whom the prime minister can have a relaxed conversation' (Jones 1985, p. 91). These functions went beyond the normally rather hum-drum functions of the Political Office.

Special Advisers

Modern prime ministers appoint Specialist Advisers particularly on economic affairs but also sometimes on foreign affairs, defence and specific domestic policies. Before 1970 it is hard to distinguish such appointments from the half-formed and emerging policy units. Lindemann and his Statistical Section under Churchill is an example, or Thomas Balogh, the Oxford economist, under Wilson. After 1974, the Specialist Advisers have to be distinguished (by observers and by themselves) as individual specialists separate from both the Policy Unit and, until 1983, the CPRS.

Balogh had been close to Wilson in opposition, and remained influential in the first years of government. But Wilson took advice from many quarters, and gave priority to political considerations. Balogh met resistance from the Civil Service. Wilson backed the Cabinet Secretary in a fierce row in 1967, and Balogh eventually returned to Oxford – an early example of the excluded amateur in Whitehall.

Mrs Thatcher preferred supportive people to advisory units, and at her peak gathered eight or nine advisers about her. In 1982 she appointed Sir Anthony Parsons as her adviser on foreign policy. Sir Anthony was a former diplomat who had come to her notice as Britain's representative at the United Nations during the Falklands War. He took more care than Balogh to fit into Whitehall. Sir Anthony was described by former members of CPRS as of 'open-minded and intellectually searching character' – as the CPRS team had found when they interviewed him in Tehran during their investigation of the Diplomatic Service. It should not be thought that prime ministers always favour open-mindedness. Mrs Thatcher did not much like the Foreign Office and was probably attracted by Sir Anthony's unstuffy and sceptical views. Nevertheless, Sir Anthony left the following year. He goes down in history as one who once told his imperious Prime Minister to shut up (Hennessy 1989, p. 646).

In appointing Sir Alan Walters as Economic Adviser, Mrs Thatcher was clearly seeking a source for a particular kind of monetarist, economic advice. She needed protection from any Keynesian back-sliding by the Civil Service, Cabinet ministers, or even Sir Robin Ibbs, at first head of CPRS and then Efficiency Adviser, who was known to have doubts about monetarism (Blackstone and Plowden 1988, p. 86). Walters was influential in monetary and taxation matters, and on transport policy and the nationalised industries. But he lacked political sensitivity, and Mrs Thatcher, whose ideology was always tempered by political considerations, did not always follow his sharp and uncompromising advice.

The Walters appointment was and remained interesting because it showed how a major new policy divide was reflected in the central executive advisory system. Surely, you might say, that might make for trouble with Cabinet or minister? It did. In the autumn of 1989 the Chancellor of the Exchequer, Nigel Lawson, resigned in protest against the continuing influence with the Prime Minister of her Economic Adviser (see Case Note, Chapter 13).

Friends: the kitchen Cabinet

comprised of friends rather than "competent" ones

Life at the top is lonely, and there is little natural and warm friendship. Old acquaintance ripens under the burdens of office and the tensions of personal and political competition into enmity – or at least neutrality. In that situation the Prime Minister needs friends. Some of these may be drawn from colleagues both senior and junior; and from the Downing Street Office, both officials and 'outsiders'. But most prime ministers have also had 'friends' who cannot be located in the Cabinet Office or Downing Street structures; but, since they are sometimes said to be part of a kitchen Cabinet, they may be located in the kitchen. Mrs Thatcher, it is said, sometimes cooked eggs and bacon for her closest advisers (this is more plausible than the television pictures showing her helping her daughter to decorate her flat). A prime minister's 'friends' do include members of the family: Mrs Thatcher has certainly sought support and advice from husband and daughter at least during an election campaign.

'Friends' enjoy an intimacy with the Prime Minister which goes beyond political advice towards personal support – a quiet chat at the end of the day, feet up, whisky in hand, giving strength in times of adversity and sharing pleasure in success. A prime minister's circle of 'friends' easily acquires a slightly sleazy reputation: 'kitchen Cabinet', 'grey eminence', crony. The easy availability of the words indicates a long history of suspicion of royal favourites. In principle, a prime minister's friends are little different from the circle of colleagues, friends and family any other executive might choose for companionship after a heavy day making decisions or money. But, of course, there is the suspicion, and indeed the possibility, that 'friends' might have undue influence (undue because unrepresentative).

A prime minister may feel that the critics of the kitchen friends would have him or her behave like a monk or a nun or a juror.

Why should the Prime Minister not talk with people other than ministers and advisers? The answer is that the Chief Executive of a democracy ought to choose his or her friends with care – not too many bankers, newspaper proprietors, mediamen, trade union barons, Oxford dons.

This prescription would soon lead to absurdity. Yet there are signs throughout history, as well as in late twentieth-century Britain, that princes and chief executives may become excessively dependent on courtiers or kitchen friends. Wilson employed George Wigg nominally as Paymaster-General, in practice to keep an eye on the security services, to alert Wilson to plots, and to offer general advice. However, Wigg was never as influential as Mrs Marcia Williams, Wilson's political secretary. Joe Haines, the Press Secretary, describes Mrs Williams's influence with the Prime Minister as 'powerful – indeed all pervasive. . . . She wielded power with the Prime Minister to a degree unequalled by any person in my experience' (Haines 1977, pp. 157–8). It is true that Wilson listened to her – she had his ear – but he took her advice mainly on party political matters, certainly not from her opposition to US policy in Vietnam. The Civil Service deprived her of early information as far as they could, but Wilson protected her to the end, rewarding her with a peerage.

Bernard Donoughue, as head of Wilson's Policy Unit, judged that Mrs Williams's influence was potentially high, but was 'only intermittently exercised . . . (especially on minor non-policy matters)' (Donoughue 1987, p. 37). Donoughue thought Joe Haines was more influential in the period 1974–6: 'effectually the prime minister's main political adviser' (1987, p. 25).

Edward Heath appointed Douglas Hurd as his political secretary. Hurd understood his job to be 'aide' and friend, but particularly to offer 'political advice'. 'The political adviser must try to relate the immediate problem to the general mood and state of the nation. He watches the strategy of the Government to see how its policies knit together and what impression they are creating. He watches the personalities of the Government for signs of strength or exhaustion. He watches the reaction to the television and radio broadcasts, some of which Ministers make but hardly any of which Ministers see or hear' (Hurd 1979, p. 36).

Mrs Thatcher appointed a 'Chief of Staff', saw a good deal of a few personal advisers including media people, and leaned on one or two senior ministers (Whitelaw, Carrington). Mrs Thatcher also treated as close friends and trusted aides, her Press Officer, Bernard Ingham, her official Private Secretary for Foreign Affairs, Charles Powell, and for a time her Parliamentary Private Secretary, Ian Gow.

Charles Powell, it was suggested, enjoyed undue influence, but the criticism focused most accurately on the alleged incompatibility between his role as trusted friend and his Civil Service status. Ian Gow, later to be murdered by the IRA for his closeness to Mrs Thatcher, earned a sharp comment from James Prior, then Secretary of State for Northern Ireland, for liaising between the right wing of the party and the Prime Minister in the cause of opposition to the Government's Irish policy. This may indeed seem an intolerable situation to a Cabinet minister. Thus it is easy for a prime minister to step outside the bounds of collective responsibility with friends. But in the main, a kitchen Cabinet of some sort is a natural development and a useful support, and harmless if there are strong colleagues to stop the Prime Minister shutting himself/herself away from Cabinet advice.

In the matter of friends and kitchen cabinets there is more smoke than fire. All prime ministers have felt the need for the company of 'trusties', advisers who are also personal friends, not officials and not political competitors. Sometimes the kitchen trusty is on the public payroll. Harold Wilson commented reasonably that 'friends' are not new in a prime minister's entourage. Indeed, the development of the Prime Minister's Office since 1970 has worked against the influence of individuals near to the throne. The political functions of 'friends' have been largely institutionalised. The heyday of the prime minister's friends was in the 1930s and 1940s. 'No-one working for Margaret Thatcher as prime minister seems to me to have fulfilled the role of guru or éminence grise to the same extent as Horace Wilson for Neville Chamberlain or Professor Lindemann did for Winston Churchill' (Pliatzky 1989, p. 11).

Consideration of the Prime Minister and his/her 'friends' focuses attention on the Prime Minister as a person. Individual personality is significant for the conduct of the prime ministership, but the Prime Minister is also a person set in an office and encased in structures which constrain simple individuality. This diminishes the influence of the 'friends' or indeed of any one factor in the total context of prime ministerial activity. The Prime Minister is captured by the role he/she has to play.

Other sources of advice for the Prime Minister

The use of special advisers may give the impression that they are the main, or even the only, source of advice. This is not true. Advice comes from many sources, in many forms, not always clearly labelled 'advice'.

A prime minister is most likely to be influenced by anyone at hand if he or she is short of policy ideas and searching for a solution, or at least a 'quick fix' to some pressing problem. The policy advisers in Number 10 have the advantage of being at hand, but there are other and competing stores and providers of policy ideas, as set out below.

1. Cabinet and ministerial colleagues formally and informally offer their advice. The departments are a major source of advice and new thinking. They would claim that there are few serious and practicable policy ideas which they have not already examined (and rejected, their critics would add).
2. Within the ministerial category are 'Ministers without Portfolio' (including the Chancellor of the Duchy of Lancaster) who hold a specific or roving brief to advise, gather intelligence, 'co-ordinate' or otherwise intervene. Harold Lever acted in this way for the 1974–9 Labour Governments. He was a trusted adviser and negotiator in financial affairs, and close enough to the top to have brought to Callaghan the news of Wilson's impending resignation.
3. The Party Manifesto sustains the government through two or three years, though the detail of the practical implementation of its prescriptions may be thin, and unforeseen problems, or unforeseen complications of existing problems, crop up.
4. The whole apparatus of party – in the country, in

Parliament, and in the national organisation, including the Research Department – reinforces and refreshes the party's general commitments (the Labour Party being more respectful of the manifesto 'mandate' than the Conservative Party). The party has a voice in the Cabinet through the Chief Whip (for the Parliamentary Party), the Chairman (for the Conservatives) and members of the National Executive (for Labour).

5. Various 'Think Tanks' make some contribution to policy making. It has always been true that the Labour Party has drawn policy ideas from the numerous left-inclined members of the intelligentsia based in London and Oxbridge, and from radical journalists and some campaigning organisations. Conservatives have fought back since the 1970s with the ideas of the 'New Right', partly based in publicising organisations such as the Institute of Economic Affairs, the Adam Smith Institute and the Centre for Policy Studies. The latter was founded by Sir Keith Joseph in 1974, with Mrs Thatcher as Vice-Chairman, to research and publicise what came to be recognised as Thatcherist economic and social thinking. It has remained influential because it was close to Mrs Thatcher and it met the need for sharp and hard-headed exposition of the policy ideas of the New Right.

    The CPS was probably most influential in the 1970s, when the Conservatives were in opposition. That is the time when politicians are free to think for themselves – free in the sense of having no-one else to do it for them and not being overwhelmed by immediate problems, and free from the centrist tendencies of the Civil Service.

6. Royal Commissions and Committees of Inquiry, usually composed of the 'Great and the Good', persons of eminence and weight, offer a way of securing 'outside' and public advice for the Government as a whole. 'Advice' may include research and submitted 'evidence', expert opinion and generalised wisdom. Such commissions do not often generate new wisdom, but re-present some part of the conventional wisdom. The Government is not committed to such advice, and it could be obtained in other ways. (See Case Note, Chapter 13).

Speech writing

Prime ministers read, write, and discuss, just like other senior executives. But the political context of their work requires much more public speaking. A good deal of this is now unscripted, for example Supplementary Questions in Parliament, or a television interview. Such public performances are carefully prepared with full briefing and rehearsals. Mrs Thatcher was known to prepare meticulously and at length for both television and Parliamentary Questions, so that she was rarely caught without a ready response, even if the question to which the response was directed had not been asked. She employed speech writers, notably the dramatist, Ronald Millar, who was responsible for the famous quotation attributed to Aquinas and read out on the steps of 10 Downing Street after Mrs Thatcher's first election victory. Millar, according to Hugo Young, 'became a worshipper and minor confidant, who occasionally even managed to make the leader laugh' (Young 1989, p. 209). Millar, with two others, worked through the night, it is said, to produce the Leader's speech to the 1990 Party Conference, greeted even by some unsympathetic commentators as unusually witty and philosophical.

There were very few major speeches in Parliament by Mrs Thatcher as Prime Minister, and her public appearances outside Parliament were carefully spaced out. Harold Wilson was more generous with his public speaking engagements:

> In three months from mid-September to mid-December 1975, I had forty-four speeches to prepare and deliver, eighteen of them major ones, involving a great deal of research, briefing and preparation. This excludes some seven or eight speeches each evening during Party Conference, on the nightly tours of dinners or receptions given by regional parties, associated organizations and trade unions.
> (Wilson 1976, p. 88)

Wilson liked to prepare his own speeches, 'sometimes writing them by hand (taking up to twenty hours), sometimes dictating; most recently preparing a full set of notes, then dictating' (Wilson 1976, p. 89). He deplored 'the transatlantic custom of using speech-writers, recently imported into Britain for the use of certain eminent politicians and others' (1976, p. 88). However, he admitted accepting help during the 1974 election, and subsequently his speeches went through a process of draft and redraft. His Press Officer, Joe Haines, an accomplished journalist, contributed to his public, and especially his political, speeches. Donoughue says: 'In my time [Joe Haines] wrote nearly every word of virtually all of Harold Wilson's public (as opposed to his parliamentary) speeches' (1987, p. 25).

Edward Heath's Political Secretary, Douglas Hurd, was much concerned with the writing of speeches. One account gives something of the flavour and perhaps the occasional futility of a major political speech. Hurd's diary for 11 May 1973 records: 'Early to Turnhouse [on way to Scottish Party Conference at Perth] . . . The ritual of many years unfolds. Listen to an abysmal economic debate. . . . Work on chunks of speech. Dinner, 6 elaborate courses . . . EH exploded (into a speech which dwelt on what Heath came to call 'the unacceptable face of capitalism').' Similarly, Nigel Lawson, then a professional journalist, wrote for Harold Macmillan in his last year.

The Prime Minister's Office: a summing up

The problem of 'outside' advice

'Advice' is a complex term. In this political context its meaning ranges from expert technical information and the analysis and presentation of policy options to simple personal support. Much of this lies within the range of official and departmental capability. Hence there is always a problem of fitting in advisers who are not officials from a department, the Cabinet Office or Downing Street. However, to the Prime Minister or a Cabinet minister the outside adviser offers the possibility of independent review of an insider's thinking. This looks reasonable enough, but it leaves the outsider with the task of beating the departments at their own game, or simply re-inforcing a minister's political judgement. For example, if the Prime Minister called for a reduction in the prison population, the Home Office might well respond with several substantial arguments as to why this could not or should not be done. An adviser to the Prime Minister would have to take on the Home Office experts, or bang the table. But banging the table is not a proper advisory function.

The structure of advice

- The Prime Minister's Private Office is now quite substantial, and provides a superb service to the Prime Minister. The service is engagingly, even addictively, supportive, and the Prime Minister can relax into a secure dependence upon it. Mrs Thatcher resisted such dependence.
- The whole structure is still pretty thin in relation to departments, both in size and in the kind of weight that counts in Whitehall (age and experience of government). Pliatzky writes: 'If Margaret Thatcher has stamped herself on her times, it is not because of the size of her immediate entourage' (1989, p. 11).
- The Prime Minister's Office is now an accepted part of the structure of government. The hostility of the Civil Service, especially in the departments, has diminished, and access and information are conceded.
- The structure is more a network of people than a formal institutional structure. This suited well Mrs Thatcher's style of management, which was people-centred (King 1985, p. 122), and little concerned with institutions.

The balance between Cabinet Office and Prime Minister's Office has shifted slightly towards the Prime Minister, and away from the Cabinet-oriented Cabinet Office. However, the Cabinet Office is by its nature committed to supporting the collective processes of British government, and so acts as a check on the extension of prime ministerial government.

The Prime Minister's Office and the Policy Unit in particular add significantly to the Prime Minister's capacity to participate effectively in the processes of argument and debate on which democratic government and the work of the central executive in a democracy must be based.

The structure of the prime ministerial element in the Central Executive Territory may be summarised as a circle or triangle of institutions surrounding the Prime Minister. The relationships implied are interactive and mutually supportive; influence flows in all directions, but most strongly from the Prime Minister. He or she alone can command the system or change it.

Whatever the shape and structure, the Prime Minister's Office works as a network of people (like all organisations), and it works in different modes, depending on individuals and circumstances. Individuals, whatever their office, cannot prosper if they are cut off from the networks. Isolation from the political, official and advisory networks is slow death, even for a prime minister. Donoughue's influence in the 1974-9 period can be attributed in part to his building of a network of contact and communication. William Armstrong's extraordinary influence in Edward Heath's administration (Pliatzky says he 'master-minded' Heath's economic U-turn, and he went on to acquire a reputation as Deputy Prime Minister) depended on Armstrong's experience as Permanent Secretary to the Treasury as well as on his post as Permanent Secretary to the Civil Service Department.

A Prime Minister's Department?

The recent development of the Prime Minister's Office has accompanied arguments for the establishment of a much more substantial 'Prime Minister's Department'. This was advocated in 1970 as part of the reforms of central government backed by both Wilson and Heath. The American example, and particularly the establishment in Washington of the Office of Management and Budget, was regarded as relevant and encouraging. Reform was advocated again in 1980, at the beginning of Mrs Thatcher's administration; but Mrs Thatcher was not interested in institutional reform, and found the existing arrangements good enough. There was to be no Prime Minister's Department, for the good reason that an adequate surrogate already existed.

A Prime Minister's Department is envisaged as much more substantial than the present two Offices of Cabinet and Prime Minister. The functions would be similar, but transformed in scale. The case was put by Lord Hunt, Secretary of the Cabinet, 1973-9, at a conference in 1984 (Hunt 1987). Hunt's diagnosis was that there had been a transformation in the scale of government since 1945, which had opened up 'a hole in the centre': the absence of a fully constructed Office of Chief Executive. The weakness at the centre related to both Cabinet and Prime Minister:

- The Cabinet 'has collective responsibility without sufficient information or power to exercise it' because of departmental overload and the absence of collective briefing (Hunt 1987, p. 67).
- The Prime Minister works under heavy pressures (the media, Parliament, summitry, Europe, big heterogeneous departments and a weaker Treasury), and must get through a massive workload and carry out crucial functions of co-ordination and strategic oversight.

The Prime Minister must therefore act positively as a chief executive. Hunt rejected the alternative view, that of 'beefing-up' the Cabinet Office. He noted the increasing proportion of his time the Secretary of the Cabinet had to give to the Prime Minister, rather than to running the Cabinet. The Cabinet Office could not go on 'riding the sort of double bicycle, providing the sort of service the prime minister wants, and at the same time preserving its neutrality policy and playing its "honest broker" role, as a collective service to departments' (Hunt 1987, p. 70).

In any case, prime ministers 'want advice from someone they regard as their own' (ibid., p. 69). This seems reasonable enough; but suppose the Prime Minister's personal economic adviser offers advice sharply different from the Prime Minister's other economic adviser, the Chancellor of the Exchequer? There are clear possibilities of conflict, with the Cabinet acting as jury – or silent onlooker. Such a case arose in 1989 when the Chancellor, Nigel Lawson, resigned. Lord Hunt was aware of the problem and recognised that the establishment of a Prime Minister's Department would change relationships between the Prime Minister's Office and the departments.

Lord Hunt's arguments for a Prime Minister's Department have failed to persuade the institutional conservatives. While the conservatives may concede the need for some further development of Number 10 and the Cabinet Office, they judge that their present scale and shape are appropriate. The 'house' atmosphere of Number 10 is regarded as helpful for informal, lively and committed communication. The Number 10 arrangements recognise that government is based in the departments, and headed by the Cabinet, a form into which a Prime Minister's Department cannot be fitted. Indeed, Professor Jones has argued that a Prime Minister's Department is inappropriate to the constitution, which provides for a collective Cabinet form of government (Jones 1987, p. 64). The present arrangements discourage presidential styles of government and are easily adaptable. Apart from the constitutional arguments, the interests of both ministers and civil servants in the departments indicate resistance to further expansion of the Number 10 complex. Further, it is possible that the interests of the Prime Minister lie with an office he can command rather than with a department which might constrain him. Thus the issue returns to the essential ambiguity of the Prime Minister's Office/Cabinet Office complex: a service for the Cabinet or for the Prime Minister? The same question arises for a Prime Minister's Department.

Part IV
The Prime Minister

Introduction: Political Leadership and the Office of Prime Minister

Prime ministers exercise political leadership among colleagues. The balance between leadership and collegiality varies with different prime ministers, at different times and on different issues. The more precise and picturesque phrases are often inaccurate. No prime minister is a 'dictator'. Similarly, the sleepy negative images mislead – Baldwin emerging from the Commons Library with an armful of personal letters, Macmillan reading Trollope and Jane Austen.

The Prime Minister is by definition the leader of a political party. He or she inherits substantial power from the apparently mechanical majority of the House of Commons. But such power has to be maintained, rebuilt, shaped and balanced. Power is inherited on a full, repairing lease. All government, including prime ministerial government, is in the last resort government by consent of the governed; at the same time, the erosion, even the withdrawal of consent, does not bring about the fall of government.

The Prime Minister is also a 'national' leader in a sense that is now widely understood. 'National leadership' implies high publicity for party and policy leadership and a strong recognition that 'the Prime Minister stands for the nation'. This is the serious regal or royal function, the monarchy itself being now politically

Prime Minister is all we have – the major personal state power. These aspects of political leadership – policy, regality – add up to a formidable potential and high vulnerability. The Prime Minister is at once the national leader and the ultimate occupant of that great office of state, Can-Carrier Extraordinary.

But already the idea of the Prime Minister has taken on a life of its own, derived from the magic of leadership. There are more mundane, day-to-day versions of the office – the Prime Minister as chairman or chief executive. These embrace the roles of chairman, director, manager, and the functions of policy development, policy implementation, co-ordination, crisis management. There is an apparent gap between the function of chief executive and the idea/image of political leadership. The gap is crossed, and idea and function are joined, by the urgencies of consent. Prime ministers and their colleagues govern by consent of the governed – mediated in the British case by Parliament and elections. To secure consent the Prime Minister must preach the word, mobilise the faithful, 'lead the people'. Thus the Prime Minister has to combine, in some proportions, the qualities of leader and manager, bishop and bookie, God and godfather (and godmother, too). The prime ministership really is a quite extraordinary job.

The Office of Prime Minister

The prime ministership is an office, not a department. This is a major distinction in British government, which is characteristically a federation of mainly functional departments. Departments are the driving force of government. The Prime Minister rides the vehicle of government, and clutches a steering wheel, but this vehicle has a dozen other steering wheels. The Prime Minister is not borne up by departmental forces; nor is he/she borne down by the burden of departmental responsibilities. The prime ministership is also an office for an individual and draws some of its character from the political nature and purpose of that individual. The prime ministership is not a presidency, but it has some of the characteristics of a presidency.

The office of Prime Minister can be analysed under three broad headings – structure, style and working relationships. Such an analysis provides the basis for an assessment of role and influence.

9

The Office of Prime Minister: Structure and Style

Constitution, authority, structure

The office of prime minister is one of the three or four basic institutions of British government; yet it has little significance in the formal constitution. This not unfamiliar paradox arises from the nature of the constitution. But the constitution may reasonably be redefined to go beyond the written-down and to include the accepted customs, practices and morality of government. It is then possible to set down the constitutional outlines of what would be generally understood as the office of prime minister. It would be on the following lines:

1. The Prime Minister is appointed by the Crown as being the leader of the majority in the House of Commons, and may retain the office and powers of prime minister while he or she has the support of a majority in the House.
2. The Prime Minister appoints (by the process of recommending to the Crown) Secretaries of State and other ministers who shall be responsible to him or her (but formally to Parliament) for the administration of the Departments of State.
3. The Prime Minister shall select from among his or her

senior colleagues a Cabinet which shall be answerable to him or her, but formally responsible to Parliament, for governing.
4. The Cabinet is a collectivity chaired by the Prime Minister and guided by him or her in the conduct of its affairs.
5. The Prime Minister shall be First Lord of the Treasury, and head of the Civil Service and of the armed forces.
6. The powers of the Prime Minister in appointment and dismissal are unlimited except in the case of judges.
7. The Prime Minister is entitled to the support of all ministers for the whole programme of government in face of Parliament and the public, unless there is special exemption from the convention of collective responsibility. The Prime Minister does not expect dissenting ministers to resign, except at his or her request, but is entitled to be angry when they 'leak' their disagreements.
8. The Prime Minister is normally entitled to the dissolution of Parliament on request. Hence, defeat of the Government in the House of Commons on a specified vote of confidence does not lead to the resignation of the Prime Minister until after defeat in a general election.
9. A prime minister who retains a majority in the House of Commons chooses the date of a general election within the limit of five years.

This statement may be compared with the provision of the Constitution of the USA for the office of President. In shortened form it is as follows:

Article I
Section 1. All legislative powers herein granted shall be vested in a Congress of the United States. . . .
Article II
Section 1. The executive Power shall be vested in a President of the USA. He shall hold his Office during the Term of four Years and be elected. . . .
Section 2. The president shall be Commander in Chief of the Army and Navy . . . ; he may require the Opinion, in writing, of the principal Officer in each of the executive Departments. . . .
He shall have Power, by and with the Advice and Consent of the Senate, to make Treaties, provided two-thirds of the Senators present concur; and he shall nominate, and by and with the Advice

and Consent of the Senate, shall appoint Ambassadors . . . Judges of the supreme Court. . . .
Section 3. He shall from time to time give to the Congress Information of the State of the Union, and recommend to their Consideration such Measures as he shall judge necessary and expedient. . . . [The President also has the right to veto bills, but Congress may override that veto.]
Article III
Section 1. The judicial Power of the United States, shall be vested in one supreme Court. . . .

Comparison indicates the superior constitutional authority of the Prime Minister. The US Constitution makes no reference to political party, but this is a factor of some significance for the President and of immense significance for the Prime Minister's power. The US Constitution attempts to regulate the relations of President and Congress; the Prime Minister is 'responsible' to Parliament, but this is a body normally controlled by the party of which the Prime Minister is the leader. The specific provision of executive power for the President is matched by the general, unspecified provision for the Prime Minister. The powers of the President of the USA are at once confirmed and circumscribed by the constitution. The powers of the Prime Minister depend on party, but party works normally to confirm rather than circumscribe the Office of Prime Minister. To summarise, the constitutional authority of the office of prime minister is based on the following:

1. The confidence of a majority in the House of Commons normally through the leadership of a party, hence a legitimate claim to popular support.
2. Occupation of the Office of Prime Minister and command of No. 10 and the Cabinet Office.
3. Management of the Cabinet system through appointing, chairing, and control of the agenda.
4. Executive authority in the broad sense. Power to intervene and steer, especially in economic and foreign affairs. (In the formal sense, executive authority lies mainly with departmental ministers.)
5. Regal or quasi-regal functions as representative of the nation in good and bad times.

6. Unrivalled access to, and capacity to manage, the media. In the case of Conservative prime ministers, the additional unquestioning support of most of the popular press.

Thus the 'Constitution' provides for a powerful prime minister. The actual extent of that power depends on the personal qualities and choice of the Prime Minister and of Cabinet colleagues, the political circumstances, including the disposition of the majority party, and the flow of events.

Prime ministerial style

Approach or stance

Structure and custom set the parameters of the job of prime minister. The political position of the Prime Minister sets some limits, but may open opportunities. Within such rough guidelines the Prime Minister is free to shape the job. Choosing and cultivating the image of national leader is only a small part of it. In the day-to-day work of the Prime Minister in governing, the choice lies between the roles of Chairman and Chief Executive. (The latter is sometimes likened to a president, specifically the US President, but that can be misleading.)

Chairman	*Chief Executive*
consensus building	decisive leadership
reactive	pro-active
'hands-off'	interventionist
looking to survival	specific objectives
gradualist	purposive
keeping convoy together	racing ahead

The two models are not mutually exclusive, and modern prime ministers choose to locate themselves somewhere in between, varying at different times and on different issues. Thus they are all 'individual leaders in a collective context', but that formulation allows a very broad range of variation. The choice has become a conscious one: Crossman invented 'prime ministerial power', Harold Wilson discoursed at length on his own prime ministership, the diarists recorded in detail his conduct of the office, and Mrs Thatcher set the commentators arguing again about prime ministerial superpower.

In practice the range of choice is not so great. Lord Hunt, former Cabinet Secretary, 1973–9, ruled out the weaker chairman role, speaking at a conference in 1984:

> The prime minister must steer, but in a direction that the cabinet as a whole supports. I do not think it is possible any more – regrettable as it may be – to think of the prime minister in this country simply as holding the ring as a neutral chairman. This has nothing to do with whether there happens to be a pushy prime minister or a less pushy prime minister.
>
> (Hunt 1987, p. 68)

The choice (such as it is) is not just about quantity of power: it is about the whole approach to government, including choice of policy objectives and broad political strategy, in particular the choice between popular and party leadership and bureaucratic management. Here Wilson and Heath provide good examples – Wilson conjuring consensus from a divided party and decaying economy, Heath believing in the application of rationality, logic and bureaucratic method to the same problems. Both failed.

The prime ministership is, then, about individual leadership in a collective context, and neglect of one or the other may lead in the long run to disintegration of the Government. This is clearly illustrated by the comments of malcontents on Harold Wilson and Margaret Thatcher as prime ministers. For Harold Wilson the constant complaint is a lack of purpose and a failure of leadership. Crossman complained frequently of the absence of a 'focus of decision-making'. Castle reported (16 Oct. 1975) that Harold 'tried to pacify everyone as usual' (1980, p. 524). Healey was more severe: Wilson, he wrote, interfered but did not lead or give a sense of direction (1989, p. 331). This is particularly true of the 1974–6 Government. In the earlier ministries Wilson had aspired to decisive and energetic action on the model of the US President, John Kennedy, in the 'First Hundred Days'. This was mainly a public show. Generally, Wilson sought consensus, not divisive decisions. There is a strong contrast between Wilson and Thatcher. Wilson was concerned to conjure agreement, dominating the process, though not always choosing the policy outcome. Thatcher started with a desired policy, did not want to know about alternatives, and did not care much about agreement.

For Margaret Thatcher the comments of the malcontents (usually following dismissal) refer to an excess of personal leadership, and unwillingness to consult and discuss. For example, Francis Pym wrote: '[Mrs Thatcher] would ideally like to run the major Departments herself and tries her best to do so. . . . [She] may have a retentive grasp of detail, but she cannot know enough to dictate the policy of each Department, as she has gradually discovered. Her response has been to expand the Downing Street staff to include experts in every major area, thus establishing a government within a government . . .' (Pym 1985, p. 34). Sir Geoffrey Howe, in his resignation speech to the House of Commons (13 November 1990), was sharply critical of Mrs Thatcher's neglect of collectivity. 'In my letter of resignation . . . I said that Cabinet government is all about trying to persuade one another from within. That was my commitment to government by persuasion, persuading my colleagues and the nation.'

Prime ministers may feel that they cannot win; and indeed it is true that like all persons in positions of power they are likely to attract complaints of excess or deficiency, too much or too little. But that is the way of the world for those in high office. Neither Wilson nor Thatcher consistently achieved a solid and loyal Cabinet, working as a collectivity. Heath did better than this, although he was not much loved. Young (1989, p. 76) describes his Cabinet as 'a genuine collective', presenting a united front ('which in later years under all prime ministers, fell out of fashion'). The 'attrition rate' of the Cabinet (ministers leaving for any reason) was much slower than for Wilson, 1964–70, or for Mrs Thatcher. Heath's Cabinet had 'a serious claim to be called the last which respected the constitutional rules defining how British government ought to work'. (If this is true, Mrs Thatcher's succession to the party leadership in 1975 was an extraordinary event, the triumph of an outsider.)

Methods, mode of work

The activities of a prime minister, like those of a professional executive, divide into broad bands:

1. Informing or briefing himself or herself through reading, talking with colleagues, and listening to them.
2. Communicating – by telephone, by a chat, or by writing (including minuting, that is, annotating papers, and issuing a Minute).
3. Deciding, and securing ministerial agreement to decisions.
4. Choosing, and managing relations with, colleagues.
5. Managing time – important for any executive, but particularly so for a prime minister, since the job is potentially overwhelming.

In addition, a prime minister must spend a good deal of time in the role of political Head of State (the Queen being the formal and ceremonial Head of State); so the Prime Minister hosts receptions and dinners and travels abroad. Mrs Thatcher made 77 official foreign trips in her eleven years as Prime Minister, as well as attending 32 'summit' meetings of the European Community and making 142 visits to regions of Britain. Such activities are good for the public 'image' of the Prime Minister as statesman and world leader, but distract from the actual work of leadership.

There is not much evidence for the study of the basic executive methods of prime ministers. Wilson was a great reader, claiming at one time that he read up to ten documents of 100 pages every weekend. He also used the telephone (and why not?) but of course the telephone is an instrument of bilateral, not collective, communication. He was also a talker (low marks on time management from some of his colleagues – 'can't end a telephone conversation', 'kept me chatting for two hours', 'wandered off at tangents'). Wilson himself claimed, as any good executive would, that he husbanded his time, dividing ministers into those who economise and those who consume a prime minister's time. But ministers with heavy departmental responsibilities do not all believe that the Prime Minister needs to work the longest hours – he or she is free of the burdensome detail of department management.

Mrs Thatcher was a workaholic, and a good night worker, as she once said as Opposition leader preparing for a long legislative session in Parliament. She read everything put in front of her, and demanded more. Much of what she read was annotated with sharp comment, and she liked to send out prime ministerial minutes not aware (so her officials thought) that a department jumps when it receives a Minute, 'The Prime Minister does not accept that . . . /would be interested to know why/does not approve . . .'. She was not a good listener, and she liked winning arguments, but did not practise the gentler art of discussion.

Harold Macmillan was probably the last Prime Minister to boast that he had more time for reading novels (Jane Austen and Trollope, by preference) than ever he had as a minister in charge of a department. Macmillan had an old-fashioned way of describing some of his work as 'fun' and some of it as a 'bore'. This is the terminology of the true amateur. Mrs Thatcher, the professional politician and chief executive, did not classify her work in this disrespectful way.

The basic executive methods shade into the more complex business of relations with colleagues and the management of the decision-making processes. Prime ministerial methods must be further pursued in the study of these decision-making relationships.

Personal style

Personal style includes qualities of character and temperament, and values. Set out below are those which most affect prime ministerial performance:

1. Stamina: the capacity to keep going, despite long hours and stress; a mental and moral capacity, as well as simple physical strength and good health (though these are essential).
2. Intelligence: an intellect strong enough to deal expeditiously with the business: at least to see that it gets done. A prime

minister does not require subtlety of intellect, and indeed a disposition to see both sides of a question may be a disadvantage.
3. Determination and courage: to face colleagues, opponents, enemies; to survive defeat and failure. Here the unfairly derided lines of Kipling's 'If' come to mind.
4. Sensitivity: to colleagues, backbenchers, voters; but also some insensitivity to them and to the media.
5. Discrimination: in choice of colleagues and friends, especially those with frequent access and significant influence.
6. Presentation: how the Prime Minister looks and sounds. Prime ministers, it seems, need to be smart-dressers: suits and ties (blue suits for a man), not T-shirt and jeans, as sometimes worn by radical members of Parliament, and never the open-neck shirt as pioneered by Israeli politicians. The voice is important too: Barbara Castle criticised Wilson for 'drawling' and 'mumbling through his pipe'. Mrs Thatcher has the voice of Southern English authority, and it seemed to do her no harm with her natural supporters.

There is one other prime ministerial quality of which Margaret Thatcher so far has a monopoly – womanliness. Those who know Mrs Thatcher only by her public appearances may find it hard to understand this side of her complex personality. She was indisputably an attractive woman, a potential prizewinner in a beauty competition for grandmothers. While exhibiting the hard disciplinarian side of matriarchy, she also exploited the softer side of femininity, coquetry, tantrums and an occasional tear. Paradoxically she is able, too, as a woman to exploit her manliness. Prior wrote: '. . . she also sometimes takes the line that "I'm the only man amongst all you lot"' (1986, p. 139). The popular press loved this ambivalent side of her personality; colleagues found it disconcerting, to say the least.

Many other personal qualities or traits are superficial, part of the 'image' of the Prime Minister presented by the media. For example, the appearance, dress, smoking habits and enthusiasm for football of prime ministers, male and female, are not significant for the conduct of the business of government, except in so far as they have a substantial impact on the reaction and opinion of élites and the people at large. But, of course, that is quite a big exception. The accepted 'image' of the Prime Minister affects the interpretation and reception of his or her actions. For example, all prime ministers aim to be 'of the people' but authoritative and decisive. Wilson did much better in the first category than the second, and Thatcher, the reverse. The 'image', no matter how contrived, has a basis in the person, and acquires a truth of its own.

Working relationships

The Prime Minister and the officials and advisers

The Prime Minister has a substantial Office, including officials and personal advisers. He or she is also supported by the Cabinet Office. These have been described and analysed above, 'in their own right', but it is necessary also to see them as available to the Prime Minister, not simply as passive instruments in her hands. For both Wilson and Heath the development of the Downing Street complex was part of a deliberate strategy of institutional reform. In Heath's case this was far-reaching and included the invention of 'giant' departments, a new system of policy analysis, and the creation of the CPRS.

To some extent Heath's approach to government was mechanical, that is, dependent on institutions and procedures, rather than people. By contrast, Mrs Thatcher was 'people-centred' and Wilson oscillated between the two. Heath's excellent intentions did not win him friends. He was later described as 'cocooned in his relationship with advisers' (Blackstone and Plowden 1988, p. 26). Such 'cocooning' happens to all prime ministers. In Heath's case it refers particularly to his disdain for the cultivation of relationships outside his immediate entourage among junior colleagues and his own backbenchers. But his position was weakened by the loss or absence of colleagues (Macleod died, Maudling resigned, Whitelaw was in Ireland, and Home in the Lords). This helps to explain Heath's appearance of solitary power, and his undue dependence on a small number of senior civil servants, including the Cabinet Secretary; but Heath, a 'Permanent Secretary manqué', in Hennessy's favoured phrase (Hennessy 1989, p. 210), probably felt at ease with Permanent

Secretaries. In any case every prime minister has close confidants apart from senior Cabinet colleagues; and all prime ministers are now to some extent immured in the 10 Downing Street complex of support services. Thus, the prime ministership has been depersonalised to some extent, put into commission.

At the same time, and paradoxically, the Prime Minister has been personalised by summitry diplomacy and media attention. Both developments – retreat to the castle of 10 Downing Street and ascent to the media layer of the stratosphere – remove the Prime Minister from easy contact with ministerial colleagues. The effect is much the same as Heath's cocoon.

The minister endeavouring to build a relationship with his newly-cocooned leader has to cope himself with the depersonalising effect of his own confinement in a department. It is not necessary here to rehearse the elements of the relationship between ministers and civil servants in the departments; nor to accept the full weight of the civil-service-as-conspiracy argument. The minister is not necessarily the prisoner of his department, but he is its representative, and to some extent both its creation and its creator. The relations of the departmental minister with Number 10 are substantially affected by this necessary transformation of the individual politician into a minister. Thus, while media commentary and ministerial writings have emphasised the personal elements in political relationships, developments in Number 10 in particular have further institutionalised the conduct of the chief executive. The Central Executive Territory is an arena for bureaucratic endeavour and struggle, not simply for the contests and conspiracies, heroism and villainy of the politicians. This does not mean that the bureaucratic struggle is to do with rational debate and persuasion: the stakes are too high, and the Central Executive Territory is still a battlefield.

Cabinet and The Colleagues

The Prime Minister's power to appoint or dismiss, and to promote or withhold promotion, is substantial, though not unlimited. The chief limitation is that some senior colleagues have to be appointed, and cannot easily be dismissed, because of their personal authority and standing within the party, the value of their contribution, and their capacity to make trouble outside the Cabinet. For example, Wilson could not dismiss Callaghan, though at one time he would have liked to. Similarly he 'reshuffled' and otherwise frustrated Tony Benn, but did not dismiss him for fear of the reaction of sections of the party.

Mrs Thatcher dismissed, or otherwise lost, a cabinet-full of ministers, but did not dismiss Michael Heseltine early in the Westland affair, despite gross provocation. Other ministers were reshuffled rather than dismissed. Sir Geoffrey Howe was isolated and provoked into resignation in November 1990, but then struck back damagingly from the back benches in a classic demonstration of the countervailing power of enraged senior colleagues.

There is a further limitation on the Prime Minister's powers. Appointing and dismissing, especially the latter, is a burdensome and stressful business. Few people with the minimal sensitivity to be a good politician make 'good butchers'. It requires nerve and insensitivity, the rare capacity to maintain good working relations with colleagues you have sacked or will sack. It is rather messy, not at all 'clean' power. Politics is at the best of times an insecure profession (for prime minister as well as the rest) and adding to the insecurity is a very uncollegial act. Even so, the prime minister's power to 'hire and fire' is theoretically absolute, and Mrs Thatcher has demonstrated that the prudential and personal limitations indicated are quite narrow. Dismissed colleagues stay dismissed and do not easily serve as a focus of opposition – though the part played by Heseltine and Howe in Mrs Thatcher's ultimate downfall will remain an awful warning to axe-wielding prime ministers.

The possibility of dismissal or promotion affects the whole relationship of prime minister and colleagues. This is always true for the boss–subordinate relationship under continuing performance appraisal. Prime ministers expect and usually get a high degree of loyalty. Harold Wilson, in a moment of anger (unusual for him), chided Barbara Castle: 'So this is all the loyalty I get. No-one would have brought you back into Government but me' (Castle 1980, p. 345, 19 March 1975). Crossman recorded a similar instance. Mrs Thatcher's hold on loyalty or gratitude seemed until the very end equally strong. Hugo Young regarded Mrs Thatcher's colleagues as forming a kind of court, created by her and energised by gratitude for 'what she has done to their lives'.

The Prime Minister's relations with colleagues are not conducted against a constant background of threats of dismissal, or promises of preferment. But 'reshuffles' occur far more frequently than in other organisations – routinely each year, with extra shuffles to fit unexpected departures. Ministers may reasonably regard themselves as runners in a perpetual race with a shifting winning post and an unreliable referee. (Mrs Castle was dismissed by the new Prime Minister, James Callaghan, one year after her angry telephone conversation with Wilson referred to above.) The minister can fight back, as Barbara Castle did, arguing her case and refusing to accept that challenging the Prime Minister is unacceptable behaviour. Indeed, most of the time it is not, though some of Mrs Thatcher's opponents believed that once she had made up her own mind, she was intolerant of opposition. No prime minister would accept continued opposition after the issue was finally resolved, or any open or public defiance. (The Westland affair showed Mrs Thatcher rather slow and reluctant to discipline Michael Heseltine's offences under these heads.) Of course, dismissal or resignation abruptly end the possibility of fighting back.

A minister who is sure of himself or herself can threaten resignation, or organise a dissident group of ministers against the Prime Minister. Neither tactic seems to work well. The tactical threat of resignation can be used in the process of negotiation to signal strong and principled disagreement. This is usually in a coded form: 'I should have to consider my position, Prime Minister'. But the minister has much to lose: his/her standing with colleagues if the threat is not serious; and if it is, his job and career, as well as the immediate possibility of influencing the outcome. (Loss of job and career seems now to be less damaging for Conservative ministers, who swiftly exchange the burden and pay of a minister for the well-rewarded comforts of jobs in finance and industry.) For a prime minister with confidence in his cabinet (he/she chose it after all) a resignation for disagreement (that is, on policy grounds, not for ministerial fault) indicates a failure of personnel management. It ought not to happen very often. But there is always consolation for the Prime Minister upon reflecting that to lose a minister generates the revitalising breath of promotion for a junior minister.

There is not much evidence about the use of the threat of

resignation. First, the threat is difficult to define: at what point is the threat serious? In moments of tension it is difficult and tactically imprudent for a minister to define precisely under what conditions he/she would resign. Second, a minister contemplating resignation, but wanting to win the argument rather than leave the Government, should not 'reveal his hand'. Since resignation removes the minister from immediate further influence in the matter, it is not a card to be played lightly, and often indicates more general dissatisfaction and tension (for example, Heseltine in the Westland affair, and Howe ostensibly over Europe in 1990, but both discontented with Mrs Thatcher's imperious ways). Resignations are quite rare. Most of the time the Prime Minister and The Colleagues take into account the firm views of the heavyweight ministers; and the truly indispensable minister knows that the threat of his resignation and the need to retain him in the team are built into the unstated collective contract on which most Cabinets are based.

Set out below are three cases of a threat of resignation: one petering out, another apparently effective, the third effective but damaging:

1. A failure to change the Prime Minister's ministerial appointments, June 1975. Tony Benn reports on a deputation which waited on the Prime Minister to persuade him to reconsider his decision to move Judith Hart from the Overseas Development Ministry. The talk, outside the Prime Minister's room, was tough: 'Look', Benn said to Mrs Hart, 'don't plead with him [the prime minister]. Go in strength and warn him about the consequences of what he is doing . . .' Later, Michael Foot told Wilson: 'It is quite reasonable to offer [Mrs Hart] Transport . . . But it must be in the Cabinet'. Barbara Castle arrived '. . . it was nearing midnight . . . By now it must have been becoming clear to Harold that we were not prepared to serve if Judith was not put in the Cabinet . . .' There was even a modest attempt to bring Right and Left together to oust the Prime Minister (Benn 1989, pp. 395–6, 10 June 1975). But in fact Benn was probably the only Cabinet Minister ready to go through with the threat of resignation. They all backed down and Mrs Hart resigned alone.

2. A senior minister successfully resists pressure from the Prime Minister to amend legislation. Roy Jenkins, a liberal-minded Home Secretary, wanted to reform the censorship of the theatre exercised by the 'Lord Chamberlain'. The Home Policy Committee, chaired by Jenkins, supported reform, but thought there was no space in the legislative programme. Wilson was anxious about the growth of satire (the disrespectful Private Eye column, 'Mrs Wilson's Diary', was about to hit the London stage), and had received representations from the Palace (early premonitions of 'Spitting Image', perhaps).

   Wilson significantly brought the matter to Cabinet which characteristically held up the Bill without denying the liberal principle. Jenkins was asked to find ways of protecting prominent persons from 'character assassination'. The Cabinet Minute was carefully drafted: 'In neither medium [stage or television] would ordinary political satire be forbidden but there should be safeguards against the theatre being used deliberately to discredit or create political hostility towards public political figures' (quoted in Ponting 1989, p. 268).

   Jenkins decided he must stand firm, and told Wilson this was a resigning issue for him. The Home Policy Committee later agreed that no safeguards were possible, and Cabinet accepted this position in December 1967 – in Wilson's absence. In any case the Prime Minister must have judged this issue not to merit a Cabinet split or 'show-down'. Crossman tried to stop the Bill in February 1968, but failed and it went through with little opposition as a Private Member's Bill, but with Home Office support in drafting (see Ponting 1989, pp. 267–8).

3. Twisting the Prime Minister's arm, 1989. In the summer of 1989 the Chancellor and the Foreign Secretary (Lawson and Howe) threatened resignation in a dispute with the Prime Minister over the 'Madrid conditions' for Britain's entry into the Exchange Rate Mechanism. The Prime Minister accepted a compromise, but the issue remained unresolved, neither side being satisfied by the compromise. Within a few months Lawson resigned and Howe lost his job. One year

later Howe played a significant part in bringing about the fall of the Prime Minister. Arm-twisting proved to be a dangerous tactic for both sides.

10

The Prime Minister and the Cabinet: Managing the System

The selection of persons and locations for the development and finalisation of decisions

The Prime Minister has some choice about the persons and locations of decision making in the Cabinet system. He or she may use the full Cabinet, a Cabinet Committee, a ministerial group, or bilateral or simply informal consultation, perhaps by telephone. The participants may include officials, personal advisers and friends, as well as ministers. The process may be consultation (tell me what you think), discussion (let us together clarify and advance our joint thinking), collective decision making (we will together make up our minds), or simple communication of a prime ministerial proposal or decision (this is what I think we should do, or this is what we shall do). Within this range the Prime Minister has some freedom to choose a decision mode, subject to the constitutional and political constraints of the Cabinet collective. In practice, prime ministers seem to mix their modes and slip from one to another, and not always with forethought, confidence and grace. Both Harold Wilson and Margaret Thatcher encountered criticism from their colleagues as well as resignations, partly in protest at less than collegial modes of decision making.

The management of communication and information

Information does not flow freely between Number 10 and ministers. Communication is on a 'need-to-know' basis, with Number 10 judging the need. The Prime Minister is not continuously or even easily accessible to ministers. Barbara Castle complained that she could not always reach the Prime Minister by phone (not at all surprising really); appointments had to be made and the Downing Street staff acted as gatekeepers.

Alongside the generally sluggish flow of information, there is a carefully managed stream of information and misinformation through briefings and leaks. Many examples are recorded. Healey reports an agreement between himself as Defence Secretary, the Foreign Secretary and the Prime Minister (Wilson) to withhold new and discouraging information about the Polaris nuclear submarine from the rest of the Cabinet, and to justify the Polaris programme on the ground that it was 'past the point of no return' (Healey 1989, p. 302). On another occasion Wilson, angered by the leaking to the press of an unfavourable meeting of the National Executive Committee, arranged to leak to the *Evening Standard* his reprimand of the erring ministers. Mrs Thatcher, similarly aggrieved that her opponents in the Cabinet leaked against her, decided herself to leak favourable information about the forthcoming Budget (January 1981). She, or rather her Press Secretary, Bernard Ingham, arranged for her to talk off-the-record to only four carefully chosen lobby correspondents. This was a blunder, since journalists excluded from the briefing soon discovered and advertised the source of the leak.

Numerous other examples of leaking can be found. Wilson frequently sought to restrain Tony Benn, a dissident member of his Cabinet, by leaking against him, in 1975-6 (see, for example, Benn 1989, pp. 358, 372, 375, 381). Ministers for their part briefed back (see Benn 1989, pp. 413, 416). 'Open government', meaning openness to the public (or even Parliament), is not an ideal cherished by those who wield power. So a strange, unacknowledged battle goes on. The battle is not primarily designed to advance the processes of rational decision making, though to be fair it may contribute to that process in the political context.

The management of the Cabinet Council: the agenda

The Cabinet agenda was analysed above (Chapter 5) in five overlapping categories: major policy, external affairs, crisis management, matters of political controversy or sensitivity, and matters of keen interest to a member or a locality. These categories are broadly based on relative significance for the Government. Some further comment on the nature and quality of the Cabinet agenda is appropriate here.

A simple answer to the question of what comes to the Cabinet is, not very much – there simply is not time. A great deal of the highest policy making – in economic and international areas – is 'ongoing', based on continuing negotiations, secret or urgent. For truly momentous matters a 'crisis' Cabinet is summoned, but for the most part Cabinet will know 'something is going on' and will expect to be kept informed, to receive a full report later and formally to authorise fundamental policy.

Trans-departmental matters involving a significant government commitment come before the Cabinet – legislation, expenditure, international relations. But relatively uncontroversial matters may be cleared in inter-departmental discussions, and in committee. The Cabinet is particularly concerned with trans-departmental issues involving inter-ministerial and inter-departmental conflict. Hence a minister pursuing a policy that is uncontroversial within the Government and acceptable to the Treasury (preferably cost-free or profitable) and not involving a significant government commitment, enjoys comparative freedom.

The Cabinet deals mainly with individual decisions rather than overall policy; hence there were complaints under Wilson that the Cabinet never discussed grand strategy, and that policy making was fragmented, crisis-dominated, lacking consideration of the overall policy context. Edward Heath had hoped to improve on this. He said of his new style of government: 'What was most important was for the Cabinet to be in a position to take strategic decisions. I had seen Cabinets which all the time seemed to be dealing with the day-to-day problems and there was never a real opportunity to deal with strategy. What I wanted to do was [to] change things so that the Cabinet could do that' (*My Style of Government*, 1972, p. 3, quoted in Hennessy 1989, p. 209).

Improvement was in practice quite difficult, as Heath's lurches into U-turns (unplanned reversals of explicit major policy) were to demonstrate. Prime ministers sometimes took their Cabinets, with or without advisers, to the Prime Minister's country residence, Chequers, for more extended reviews of policy. These relaxed outings were better for team spirit than for serious forward planning. Barbara Castle reports one held in November 1974, when the discussion was based on a gloomy account of economic prospects by the CPRS (Castle 1980, pp. 219–24). Years later Wilson commented to Hennessy: '. . . [they] all had a little bit of fun and expression and there was no change in policy. I was quite pleased with it' (Hennessy 1986, p. 86). Wilson's remark suggests a somewhat cynical attitude to such Chequers gatherings, if not to strategic reviews. But the case for strategic thinking is less attractive in practice than in rhetoric. A government should have developed its strategy in opposition; thereafter its job is to cope with the day-to-day press of events; a revised strategy is formed 'on the hoof', until the imminence of the next election generates new thinking.

While the Cabinet is concerned about politically sensitive rather than objectively significant matters, it may be excluded from both. Some sensitive issues do not go to Cabinet, a notable case being the ban on trade unions at GCHQ in 1984. The decision was taken initially by the Prime Minister, the Foreign Secretary and the Defence Secretary. It might be argued that the decision was a special case, concerning national security, and too sensitive to go to Cabinet where it might run into expressions of disquiet at least and calls for further delay or compromise. The Prime Minister required a quick and firm decision in the interests of national security and Anglo-American relations; so Cabinet was excluded, and no political repercussions were expected. However, it is also true that exclusion of the full Cabinet from decision making was normal and routine. The Foreign Secretary, Sir Geoffrey Howe, was reported in the *Daily Mail* (6 February 1984) as saying: 'It was discussed, as almost every government decision is discussed, by the group of ministers most directly involved. . . . There are very few decisions taken by full Cabinet' (quoted in Hogwood and Mackie 1985, p. 55). Moreover the political repercussions – outrage in the Labour Party and the trade unions – were acceptable, though later court decisions damaged the Government's reputation.

Hogwood and Mackie point out that a few months later James Callaghan raised in Parliament the question of the Metropolitan Police's being permitted to acquire sub-machine guns – only to discover that the original permission had been given under his prime ministership, entirely under the authority of the then Home Secretary, without the knowledge of Prime Minister or Cabinet. So a potentially sensitive issue slipped by unnoticed. This is useful evidence indicating one limitation on the theory that the Prime Minister dominates and manipulates the Cabinet system. In the welter of issues pressing for resolution, the simple need to shift government business determines the location of many decisions, and moves them down from the top.

Cabinet Committee decisions may not go to full Cabinet as a matter of routine. Cabinet committees dealing with central or 'higher' policy are certain to include most senior ministers, and to be chaired by the Prime Minister (who normally chairs about half a dozen committees). Hence they carry much of the authority of the Cabinet itself, quite naturally, and without any implication of deception or manipulation. Gordon Walker, writing from experience as a Cabinet minister under two Labour Prime Ministers (Attlee and Wilson), concluded: 'Cabinet Committees are parallel and equal to the Cabinet itself. In matters within their terms of reference, committees can come to a decision that has the same authority as a Conclusion of the Cabinet: it will be accepted and acted upon as if it were a Cabinet decision' (1972, p. 119). Gordon Walker's view is discussed above (pp. 77–8).

This is a strong statement, but it is only unusual in its comparative precision, and its matter-of-factness. There is no hand-wringing about the erosion of the collectivity of the Cabinet. Similarly, Lord Butler, in an interview in September 1965 (Herman and Alt 1975, pp. 193–209), seems to accept the fragmentation of the Cabinet with remarkable and characteristic calm: '. . . if you take the Cabinet as covering the Cabinet committees and the committees of Ministers under it, you get a rather better conception of what the Cabinet is. If you just take the Cabinet meeting itself . . . unless the people are very alive that day, and very political, much of the decision has already been taken before it reaches them' (*ibid*, p. 207).

The procedures for public expenditure decisions are a special example of the potential high status of Cabinet Committees. In 1976 the right of Treasury ministers to take an issue from committee to full Cabinet was replaced by a right not to be overruled on financial matters in committee. This shows at least some fluctuation in the application of the Gordon Walker rule. In the 1980s expenditure decisions were sometimes processed through the special Cabinet Committee known as the Star Chamber, from which appeal to Cabinet was severely discouraged or forbidden. This was not an assertion of prime ministerial power but a recognition that the full Cabinet was notoriously ineffective in imposing discipline on the high-spending ministers.

Altogether, the Gordon Walker rule looks to be a tendency confirmed by custom and practice, rather than a rule. The Cabinet retains its ultimate right to review a committee decision, but normally the committee will have conducted its deliberations with some regard for the approval or at least acquiescence of the Cabinet. It would be misleading to interpret the 'rule' literally and perversely, without regard for the likely context of committee decisions. It is unlikely that committees can often come up with a controversial decision and enjoy the happy concurrence of their Cabinet colleagues. It is more likely that a committee enjoys full autonomy only where it exercises an acknowledged authority and capability alongside a sensible regard for the policy inclinations of Cabinet and party. This amounts to an enlarged interpretation of 'within their terms of reference' in the Gordon Walker formula. The rule might be reformulated as follows: (a) some Cabinet committees are virtually equal in status to the Cabinet; (b) specifically, a review of committee decisions in full Cabinet is unusual unless the matter has been specially reserved for further reference to Cabinet; (c) a committee is always in a good position tactically to 'bounce' its decisions through and (d) a committee including the Cabinet 'heavies' and chaired by the Prime Minister has effectively full freedom of action.

The autonomy of Cabinet committees varies according to the choice of the Prime Minister and within the limits of his or her senior colleagues. It is open to a committee under the pressure of events, led by a decisive Prime Minister who 'knows his own mind', to exploit the Gordon Walker formula in the service of prime ministerial dominance. But prime ministers do at times make intensive use of the full Cabinet because it is constitutionally right and proper, because they feel comfortable with a collegial system, and because their colleagues insist. Thus the Prime Minister's choice is not without constraints. Nor does the movement of decisions away from the full Cabinet necessarily enhance the Prime Minister's power, for he or she may be constrained just as easily be a few colleagues as by the many.

The timing of Cabinet business

In a well-designed and rational decision-making system issues would arrive on the Cabinet agenda when a decision was timely and fully prepared in the form of reasoned and researched options. But this is to expect rather a lot from an overloaded system. The orderly flow of Cabinet business is interrupted by a critical movement of events or opinion, or the obsession of the Prime Minister, or the persistence of a forceful minister. The absence of items on the agenda is frequently of more significance than their presence. The Cabinet is not very good at dealing in any depth with more than one issue at a time, so issues are postponed for lack of time and will. Thus the discussion of economic and industrial policy was pushed off the agenda in 1974–5 by the EEC and Devolution issues which were of course pressing, but not as potentially calamitous for the Government and the country as economic and industrial matters eventually proved to be.

There was, too, an element of what might be called reverse Micawberism in the evasion or postponement of the consideration of economic strategy – not just waiting, like Mr Micawber, for 'something to turn up', or hoping that the problem would go away; but waiting for matters to get worse, so that harsh remedies might be more acceptable. This was Bernard Donoughue's view of what amounted to strategy in 10 Downing

Street in late 1974 and the first half of 1975: '. . . the Treasury, like the Prime Minister, was sitting in wait for the eruption.' 'It was perhaps cynical, but certainly realistic, to assume that politicians deal honestly with a crisis only when there is no alternative and it is impossible to avoid it (a characteristic that most human beings share with politicians)' (1987, p. 60). This might look like prime ministerial desperation rather than dominance. Yet there were members of the Cabinet who wanted an open discussion of economic strategy. The power of the Prime Minister lay in his capacity to keep matters off the agenda, the power to mismanage if he so chose.

The management of the Cabinet Council

A large part of the management of Cabinet business is done outside meetings of the full Cabinet (the Cabinet Council). Skilful chairing of the meeting cannot fully make up for defective preparation. But the Cabinet Council is still a necessary part of the government process and, for disputed business, meetings require good chairmanship.

The management of the meetings of the Cabinet depends on the personal style and approach of the Prime Minister – what he or she aims to do through Cabinet. Harold Wilson and Mrs Thatcher offer contrasts: Wilson was concerned with agreement and compromise, enveloping and indirect in his approach; Mrs Thatcher was direct in her attack, concerned to push through policies.

Styles of chairmanship

There appear to be four styles of chairmanship, located on scales relating to the consumption of time, the production of decisions and the amount of talking by the Prime Minister.

1. The ideal chairman: the model here is Attlee, by reputation

and as portrayed by himself. There are many reports of Attlee's laconic and businesslike style, for example determination to stop talk; brevity to the point of discourtesy in dismissing a minister; lack of interest in the media; brusque 'put-down' of Laski's pretensions as Chairman of the National Executive Committee of the Labour Party in 1945; and brisk chairing of meetings. The style is conveyed in this extract from Attlee's interview with Francis Williams – both by what it says and how it is said:

> A Prime Minister has to know when to ask for an opinion. He can't always stop some Ministers offering theirs, you always have some people who'll talk on everything. But he can make sure to extract the opinion of those he wants when he needs them. The job of the Prime Minister is to get the general feeling – collect the voices. And then, when everything reasonable has been said, to get on with the job and say, 'Well, I think the decision of the Cabinet is this, that or the other. Any objections?' Usually there aren't. I didn't often find my Cabinet disagreeing with me. I was always for getting on with the job, you know. To get through the agenda you must stop people talking – unnecessary talk, unnecessary approval of things already agreed, pleasant byways that may be interesting but not strictly relevant. You have to be pretty stern because business is very heavy. And you shouldn't talk too much yourself however good you are at it, in my view.

> [Attlee went on to criticise Churchill's discursive style.] We used to have very good talk from Winston in the War Cabinet of course. Excellent talk. I remember he complained once in Opposition that a matter had been brought up several times in Cabinet and I had to say, 'I must remind the Right Honourable Gentleman that a monologue is not a decision'.
>
> (Williams 1961, pp. 83–4)

Lord Woolton complained of Churchill's style in his 1951–5 Cabinet, sometimes taking up the whole time of the Cabinet in personal, historical reminiscence and neglecting the agenda entirely (Woolton 1959, pp. 376–7). See also Hennessy 1989, p. 498 for a comparison of Attlee with Churchill, very much to the advantage of the former.

Attlee's reputation is no doubt somewhat inflated, and he

may be, like Baldwin, a good example of the creation of the appearance of wisdom through silence and pipe smoking. The young Gaitskell, fresh from civil service experience, wrote about Attlee's Cabinet in his diary in October 1947: 'Cabinet Meetings horrify me because of the amount of rubbish talked by some Ministers who come there after reading briefs which they do not understand.' He thought a smaller Cabinet, mostly of non-departmental ministers, would be better (Williams 1982, p. 118). Attlee's Cabinet was based on the influence of four or five political heavyweights (see Morgan 1984, pp. 46–59), and his silences contributed to the Labour Government's disastrous public relations.

2. The non-directive seminar: Wilson in one of his modes treated the Cabinet like a seminar. There was much talk but few decisions. Sometimes he seemed obsessively to monopolise Cabinet. Barbara Castle wrote that he 'spins things out something terrible, interjecting a commentary of his own between every speech' – and, more kindly, 'he conducted Cabinet like a don at an interesting tutorial' (1984, p. 261, 1 June 1967). In Wilson's absence, George Brown was regarded as better, at least quicker, than Wilson.

The seminar method consumes time, but contributes substantially to collective information and understanding and even to decision making. Talk has a cathartic or 'dumping' function, and the Prime Minister and the Cabinet may need to 'talk themselves out'. Callaghan used the Cabinet in this way, but more purposively, in the IMF crisis, holding seven meetings in two weeks in July, and 26 meetings in October to December in 1976 – 'perhaps the first recent exhibition of classic collective Cabinet government' (Hennessy 1989, p. 259).

Mrs Thatcher's earlier Cabinets, 1979–82, seem to have had some of the qualities of these first two categories. She was in a minority in her Cabinet, and was not able to dominate them (or side-step) as she did later, when her own political position was more assured. Prior, characteristically trying hard to be fair, wrote: 'In those early days Margaret was better than Ted at allowing everyone to have a say – her Cabinet tended to be far more argumentative . . .' But he adds that she was 'very much more determined and gave a far stronger lead than she ever gave in Opposition' (1986, pp. 117–18). So overall Mrs Thatcher belongs in a different category.

3. Prime ministerial briefing and counter-briefing: this includes the Duke of Wellington at one end ('I gave them their instructions and some of them wanted to stay and discuss them!') and Mrs Thatcher along the scale. In fact Mrs Thatcher, like other prime ministers who have spent some years in office, operated in several modes, always aiming to dominate the processing of business, but facing vigorous opposition in her early years.

Jim Prior, a member of Mrs Thatcher's Cabinet for over four years, contrasted her Cabinet with Heath's. The latter was cohesive, and 'a good deal happier than Margaret [Thatcher's] . . . Ted always listened attentively in Cabinet, generally reserving his own position till he heard the discussion. Margaret's approach was nearly always the opposite, making her own view clear as soon as the relevant Minister, depending on which issue was being discussed, had said his piece. If a Minister tended to be one slightest bit long-winded, or if she did not agree with his views, Margaret would interrupt' (Prior 1986, p. 66). Another, less productive, version of this mode is Churchill's addressing the Cabinet like a public meeting, and deferring business to another time or place (see Hennessy 1989, p. 498).

4. Austere and ambiguous silence: this is the less productive version of the Attlee ideal, and is associated with the style of Edward Heath. 'One could not always be sure about Ted's position even by the end of Cabinet', Prior wrote; 'he would quite often go his own way afterwards. But, if Ministers were never quite sure in Ted's day what Cabinet had decided until we saw the Cabinet Minutes the next day, with Margaret it generally seemed that every one in the country knew as soon as they opened their Friday morning papers' (1986, p. 66). Despite Heath's silences, and his

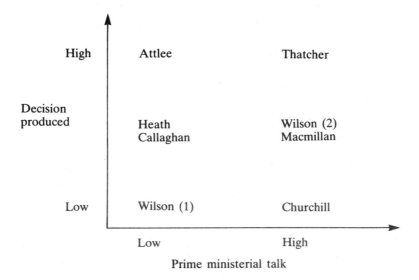

Figure 10.1

notorious unclubbability, his Cabinet remained solid and apparently united through the U-turns of 1971–2 until the disastrous winter of 1973–4.

The above categories relate to decisions and prime ministerial talk. They can be represented diagrammatically as in Figure 10.1.

Bringing Cabinet business to a conclusion

It is well known that the Cabinet does not vote, except occasionally on superficial matters such as whether to take a break. But, on matters of substance and significance, where there is no clear agreement the Prime Minister takes account of the balance of opinion, sometimes quite directly. He or she may weigh rather than count the votes, and rule against a small majority. At this crucial point the Prime Minister clearly aspires to be first and not equal. However, a prudent chairman may well defer a final decision, as many chairmen do in face of apparently irreconcilable division. Otherwise, the chairman puts prime ministerial authority 'on the line' by following his or her own rather than the majority's line, and his or her bluff may be called. Mrs Thatcher, more confrontational than Wilson, suffered many defeats in Cabinet in this way.

Prime ministers and the Cabinet

Harold Wilson normally expected to engage in some struggle to achieve his desired ends. The complaints of the diarists of his much-recorded Cabinet are not about the imposition of his views, as later sometimes in the case of Margaret Thatcher, but about the agility, finesse, lack of openness (to go no further) by which he achieved his ends. It is unlikely that Wilson's skills in these arts are totally unknown to or foresworn by other practitioners of the office. Though style may differ, there are only two main approaches to the conduct of the business of Cabinet: the soft but agile Wilson's or the hard imperiousness of Thatcher.

The Wilsonian skills (or black arts) for getting your own way short of clubbing your colleagues were as follows:

- Obfuscation and delay: the 'familiar technique of getting his own way by obfuscating the atmosphere' (Castle 1980, p. 568, 27 November 1975); no final position until there have been further consultations; no decision on timing; setting up a small committee; leaving negotiations to us.
- Concessions and verbosity: 'Trying to pacify everyone as usual' (Castle 1980, p. 524, 16 October 1975). For example, 'This apparently innocent report on EEC accession issues started a debate which lasted one-and-a-half-hours, during which Harold twisted and turned, played down every anxiety, gave way on this point and that, while achieving the substance of what he wanted – another triumph for his art of wearing down every obstacle by sheer verbosity (Castle 1980, p. 333, 6 March 1975).
- Skilled drafting: evasive and ambivalent forms of words. For example, the controversial Reserve Powers Bill (on prices and incomes, July 1975) was approved 'on a contingent basis and without prejudice'.
- Evading the issue of principle by presenting a series of

practical decisions, further investigation or negotiation, looking at the detail, building the jigsaw of principle in little pieces (EEC entry was the classic case).

In a debate on public expenditure (March 1975) Barbara Castle pointed out that the defence figures were provisional, so why did the Defence White Paper refer to a firm ten-year plan? The Prime Minister supported (so it seemed) Castle's strong objections and agreed that 'the point about provisionality should be looked into further' (Castle 1980, p. 324). A few days later Wilson circulated a minute explaining that 'provisional' did not mean provisional in the economic sense but referred only to consultations with allies (ibid., p. 333). Barbara Castle was thus beaten 'behind the scenes'. She noted that sympathisers in the Cabinet failed to speak in her support since they 'had not had time to gen up on this'.

The Thatcher approach to Cabinet was less complex than Wilson's, because less personally involved. Partly her method was to side-step Cabinet altogether, 'ruling through a web of ad hoc committees manned by trusties' (Jenkins 1987, p. 183). If opposition persisted as an issue was moved towards resolution, then the struggle would be carried on outside the Cabinet system, by news management and in public speeches and briefings. For example, when Prior was following his step-by-step approach to trade union legislation in 1980, both the Prime Minister and Sir Geoffrey Howe called in public speeches for a tougher approach, without informing Prior in advance. In that perspective, the highly public squabble over Westland was not untypical of a Cabinet which was not treated as, and could not act as, a collectivity.

In the Cabinet itself there were sometimes great rows, but mostly ministers 'kept their heads down', and went along with Mrs Thatcher's brisk and authoritative conduct of Cabinet; she made known her view and waited impatiently for the concurrence of the lead minister and colleagues. It is difficult to imagine Mrs Thatcher heading Wilson's Cabinet, but the experience would certainly have led the complaining diarists to a warmer appreciation of Wilson's consensual Cabinet style.

Callaghan earned higher marks from his colleagues as a good chairman, genuinely seeking collectivity. Benn early expressed admiration in his diary: Callaghan was 'a much better prime minister than Wilson. He is more candid and open with people and he does not try to double talk them as Wilson did' (1989, p. 693, 28 December 1976). But there was a hard political and managerial edge to Callaghan's approach to Cabinets. Healey appreciated his skilful but directive chairmanship – 'never content simply to preside over a Cabinet committee' (1989, p. 448). Callaghan, like Wilson, worked through the Cabinet: it was politically safer as well as constitutionally proper. Callaghan made a point of careful preparation, reading his briefs, consulting senior colleagues (especially the Chancellor), steering the Cabinet to his preferred position (Donoughue 1987, pp. 35–7).

It is evident that there is no persistent pattern of Cabinet politics. The Cabinet's role is unsystematic and variable. Its solidarity is fragmented by the committees and bilaterals so that the Cabinet as a whole, hence many members of Cabinet, are excluded from influence and significant decisions. The Cabinet is both the constitutional source of the system and an actor in the system; but it derives more status than force from its constitutional history.

Prime ministers manage the Cabinet, but management does not consistently amount to domination. The management of the Cabinet is an all-embracing role – in sporting terms, the Prime Minister is manager, captain and referee, a formidable combination, even without adding that he or she prepares the pitch, shifts the goal posts and writes the rule-book. Members of the Cabinet are still players in the game, and if – which does happen – three or four of them decided to stop the game, the Prime Minister would find himself or herself for the moment to be just another player.

Prime ministers, departments and departmental ministers

Prime ministers do not intervene in departments routinely and persistently. There are good reasons for this. First, it would be very difficult. The Prime Minister lacks the time, the information and the understanding to intervene effectively. Second, he or she has the clout but not the grace to intervene persistently without causing resentment, and provoking obstruction and counter-measures. The civil service machine will not run smoothly in face of prime ministerial intervention. Finally, such intervention runs counter to the constitutional framework of ministerial responsibility to Parliament and, equally important, to the political imperative on the Prime Minister to avoid public responsibility ('can-carrying') for policy initiatives which go wrong.

Harold Wilson's persistent attempts through officials and the media to frustrate Tony Benn's initiatives at the Department of Industry show how hard it was for the Prime Minister to make a direct intervention. Prime ministerial action of any kind was inhibited by the support Benn enjoyed in sections of the party. In the end Wilson was driven to 're-shuffle' Benn to another ministry.

The rule of prime ministerial non-intervention (in fact no more than a tendency) rests on a fundamental perception of the role of the Prime Minister. He or she is concerned with strategy, the totality of the government's work, with popular and party political matters, and only with 'micro-policy' in moments of crisis. Bernard Donoughue wrote:

> The Prime Minister's basic policy role, when he or she chooses to exercise it, in the face of all the constraints, is not related to a specific policy area, but is rather to sustain and co-ordinate the coherence of government policy-making as a whole. In addition, frequently his or her contribution is to introduce a dimension which is wider than departmental. It may often be seen as a national dimension, something called the national interest, difficult though that may be to define. A prime minister may feel that a department is, understandably, taking too narrow a departmental view, or, even more understandably, that a departmental Minister is taking a view that is too politically partisan. The Prime Minister may then intervene to interpolate a wider governmental or national perspective. Conversely, of course, Ministers sometimes 'go native' in their departments and the prime minister may feel compelled to introduce a degree of party political realism into that Minister's proposals. Such, on my observation, were the kinds of wider dimensions and horizons most regularly introduced by a prime minister into the policy-making process, whether from the Cabinet chair directly to a Minister in conversation, or by a prime ministerial minute.
>
> (Donoughue 1987, p. 6)

There are quite substantial exceptions to the rule of non-intervention. The rule (or tendency) applies most clearly to routine micro-policy. It applies hardly at all to economic and foreign policy, which usually has a strong 'national dimension', so that policy is not so much subject to prime ministerial intervention as normally based on close consultation and joint development – the Prime Minister does not intervene from outside but is already fully involved on the inside. There are numerous illustrations of this point under all recent prime ministers. Nor does non-intervention apply when aspects of domestic micro-policy are magnified, by mistakes, costs, impact on articulate people or media coverage, into matters of national interest.

Bernard Donoughue follows the paragraph on non-intervention just quoted with another on prime ministerial intervention:

> ... it is open to a prime minister to intervene with personal initiatives in specific areas of micro-policy. The ensuing descriptions of the crises on pay and the IMF, on the planning to exploit North Sea Oil, and the discussions of the Winter of Discontent show this. Mr Wilson took other initiatives over Ireland, the sale of council houses, commodities pricing and the film industry, as did Mr Callaghan in the fields of education, hospitals, personal tax reform, nuclear policy and aircraft purchasing policy. In each case it involved intervention in the normal Whitehall processes and often upset the respective departmental Ministers and officials who believe that prime ministers should not trespass on their cabbage patches (the Department of Education's reaction to Mr Callaghan's 1976 Ruskin speech was the worst example of this, whereas the Treasury, being of a much higher calibre, was often commendably relaxed about much more disruptive economic interventions from Downing Street). Although the general public may view the Prime Minister as having supreme power in government, Whitehall certainly assumes and prefers that he or she (as Mrs Thatcher presumably learned) does not exercise it.
>
> (Donoughue 1987, pp. 6–7)

The extent of prime ministerial intervention is determined, according to Donoughue (1987, p. 7), by four factors:

1. Personal: the Prime Minister's temperament, background and style.

2. Political: the Prime Minister's power and standing in relation to his or her colleagues.
3. Administrative: the scale and competence of the advisory services in 10 Downing Street.
4. The opportunity of events.

There is plainly a large area of policy making in which the Prime Minister regularly and actively participates, and a potential for intervention in almost every issue, not excluding traffic jams in Whitehall, litter in the park or on the road to Heathrow Airport, and the grounding of an oil tanker off the Scilly Isles (these are all matters on which prime ministers have intervened, at least to the point of demanding, 'Something must be done!'). Nevertheless, prime ministers do refrain from intervention more often than not, for the reasons indicated above. A prudent prime minister calculates the profit and loss of intervention, and may often conclude that intervention is likely to increase his or her responsibility and share of the blame without substantial impact on the policy.

Margaret Thatcher's interventionist style as prime minister seems to have given intervention a bad name: 'prime ministerial intervention is increasing and ought to be diminished'. However, much of British government goes on without prime ministerial intervention. The departments are the operating centres of British government, responsible for implementation of policy and, as a consequence, a major source of policy innovation. Normally, prime ministers see the departmental ministers as necessary and supportive colleagues; and the minister sees the Prime Minister as an essential and even welcome and appreciated ally.

11

The Prime Minister and Party, Parliament and People

Beyond the Central Executive Territory

The role of the Prime Minister beyond the Central Executive Territory is a powerful adjunct or complement to his/her conduct in office. The most skilled operator in the Central Executive Territory would be ineffective if he/she were not an adequate performer with Party, Parliament and People. Conversely, a popular political hero who could not operate in the Territory would not be an effective prime minister.

The validity of this statement can be tested by reference to diverse prime ministers. All prime ministers are vulnerable to the criticisms and intrigues of their colleagues if they lose support outside Downing Street. Attlee and Edward Heath have both been adjudged good at the Downing Street function, but they wasted or failed to cultivate popular support with politically disastrous consequences. Similarly Churchill and Macmillan retained popular support but lost their way in Downing Street. Parliament, party and people need an effective prime minister; and he or she needs their support. The dual demand of democratic leadership is for effectiveness and consent.

Prime ministers are well placed to mobilise consent. Their actions in office generate massive publicity. Using mentions in *The Times*, Headey calculated that the Prime Minister in 1960 (Macmillan) generated far more publicity than the next three most publicised ministers; and in 1969 Wilson scored more than the next two most publicised colleagues (Headey 1974, pp. 233, 237). On another measure, in the elections of 1983 and 1987 the Prime Minister and the Leader of the Opposition appeared in one third or more of the photographs of their party used in national daily newspapers.

The media, and especially television, focus public attention on the Prime Minister, offering easy opportunities for charismatic leadership. The Prime Minister is able to preach and proclaim, and no prime minister after Attlee has disdained the opportunity. The process is much intensified if the Prime Minister can promote a few simple and large ideas. These are most easily marketable if they can relate to national pride and triumph over an enemy. Margaret Thatcher's exploitation of her remarkable victory in the Falklands war is the best example of this. 'We have ceased to be a nation in retreat', she declaimed. 'We have instead a new-found confidence – born in the economic battles at home and tested and found true 8,000 miles away.' It should be added that no prime minister would have refused the promotional possibilities offered by the Falklands victory (though other prime ministers might have approached the war differently). Harold Wilson was a skilled exploiter of the propaganda possibilities of the memory of Dunkirk, a tanker disaster, a summit on a battleship. The saintly Victorian, Gladstone, was good at this too, curdling the blood of Scottish electors with talk of atrocities in faraway places.

Politicians of the Left and Centre have found great difficulty in promoting their rather less blood-curdling ideas in the same way; though the occasional victories of the Labour Party, especially that of 1945, show that such promotion is not impossible. (But the 1945 formula is difficult to replicate – two decades of depression followed by a world war.)

More sophisticated ideas are harder to sell. The Labour Party has found Socialism to be unmarketable; and it may be conjectured that the free market ideas of the New Right would attract very few buyers, had Margaret Thatcher not been a super saleswoman, well able to distinguish the saleable from the unsaleable.

These considerations raise at last the matter of political leadership. In this public sphere – Parliament, Party, People – political leadership is the mobilisation of support and consent. In the conduct of the office of prime minister within Downing Street leadership is to do with effective management, or executive direction. The office of prime minister is at the apex of these two streams of politics. Within this general context of the public relations of the Prime Minister, the three most important arenas will now be briefly examined.

Prime minister and party

Since the days of Gladstone the Prime Minister has been a leader of a national party, as well as a Cabinet and parliamentary leader. Indeed, the party is the support of the Prime Minister's position, and the source of his power. Hence a prudent prime minister (and no prime minister having climbed so far lacks this kind of prudence) gives high priority to the management of his relations with the party. These can easily be misunderstood; a concern for the support of the party is a proper priority for a democratic chief executive. It is not ignoble, unless principle is entirely subordinated to the winning of party and electoral support; and even that may be justified in a democracy.

A prime minister normally starts with the advantage of being the elected leader of the party which has just won a general election with a high personal profile. This was the case for most post-war prime ministers – Attlee, Churchill, Eden, Macmillan (1959), Wilson, Heath and Thatcher. There are exceptions: Macmillan (1957), Home (1963), Callaghan (1976) and Major (1990) – but both Callaghan and Major had won elections for the party leadership. Three times for Wilson, and once for Attlee (1950) the electoral victory was insecure, but that does not diminish the party's dependence on the leader. Thereafter the relationship of prime minister and party is nourished through the Party Conference and in continuing relations with backbench members of Parliament (who in turn are in touch with their constituents); but it is sustained above all by the leader's standing with the people.

This looks like an easy ride for the Prime Minister; and certainly the party leadership does normally ensure for the Prime Minister both impregnability and a basic minimum of force. Yet no party confers such power unconditionally: the condition is that the leader delivers success, attractive policies and the assurance of victorious elections. Neither is easy. The Conservative Party by its ethos and its constitution is loyal to its leaders; but the appetite for power is sharp and failure can lead to an unsentimental withdrawal of support – Heath being a clear example of the dumping of a failed leader, Mrs Thatcher a striking example of a leader 'defenestrated' when it became clear she might lose the next election.

The Labour Party by its ethos and constitution is a more troublesome party to lead. The party is self-consciously a party of intellectual and moral commitment and watches anxiously as its prime ministers trim, dilute, and compromise in face of harsh reality. The party is in effect a federation of trade unions, constituency parties and the Parliamentary Party. Votes in the electoral college are shared between these three, with 40 per cent in the hands of the trade unions. These elements are represented in the National Executive Committee. Some members of the NEC (who may also be ministers in the government) believe that the government should follow instructions given by the NEC in interpretation of the party manifesto. All Labour prime ministers have found the relationship with the NEC difficult, sometimes intolerable. Wilson and Callaghan at times virtually abandoned the relationship. For them the party to which they owed their position was a constraint, not a support.

A prime minister is not without resources in the face of his or her party. Success in government warms all but the most ideological party heart. Patronage also soothes sensitive consciences. Appeals to reason, sentiment, loyalty may not be in vain. This is political leadership. The party leader should know all about this side of the business, and do it very well. But it is a distraction from the serious business of the Prime Minister: governing the country.

Prime minister and Parliament

Prime Ministers' relations with Parliament are largely a reflection of their relations with the party. It is their own side which gives them the most support (of course) but also the most trouble. This is easily demonstrated. There is a short list of measures on which governments have retreated, and the legislature appears to have made a significant impact on the policy of the executive: for example, the Rent Act 1957, steel nationalisation 1965, trade union reform 1969, student grants 1984, the sale of Land Rover 1986, the Sunday opening of shops 1986, the Community Charge (poll tax) from 1989. In each case, it is the Government's backbenchers, not the Opposition, who have moved the Government.

This does not mean that government backbenchers have substantial power: the list of measures they have influenced is not long and the effectiveness of their pressure usually indicates that they were voicing the concern of others besides themselves – constituency parties, interest groups, dissident members of the government even. In addition to this continuing modest influence, government backbenchers carry the ultimate weapon, the withdrawal of support from the Prime Minister. In the ousting of a prime minister (a once-in-fifty-years event) the decisive opinions are those of the Parliamentary party, as reported by the Chairman and the Chief Whip. This possibility adds a little iron to the continuing relationship.

The intra-party relationship is by far the most important of the Prime Minister's relations with Parliament. Little of it is conducted on the floor of the Chamber. But the Prime Minister needs to deal masterfully with the Opposition in the Chamber, because by dominating the House he dominates his own party. This is the function of the Opposition, to test the Prime Minister's mettle, and establish his standing with his own side.

The prime minister's most frequent activity in Parliament is the twice weekly appearance to answer Parliamentary Questions (about 15 minutes each Tuesday and Thursday). Mrs Thatcher answered 7,500 oral questions in her eleven years as prime minister. Wilson devoted 12 of his 29 pages on 'Prime Minister and Parliament' to questions, and both he and Mrs Thatcher spent hours preparing themselves for this curious test of the Prime Minister's capacity for well-prepared spontaneity.

The restrictions on acceptable subjects for Parliamentary Questions are evaded in the case of the Prime Minister by the use of questions about the Prime Minister's activities and itineraries, leading to Supplementary Questions about the problems of the area visited, the views of its businessmen, unemployed, farmers;

or, on a wider scale, the problems of Latin America, Western Europe, the Eastern Mediterranean . . . A question about a ministerial speech – did that represent the Government's policy? – can be particularly awkward to handle.

The Prime Minister is more exposed than departmental ministers. He or she offers a politically attractive target: there are no deputies to share the answering of questions, and the topics raised concern broad policy as well as specifics, and are of course designed not to seek information but to trap the Prime Minister. The introduction of television has made Prime Minister's Question Time a great opportunity to impress the nation – for both Prime Minister and Opposition. It is less rumbustious, an opportunity to show statesmanship, always easier for a well-briefed prime minister, concerned to govern the country, than for a Leader of the Opposition. Both are trying to score political points, but the Prime Minister can deploy his undoubted heavy responsibilities and make point-scoring look a virtue.

The Prime Minister needs to be well-briefed, quick-thinking, agile. Great care and much time is taken on briefing, including the spotting of possible supplementaries. Prime Minister's Question Time is plainly a stiff test for the Prime Minister. Humiliation is unlikely but a weak, dull performance diminishes standing with the party, if not with the nation. A triumph shown on the evening news programmes is enticing. Whether so much of the Prime Minister's time and thought should go into Question Time is debatable. Its success on American television channels does not validate its contribution to good government in Britain – and raises serious doubts about the quality of American television.

Question Time is the Prime Minister's major contribution to Parliament. Until 1940 the Prime Minister also acted as Leader of the House of Commons, with regular responsibility for the conduct of its business. Since then, the Prime Minister's contacts with the House have diminished. On average, since 1940, prime ministers make statements or speeches about once a month, with little variation. However, Mrs Thatcher is notable for the infrequency of her speeches compared with her predecessors since 1940. In three sessions, 1985–8, she made no contribution to debates at all. Parliamentary Questions accounts for only half an hour each week. Mrs Thatcher was, according to recent research, 'far and away the least active prime minister in the Commons for the last hundred and twenty years. Her abandonment of debating interventions, and her very infrequent speeches, set her strongly apart . . .' (Dunleavy et al. 1990, p. 137).

Mrs Thatcher's retreat from Parliament broke with the traditional perspective in which the Prime Minister was most characteristically on the Front Bench in the House, speaking to and for the nation at the very centre of British government. The traditional view was expressed for all ministers by Roy Jenkins, who took great pains over his set speeches: 'Parliamentary speaking . . . is of vital importance to a Minister' (*The Observer*, 20 June 1971, quoted in Campbell 1983, p. 217). Mrs Thatcher, never quite at ease in this male-dominated debating chamber and club, had better things to do with her time. Her attitude to the House of Commons was consistent with her attitude to Cabinet: we cannot waste time having unnecessary arguments.

Prime ministers and the media

'Parliament is the chief constitutional forum for the presentation of self [i.e. the prime minister] to politicians, and the mass media is the chief electoral forum' (Rose 1980, p. 11). Prime ministers may neglect the constitution, but they can never forget the political imperative – to win the next election. The television interview and the photo opportunity come ahead of Parliament in priority, as the Castle Diaries confirm.

Prime ministers have always been concerned to be well-reported and well-presented in the media. Gladstone and Disraeli expected verbatim reports in sympathetic newspapers. Lloyd George assumed that a serious politician needed to own at least one newspaper, and to influence the proprietors and editors of others by honours and favours. Baldwin took to radio with alacrity. Chamberlain returned from his visit to Munich in September 1938 to wave the notorious piece of paper ('Peace in our Time') before newsreel cameras from the infant BBC Television. Churchill famously rallied the nation in his war-time broadcasts.

That marked the peak of radio political broadcasting. Both

Attlee and Churchill stood by the old tradition that prime ministers speak to the nation in Parliament. Attlee disdained all publicity (not at all a virtue in a political leader). Churchill was suspicious of television, with its novel technical demands. Macmillan likened the early television studio to a torture chamber. Until the mid-1950s political leaders conspired with the broadcasters to keep politics, as far as possible, out of broadcasting. The first television news bulletins were read behind a picture of the BBC clock. In the mid-1950s the extraordinary '14-day Rule' prevented the discussion on radio or television of any topic within 14 days of a parliamentary debate.

This restrictive approach, particularly to television, was swept away by the end of the 1950s. Prime ministers and politics entered the age of television. Television rapidly became the main and universal source of political news and information. The impact on politics, including government at the centre, was greater than any other change, institutional, procedural or personal. Henceforth politics became a media show and the Prime Minister, for better or worse, a media star. Proper concern for the 'presentational aspect' of a policy decision raised the specific question, 'How will it play on the Nine O'Clock News?' Prime ministers struggled both to use television themselves and to control its uses by others. Examples abound of the exploitation of television for the promotion of political leaders. This is a continuing process, but it is most evident, and most flagrant, during general election campaigns. These have become the stringing together of a series of 'photo opportunities' and 'sound bites', cleverly orchestrated by media specialists, in a relationship with the broadcasters which is partly adversarial, partly conspiratorial. Similarly the annual Party Conferences are designed for television.

The television highlight of the 1983 election campaign was a film of the Prime Minister nursing a calf in a Suffolk field, surrounded (off-screen) not by Suffolk farmers but by a score of camera crews. The highlight of the 1987 campaign was the short film about the Leader of the Opposition, Neil Kinnock, his background, family life, values, all against a background of the Welsh coastline and the music of Brahms and Beethoven. The discovery of truth is not a prime objective: this is advertising. Minor deceptions are routine – the prime minister appears to use the telephone in her campaign bus to learn of the release of a British hostage in Iran – but the news was two days old, and the secretary at the other end of the line could not understand Mrs Thatcher's strange exclamations of satisfaction. This is not an argument to be pursued here, but it has to be appreciated that the Prime Minister, in carrying the responsibilities of government in the Central Executive Territory, is also performing in show business. Hence the Press Officer is transformed from a messenger at the margins into an influential adviser on policy, since policy is shaped by the message by which it will be transmitted.

The manipulation is not all on the side of the politicians. The media are voracious for news, visual, immediate and exciting. A manageable political problem can be converted into a crisis by the media, whether the politicians like it or not. The Conservative leadership crisis of November 1990, which led to the fall of Mrs Thatcher, was a striking example of a week-long orgy of media coverage, endlessly reporting, interviewing, commenting, with cameras and microphones in the House, in the streets, on doorsteps, almost everywhere except the Cabinet room itself. Politicians and media-men manipulated each other, and both manipulated the public. It was an extraordinary example of unscripted national soap opera or situation comedy. Ironically, it demonstrated the advantages, even in a democracy, of the unreformed, secret processes of the old Conservative 'magic circle' which arranged the succession in 1957 and 1963.

The Prime Minister is condemned to perform in show business whether he or she likes it or not. The performance of the Prime Minister as media star is influenced by five factors:

1. The organisation of television broadcasting (so far) has to provide non-partisan and 'balanced' coverage of political news and opinion. The overall balance does not always satisfy the parties. Radical and marginal opinion is seriously under-represented and major pressure groups, such as the farmers, are generously treated. Nevertheless, in contrast with the press, television certainly makes a serious effort to give a hearing to more than one side of the question.
2. The press has a heavy Conservative bias. Only one popular, high-circulation newspaper is sympathetic to Labour (*The*

Daily Mirror) and that is a wayward supporter. A Conservative prime minister can normally count on the enthusiastic support of three-quarters of the press (as measured by circulation).

Mrs Thatcher was generous in patronage and privilege and assiduous and skilful in managing the press. Prior quotes ruefully a story in *The Sun* in October 1980: 'Premier Margaret Thatcher routed the "wets" in her Cabinet yesterday in a major showdown.' The report was not true, and when, a month later, this became evident, *The Sun*'s headline was 'MAGGIE AT BAY' (Prior 1986, p. 135). Mrs Thatcher rewarded the proprietors and editors of her loyal press with privileged access, honours and a tolerant view of growing monopoly. There were elements of corruption in the relations of government and press. All other political leaders compete under a grave handicap. This massive bias is too big to be wholly counter-balanced by television; in any case, the press often sets an agenda for television to pick up.

3. The promotional possibilities of the Prime Minister's public personality mean that the Prime Minister simply has to be good on television – appearance, voice, style, quickness of mind, clarity and effectiveness of speaking.
4. The government has a built-in advantage in the competition for 'good television'. Government naturally dominates the news, can easily produce high news values, and has a massive advantage in the management of news, in timing and presentation. It is especially easy to present the Prime Minister as a world leader, thus lifting him (or her) above domestic problems to a world stage where apparent success overlays actual impotence.
5. High exposure to the media is very risky for all political leaders, even for Conservatives. To adopt a phrase from the media, the banana skin count is high. Again there are many illustrations, especially for the Labour Party – Wilson's reference to the 'pound in your pocket' not being devalued (after devaluation in 1967); Callaghan's airport interview on his return from the Carribbean during the 'winter of discontent', when *The Sun*'s headline ran: CRISIS? WHAT CRISIS? (This was strictly incorrect but a fair indication of

the gist and tone of Callaghan's remarks.) Kinnock slipped on the seashore (not on a banana skin), and the pictures were cheerfully broadcast (after all, he was there to be photographed). Mrs Thatcher usually avoided banana skins; and enjoyed the advantage that her slips would not be repeated and amplified in the popular press.

Thus the rule that those who live by the media may perish by the media does not apply fully to Conservative prime ministers. This has not lessened their determination to impose their concept of impartiality on the broadcasting organisations.

Prime minister and people

The Prime Minister builds a relationship with the people mainly through the media, and to some extent through the party. Poll evidence seems to show that some prime ministers are significantly better than others at building popularity, no matter what they do as prime ministers. This was true most of the time for Wilson and Thatcher, while Heath and Home were losers. Such personal popularity or unpopularity has a 'coat-tail' effect on the fortunes of the parties. However, the British political system is very far from being fully presidential, and parties perform in elections to some extent independently of the leader. The leader component of electoral performance is substantial, but not dominant.

This can be explained mainly by the adversarial nature of British politics. Party conflict teaches the voters to dislike the other side, its policies and its leaders. So a British prime minister can normally expect to be much hated as well as much loved. Mrs Thatcher was at one time the most unpopular Prime Minister in polling history. Further, it is unlikely that the Prime Minister's supporters (those who voted for him or her) amount to more than 50 per cent of the actual voters, and rather less of the whole electorate. It is not surprising that some prime ministers seem to suffer from paranoia – they have a lot to be paranoid about.

Part V
Cases

12

Two Prime Ministers: Harold Wilson and Margaret Thatcher

HAROLD WILSON: PRIME MINISTER, 1964–70, 1974–6

The character of a prime ministership arises from a unique combination of personality and political circumstance. There is no prime minister wholly representative of the office, yet none who does not illuminate the variable nature and quality of the office. Thus Harold Wilson exemplifies the operation of a prime minister leading a heavy-weight Cabinet and a disputatious party, and having some regard for the building of agreement ('consensus') in government, party and nation.

Structure and style

Harold Wilson may reasonably be given some part of the credit for the recent expansion of the 10 Downing Street Office to its current size and significance. This was deliberate and planned. Wilson wanted a strong prime ministership, changing Number 10, as he said, from a small village, or a monastery, into a power house. This was probably intended as a complement, rather than counter to, the Cabinet. Such an approach was evident in his first two years, when he had a precarious majority and a relatively inexperienced Cabinet. Major economic strategy was decided by Wilson, Brown and Callaghan; the crisis economic package of July 1965 was 'dumped without warning on the Cabinet table the morning it was due to be announced and ministers were given three hours to discuss and agree it' (Ponting 1989, p. 33). Foreign and defence policy depended mainly on Wilson's relations with the US President, Johnson, not with the Cabinet.

Nevertheless, Wilson was in principle a Cabinet-man: the Cabinet was the base from which he pursued his tactical alliances. For all the complaints about Wilson's independent and bilateral activity behind the Cabinet's back, Wilson worked within the Cabinet framework. However, he made much use of advisers, inner Cabinets and a kitchen Cabinet. His first government was initially dominated by the triumvirate, all anti-Bevanites. To his Cabinet colleagues he seemed elusive and unreliable, but in the long run Wilson was never able to distance himself from them. He aimed to dominate the Cabinet, not to banish it from the inner circle of policy making.

His approach changed somewhat in his second ministry. The approach was more relaxed, not to say dilatory, even though the parliamentary and the national situation were equally worrying. There was no more talk, as in 1964, of a dynamic 'first one hundred days'. He adapted his favoured football analogies to a less prominent role, 'an old-fashioned deep-lying centre-half' rather than 'in every position on the field' (Wilson 1976, p. 78).

Through both his governments Wilson's approach was interventionist. He was active in economic and foreign affairs, including industrial and trade union policy, public expenditure, the constitution, Vietnam, Rhodesia, the EEC and Northern Ireland. No prime minister could reasonably neglect these issues and there was little of significance left in which he could pursue non-intervention. Foreign affairs attracted him as it does most prime ministers.

Working relations

Wilson's style as chairman of the Cabinet has been referred to above (Chapter 10). Wilson's relations with colleagues were shaped by the Cabinet framework, and within that by the political weight of some of his senior colleagues, and by disagreements and divisions within the Cabinet. Of his colleagues, none had an automatic veto, but two or three had to be appeased, and their agreement built in. For example, Crosland complained that a Cabinet had spent two hours and more on Overseas Aid (in deference to Barbara Castle) and only five minutes on Education (Castle 1984, p. 53, 29 July 1965). This is a minor (but hardly trivial) illustration of the Government's inability 'to put aside or transcend the personality clashes and political rivalries inherited from thirteen years in opposition. . . . [T]he peculiar intensity of the battles in the 1950s between the Bevanites, Gaitskell's supporters, the unilateralists and the group around Wilson left lasting wounds. Trust and mutual respect between the groups were missing, so that almost every move was regarded with suspicion and at the top of the party there was persistent rivalry' (Ponting 1989, p. 401).

Apart from the pressure of such rivalries, Wilson recognised the need to hear about alternative lines of policy, and liked to conjure agreement out of division. The diaries give accounts of long Cabinet meetings (not always welcomed by The Colleagues), sharp divisions, and, quite often, a collective decision conjured by Wilson from his warring colleagues (e.g. Castle 1984, pp. 238–9, 4 April 1967). Like most prime ministers except Attlee, Wilson enjoyed the illusion of power so easily available on the international stage, the first and sweetest corruption of power – *folie de grandeur*. Wilson also used protracted Cabinet discussion to smother his colleagues and obscure an issue. For example, four Cabinet meetings in one week in November 1974 were used to 'disarm the disarmers', and secure support for a continued heavy nuclear arms policy. Barbara Castle moaned that he could 'never resist filling a Cabinet vacuum with words' (1980, p. 333, 6 March 1975). What she called 'garrulity', 'talking us down by sheer repetition' was one of Wilson's secret weapons. To be fair to Wilson (as the diarists are not) Mrs Castle, always eager to fight her own corner, often seemed unaware of the difficulties of holding together a divided Cabinet.

Wilson's apparent commitment to Cabinet collectivity was weakened by his use of bilateral communication, 'ringing some ministers about some things, others about other matters'. Castle, Crossman, Crosland and Brown all complained at some time about the lack of collectivity – unless the minister was actually gaining by prime ministerial support against the rest of the Cabinet. But Wilson did tolerate open rows in his Cabinet, partly because the heavies and the radical dissidents insisted, partly, to Wilson's credit, because he accepted, in the best if damaging tradition of the Labour Party, that his colleagues were entitled to argue their case.

One notable feature of Wilson's relations with his Cabinet colleagues was 'leaking'. Although leaking was not invented by Wilson and his colleagues, it seems to have come of age in his governments, increasing in quantity and developing as a regular, routine tactic in interministerial conflict. Wilson himself subjected his colleagues to regular denunciation of their alleged leaking habits. Crosland drew attention to the practice in August 1966, following a warning by Wilson against leaks and the airing of differences in the press. Barbara Castle wrote: 'Crosland leant forward deliberately and said very politely what a lot of us had been longing to say for a long time: "Prime Minister, I have listened with great humility to your weekly lectures about leaks, but I must point out that there is evidence that these leaks are not coming from those of us who raise these matters here but from the most senior members of the Cabinet"' (Castle 1984, p. 159, 4 August 1966).

Wilson's prime ministership is unusually well covered in his own writings and those of the diarists. His terms of office span years of growing awareness of economic failure in Britain. These two points colour the picture of Wilson, and have damaged his reputation. One of his major concerns was to hold his fissured party together. His Cabinet included political heavyweights, and in some cases they led sketchily organised factions – Bevanites, Jenkinsites. Wilson's long-term achievement as party leader was limited; the party came near to collapse in the 1980s.

His concern for the party was crossed and complicated by his bureaucratic leanings. Temperamentally and by early experience he was, like Gaitskell, and Heath too, a good civil servant, another Permanent Secretary manqué. 'He became absorbed into the Whitehall ethos: like the civil servants he too came to regard the efficient conduct of business within Whitehall as equivalent to successful government' (Ponting 1989, p. 173). This had some effect on his conduct of the prime ministership. Wilson's initial deliberate attempts to strengthen 10 Downing Street were based on careful reflection, not just the excitement of high office. He favoured a positive move towards a more powerful Number 10 as the driving force of Cabinet government (Wilson 1976, p. 77).

Wilson quotes with approval Professor Jones's statement that: 'The Prime Minister is the one minister who stands on the peaks of both politics and administration' (Wilson 1976, p. 80). In his early career, Wilson had proved himself an able manager. But he was fascinated by the personal and party side of politics too, the necessary but messy business of building assent. He was pre-eminently a fixer, good at arranging, distilling, conjuring agreement. This was not always the path of least resistance: it required patience, and courage; as Barbara Castle inelegantly wrote, Wilson had 'guts of a rather devious kind' (1984, p. 291). But fixing had its 'downside'. Wilson's critics claimed that his approach lacked strategic purpose: the objective was to fix – he did not distinguish between concessions on matters of central principle and marginal adjustments. Sometimes he saw the objective in terms of personal political competition: 'downing the Tories or embarrassing Heath' (Benn 1988, p. 166, 8 May 1969, who calls him 'a small-minded man').

Wilson's achievements as prime minister were not substantial. He held the Labour Party together, and negotiated some politically difficult issues, notably Britain's membership of the EEC; but the party's unity was short-lived. The Government's conduct of the economy was wrecked by the unreformed trade unions, with whom the Labour Party claimed a special partnership. One lesson of Wilson's prime ministership was that there is no substitute for effective political leadership outside the Central Executive Territory: it is never enough just to avoid upsetting one's political friends.

Cases

A Middle East Crisis: the Cabinet meeting of 27 May 1967

An emergency Cabinet was held to consider a crisis in the Middle East at the time of the Six-Day War, and the closing by Egypt of the Straits of Tiran to Israel. The Prime Minister and Foreign

Secretary (George Brown) wanted immediate Cabinet support for firm action, specifically joining with the USA in an unequivocal statement of intent to enforce rights of free passage. It appeared that military action was intended. The situation was critical; the Foreign Secretary was flying to Moscow that night and wanted a clear and strong position.

The Cabinet was not impressed by what looked like a 'bounce', which seemed to reflect the Prime Minister's fondness for the Anglo-American 'special relationship'. The rest of the Cabinet preferred to wait for the UN Security Council to meet. The Chancellor was hostile, and the Defence Secretary, having consulted his military advisers, did not like the proposal. The meeting grew angry. 'There was a moment when [Wilson] and Jim [Callaghan] came to verbal blows in a way I have never seen in Cabinet before. Said Jim, "Some of us won't have this policy". At which Harold snarled back, "some of us won't have this constant obstruction". But gradually the weight of [the Chancellor's] arguments, and the overwhelming preponderance of view in the Cabinet, wore him down' (Castle 1984, p. 258, 23 May 1967).

The case had resonance for the Gulf crisis of 1990, and counts against a simple view of prime ministerial power. It is possible that the Cabinet could have been persuaded by different tactics – or perhaps by a *fait accompli*? But the opposition of the Defence Secretary and, to a lesser extent, the Chancellor, was crucial. This Cabinet is not recorded in the diaries of Crossman and Benn, who were both away at the time. But Gordon Walker's 'Imaginary Cabinet Meeting' (1972, pp. 138–51) is partly based on this meeting, and gives a good impression of a calmer, more rational debate.

Postponement of the raising of the school-leaving age, January 1968

In January 1968 the Wilson Cabinet was looking for cuts in public expenditure of up to £850m. A politically-balanced package was proposed: the postponement of the raising of the school-leaving age; the abandonment of the East of Suez role; and the cancellation of the purchase of F-111 aircraft.

The raising of the school-leaving age was a long-term

educational goal, and had featured in the 1964 and 1966 Labour manifestos. There was little disagreement that this reform was justified, though room for misgivings about the kinds of education required and about practical implementation. The Cabinet of 5 January is recorded in three diaries (Castle, Crossman, Benn) and Susan Crosland has an account in her biography of her husband. Crossman and Castle analyse the motives of the Cabinet discussants: trade unionist, socialist ideologist, working class. The Defence Secretary was concerned to see cuts in domestic programmes equivalent to projected defence cuts ('trying to get his own back', Benn commented). Barbara Castle was torn between 'left-wingism' and her roads programme. Callaghan when Chancellor had favoured postponement but now followed the working class line. The Secretary of State for Education, Gordon Walker, sat silent and trembling and, when asked, 'mumbled acquiescence'. Benn said his arguments were 'quite disgraceful'.

The analysis illustrates how a choice of this kind (admittedly difficult) may be made by members of a Cabinet. But the discussion was also notable for a moment of drama when Crossman put a sharp question and George Brown launched an attack which the upper middle-class Crossman found 'unpleasantly class-conscious'. The episode is best reported by Susan Crosland, based on a conversation with Anthony Crosland that night (which was evidently noted). 'Crossman supported the Chancellor and postponement, but expressed concern about who would be affected:
"Only 400,000 children. But they're not our children. It's always other people's children. None of us in this room would dream of letting our children leave school at fifteen."
The Foreign Secretary, George Brown, said to the Secretary of State for Education: "I want a straight answer to a straight question. If you had to choose between these 400,000 fifteen-year-olds and university students, which would you help?"
"If I had to make such a choice, I suppose I'd help university students", Gordon Walker replied.
"May God forgive you", said George Brown. It was very effective, Tony told me that night.' (Crosland 1982, p. 194). The Cabinet was divided 11 to 10 in favour of postponement. Castle commented: 'We don't vote in Cabinet, of course, but Harold

collects the voices very carefully on issues that divide us as acutely as this' (Castle 1984, p. 351, 5 January 1968).

The F-111 fighter aircraft, January 1968

In a meeting of Cabinet lasting altogether four hours cancellation of the F-111 was decided by the Prime Minister's vote. However, the Defence Secretary, Denis Healey, was powerful enough to threaten 'reconsideration of his position' (i.e. resignation). He was able to secure a second round of debate a week later, when he argued for alternatives. He lost by 12 to 9. Benn was impressed by Healey's courage and dignity, and by Roy Jenkins, the Chancellor, who won. Benn thought Wilson 'never quite equal to the occasion'.

'In Place of Strife', 1969

In 1968–9 the Labour Government published a White Paper, 'In Place of Strife', proposing legislation to regulate trade unions. A new legislative framework would constitute 'a charter of trade union rights', but – and this was the point – there would be some limitation on the right to strike, including fines on employers and unions for breaches of the law. The trade unions, a large number of Labour Members of Parliament, and some members of the Cabinet, opposed the proposals, and the Government was eventually forced into a humiliating climb-down. In place of the proposed legislation the TUC signed a 'Solemn and Binding Agreement', making promises that could not be delivered.

This was one of the most substantial cases of a government climb-down in recent history and is significant in a number of ways.

1. The White Paper was prepared by Mrs Castle, the Secretary of State, with the support of the Prime Minister, and following the Report of the Donovan Commission on Industrial Relations. However, the White Paper went beyond the largely 'non-interventionist' proposals of Donovan. That report had not paved the way, as the

Government had hoped, so there was an inadequate basis for the radical proposals (radical in the British trade union context) of the White Paper.
2. Some members of the Cabinet felt that they were being bounced. Tony Crosland believed it was too late in the Parliament for such controversial legislation, which in any case could not be made to work. The Chancellor, Roy Jenkins, a key figure, thought a quick, short bill might have passed; he gave his support initially, but weakened as the months dragged by. James Callaghan, then Home Secretary, fought the proposals quite openly and defiantly, and in total disregard of collective responsibility or simple collegiality.
3. The Government negotiated as the weaker party with the trade unions, and the authority of the state dissolved.
4. The Parliamentary Labour Party would not support the Government. The Labour Party appeared for what it partly is, the parliamentary wing of the trade unions.
5. At the height of the crisis in the summer of 1969 the Central Executive Territory fell apart. Cabinet met four or five times a week, the Prime Minister's self-control gave way to petulance and threats of resignation, Callaghan was excluded from the new Inner Cabinet, and Tony Crosland told Wilson, complaining of leaks, that most of them came from 10 Downing Street (Crosland 1982, pp. 202–3).
6. At the end the Prime Minister climbed down with grace, and congratulated Mrs Castle on her achievement. It is clear that prime ministers need to be able to cope with disaster: they need resilience, courage, insensitivity to embarrassment. A blushing prime minister is a contradiction in terms.

The story of 'In Place of Strife' can be followed in the diaries (Benn, Castle, Crossman); also in Susan Crosland's biography of Tony Crosland (1982) and in Peter Jenkins's *The Battle of Downing Street* (1970).

Public sector pay claims, February 1970

This case offers a good illustration of the process of Cabinet decision making (Castle 1984, pp. 761–3; but see also Benn 1988, pp. 236–7; Crossman 1977, pp. 815–16).

Department ministers had put in claims for their own 'clients': nurses, teachers, postmen, armed forces. Castle, not herself directly concerned on this occasion, commented: 'It certainly was a grimly inflationary retinue'. The Chancellor of the Exchequer 'opened with a typical Chancellor's sermon' – he said: 'This is the last moment we have a chance to stop the avalanche and do something about it.' Department ministers spoke to their claims: the armed forces were near to mutiny, the nurses would bring about a political crisis, the teachers were demonstrating, the postmen would strike. Both Crossman and Benn, in their accounts, say that Denis Healey 'went on and on', 'bored the Cabinet', but this seems to have been an effective technique. Mrs Castle, in this case an independent voice, argued that the Government, having abandoned a prices and incomes policy, ought not 'to try to resurrect the policy against those who were not in a position to wreak so much economic damage'. Other accounts do not feature Mrs Castle so prominently.

The Prime Minister 'then came in with his favourite theme: we must look at it politically. Timing was the essence of our problem, particularly as events had now made a spring Election impossible. We should aim to postpone the results of some of these claims as far as we could: he would rather win the Election and have a November Budget than have July measures and lose the election.' Phasing was the answer. 'It was all pretty crude and Roy reacted loftily: "I would rather lose the Election than jeopardize our economic success". Castle commented, 'That didn't sound sense either'. Benn was especially uneasy about the Prime Minister's political approach. 'It was the crudest political statement I had yet heard. . . . My opinion of Harold dropped to its lowest. Crossman seemed unconcerned.'

Phasing was adopted. The Prime Minister intervened to improve the proposal for the armed forces, and the Defence Secretary made a further deal later with Mrs Castle (as Employment Minister). The Defence Secretary, Denis Healey, 'could hardly conceal his satisfaction at having got away with so much'. In the next Labour Government Healey, as Chancellor of the Exchequer, took the usual Chancellor's line. Crossman made the mistake of leaving before the summing up, which did not accord with his views.

Consultants and paybeds, December 1975

Barbara Castle, Secretary of State for Health was negotiating to reduce and eventually abolish 'paybeds' in the National Health Service hospitals. These were used by 'private' paying patients thus, so it was argued, giving privileged access to largely state-supported facilities. In the negotiations Lord Goodman acted as an intermediary between the doctors and the Government, though without official status. After a long meeting with Castle, Goodman went directly to the Prime Minister (without informing Castle) and got much of his own way. Barbara Castle was, not surprisingly, annoyed.

Three points are notable: (a) Lord Goodman seems to have been closer to the Prime Minister than the Secretary of State. (b) Values affect procedure. For the minister, paybeds represented an issue of socialist principle and a manifesto commitment; for the Prime Minister, this was a matter for compromise, especially because numbers and timing could be negotiated. (c) Barbara Castle had acquired a reputation for toughness. Paradoxically, this made it more difficult for her to act toughly.

Pay policy, 1975

The adoption of a pay policy in 1975 offers a good example of Harold Wilson's collective mode of prime ministership. The economic crisis of mid-1975 compelled the Government to 'do something' about wages. Annual inflation was near to 30 per cent. The pound was expected to sink from over $2 to $1.65 by the end of the year. Wages were about to 'explode': Cabinet approved a 30 per cent pay increase for railwaymen. Severe cuts in public expenditure had been rejected. The Government had made commitments against unemployment and a statutory wages policy. The Government finally adopted a voluntary pay policy backed by sanctions against employers. The process by which this outcome was achieved was complex. The Prime Minister took a policy proposal from the Policy Unit, resisted the Treasury's demand for a fully statutory policy, and persuaded Cabinet (in an open discussion at a full-day meeting at Chequers) to accept a pay policy in principle.

Three committees then worked on the policy – an Official Committee on Prices and Incomes, a Standing Cabinet Committee on Economic Strategy, and a new and secret *ad hoc* committee on pay policy (Donoughue 1987, pp. 64–5). The latter invention was justified, according to Donoughue, because the issue was highly sensitive, likely to split the Cabinet on a familiar Left–Right basis, and the Prime Minister needed to carry his senior colleagues with him. The Prime Minister wanted to avoid 'daily leaks to *The Guardian* of sensitive policy papers'; and to include in the Committee 'senior Ministers who were not normally members of the regular ministerial Economic Strategy Committee as well as to exclude some Ministers who were regular members' (ibid., p. 65).

There followed (in Donoughue's account) a battle for the Prime Minister's mind and will between the Chancellor and Treasury on one side and Donoughue (of the Policy Unit) on the other. The Prime Minister wavered, but finally came down in favour of the Policy Unit's non-statutory voluntary policy with sanctions. The Prime Minister conveyed his choice to the Chancellor, who immediately accepted that position.

In Healey's briefer account, the Chancellor was the initiator of the policy, and persuaded the Prime Minister, the relevant Cabinet committee and then the full Cabinet to accept a policy which Healey regarded as effectively (through the reserve powers) a 'statutory' policy. (The Cabinet Healey refers to occurred ten days after the crucial decision in principle taken at the Chequers meeting.) The Reserve Powers were initially approved neither in principle nor in practical detail, but 'on a contingent basis and without prejudice'. So they were approved, but not finally approved – or perhaps not yet approved. It is evident and significant that much depended on the interpretation of forms of words, and on the assumption of participants that they were all getting their own way. This was true for the Prime Minister, too.

Further, the crisis demonstrates that a fully collective agreed policy on a controversial matter cannot be achieved by a single prime ministerial decision, nor by one Cabinet meeting. The work of the Policy Unit seems to have been effective in this case (even allowing for some bias in Donoughue's account) particularly in holding off the Treasury. The committee structure was then plainly inadequate, until supplemented by Wilson. (After this episode the structure of economic policy making was improved by the establishment of a single Economic Strategy Committee, and the Treasury acquired a second minister in the Cabinet.) The Wilson Cabinet was, as usual, disturbed by deep disagreements on 'socialist strategy', and obsessive concern to please the TUC.

The Cabinet included several political heavyweights, so Wilson had little choice but to work collectively. But this was in any case his preference, and his conduct of this issue offers a classic illustration of prime ministerial leadership in a Cabinet framework, building consensus where none initially (and even subsequently) existed, and developing a policy from unacceptability to acquiescence.

MARGARET THATCHER: PRIME MINISTER, 1979–1990

Introduction

Like all substantial historical figures, Margaret Thatcher is likely to distort our understanding of her office and her times. In the 1980s 'an ordinary politician, labouring under many disadvantages, grew into an international figure who did some extraordinary things to her country' (Young 1989, p. 135). It is not an objective of this book to present an assessment of 'the Thatcher decade' and 'Thatcherism'. Nor is it necessarily true that Margaret Thatcher has brought about fundamental changes to the office of prime minister and to the Central Executive Territory. She did not permanently extend the office of prime minister, but she certainly demonstrated its potential for personal power, stimulated a re-examination of the place of collectivity, and inspired a reciprocal re-affirmation of the primacy of the Cabinet.

Margaret Thatcher's tenure of the office of prime minister was indeed unique in many ways: the first woman to hold the office (in a profession still dominated by men); tenure longer than any prime minister this century; an unusually strong personality; an Opposition in disarray; and critical challenges to the authority and power of the state (the miners' strike, the Falklands war, the Gulf crisis). Mrs Thatcher was unique as a prime minister, but her tenure of the office tested it under stress and revealed both its extreme possibilities and its enduring characteristics.

Structure

Unlike some of her predecessors, Margaret Thatcher cared little about the structure of the office of prime minister (though much about its capabilities, authority and dignity). 'Hers is an almost exclusively people-centred style of government. Her interest in the structure of government is minimal' (King 1985, p. 122). The Prime Minister's Office and the Cabinet Office did not change much in her time, apart from the abolition of the CPRS in 1983 and the assumption by the Cabinet Secretary of the headship of the Home Civil Service. These two Offices, Cabinet and Prime Minister's, constitute the basic structure of prime ministerial government, and the Cabinet Secretary continued to serve in effect as the Prime Minister's Permanent Secretary. But the less formal elements of Number 10 fluctuated. There were always 'friends', confidants, advisers close to Mrs Thatcher, though never quite forming a group or a kitchen Cabinet. The friends included at various times the head of the Policy Unit, personal advisers, her Parliamentary Private Secretary, the Press Secretary and one or two officials from the Private Office, as well as sympathisers from business and the media. Some of Mrs Thatcher's appointments seem to have been quite casual, though no-one became a close 'friend' who did not meet her personal standards of vigour and purposiveness (see Young 1989, pp. 164–6).

These were the people of Margaret Thatcher's people-centred 'Number 10'; but overwhelmingly the structure and force of Number 10 centred on the Prime Minister herself. She demonstrated beyond question that prime ministership is a combination of office and individual, in which the individual is potentially the dominant force, transforming the structure. This approach to government – personal dominance aiming to get things done – inevitably diminished the role of Cabinet and collectivity. She sidestepped the Cabinet when she could, ruling through a network of 'trusties' manning *ad hoc* committees. This was 'government by herself in concert with selected ministers . . . brought together only semi-formally under her aegis' (Young 1989, p. 430). The exclusion of senior ministers from the inner councils of her government was remarkable. For example, 'Prior and Pym were kept off the key economic policy committee, and John Biffen . . . was virtually excluded from government while still Leader of the House (Jenkins 1987, p. 183). This constitutional choice was perverse but not necessarily authoritarian: it is normal in business, and would be the preferred system (if they could get away with it) of many people in high public office. But it certainly lay outside, or at the margins of, the constitutional tradition of Cabinet collectivity.

Style

Margaret Thatcher's approach to the office of prime minister derived directly from her political stance. She had 'a mind of her own' and a set of policy ideas taken from her 'right-wing' associates and mentors, both in and outside the party. These ideas formed for her a policy agenda for immediate implementation – rather as 'left-wing' Labour politicians regard the pledges of the party manifesto. For Mrs Thatcher there was urgent work to be done, and no further time to be wasted waiting for 'consensus' (a word she particularly mistrusted). By constrast, other prime ministers have chosen first to build agreement on what is to be done, or to await quietly the persuasion of colleagues or the emergence of a crisis.

Mrs Thatcher was, in her own estimation, a 'conviction politician' – which, as a former Chief Scientist to the CPRS said, is not the same as being 'a rationally-guided politician' (quoted in Hennessy 1989, p. 312). Her ideas were simple, sturdy maxims, admitting neither doubt nor subtle shading: taxes and trade unions were bad; the national economy could best be run by the homely wisdom of a provident housewife; Britain was great; and the authority of the British state must be preserved and enhanced. Such ideas ran with the times and were politically astute – far more than the more sophisticated and subtle formulations of more intellectually inclined politicians. Mrs Thatcher's strong convictions were shaken in her first two years of office, but were confirmed subsequently by her apparent successes, notably over the miners and Argentina. Faith was confirmed by works; there was no alternative, and no turning back (in the detested U-turns of her Conservative predecessor).

The main weakness in such a hard approach to the office of prime minister lay in the high risk of failure. Mrs Thatcher was indeed lucky to 'get away with it' – lucky to defeat Argentina at comparatively low or bearable cost, lucky again that her defeat of the miners was so dramatically complete, if costly. But Mrs Thatcher also earned her good fortune by her concern for the political and presentational side of the office. She had learned from her ministerial experience that blame was easy to come by, and credit needed to be grasped; she also learned to evade or postpone the harder consequences of her convictions (for example, in avoiding a premature confrontation with the miners). High moral principle was eased by political calculation; and a great deal of time was spent (not least with the hairdresser) on the presentation of herself as prime minister.

Mrs Thatchers's methods of work matched her approach to the prime ministership. She was truly a 'workaholic' in the sense of a consuming addiction to work, excluding what most other senior executives, and other prime ministers, regard as pleasurable activities (including sleep). Jenkins says 'she was still the scholarship girl attending to her homework' (1987, p. 86) – as if girls and homework and scholarships were not quite right for a prime minister. When she was a minister, her Permanent Secretary, with whom she did not get on at all, said of her 'She worked all hours of the day and night. She always emptied her box, with blue pencil marks all over the paper. . . . She was always a very good trouper, always meticulous about turning up for meetings. If she said she'd be there at two minutes past six, she'd be there at two minutes past six' (quoted in Young 1989, p. 72).

Mrs Thatcher was good – both skilful and industrious – at mastering briefs, and rarely uncertain of the detail of policy, even in stressful and complex international negotiations. This was masterful leadership in detail, not broad brush leadership with much delegation. Her approach to colleagues and officials was characterised by her first encounter as a minister with her civil servants at the Department of Education and Science. They were presented with eighteen instant demands. She meant to have her way, no matter what courtesy or reasoned argument might indicate. Most of her colleagues had no defences against her dynamism.

Margaret Thatcher's style as prime minister was evident in her approach and methods of work. There is little more to add about 'personality'; though a great deal has been written and spoken, much of it at second hand (including of course by the present writer!). Some commentators believe Mrs Thatcher cannot be fully understood as a politician without reference to her gender and class – a woman from the lower middle class who did not fit easily into the male-dominated, upper middle class culture and assumptions of the old Conservative Party. Her insecurity was evident in her comparatively deferential attachment to two Tory 'grandees', Whitelaw and Carrington, and in the rather 'governessy' manner she developed as armour against both her colleagues and her opponents. (Her truly dreadful experience of IRA terrorism must also be taken into account for its effects on her outlook and life style.)

This interpretation is plausible, though it undervalues the remarkable way in which the young Margaret Roberts made her own way from the Grantham grocer's shop via Oxford to substantial professional and personal success by her early thirties. Margaret Thatcher was an extra-ordinary personality. She used both her gender and her class background as positive political assets – which put her in touch with the common people of England (if not Britain) in a way which Labour leaders, in their intellectual and trade-union oriented (and of course male-dominated) culture, should have envied. She was also blessed politically with strong self-belief, though that is always a mixed blessing. She had faith in herself and in the contribution she could make to the salvation of the nation: 'If I give up, we will lose' (Young 1989, p. 207). Like Cromwell, she was a zealot, believing in her destiny; like her admired Churchill she saw herself romantically as a national leader – but she lacked Churchill's wit and sense of history. In any assessment of individual personality against institutional structure in the office of prime minister, Mrs Thatcher's tenure weighs heavily on the personality side.

Working relationships

Mrs Thatcher's 'people-centred' approach to the organisation of Number 10 was complicated by the nature of her personal relationships and their shifts during fifteen years as leader of the party. Hugo Young proposes a magnetism/aversion explanation of her personal political relations. 'Intimacy', he wrote, 'was one of the tools of mastery' (1989, p. 160). For a favoured circle there were strong bands of intimacy; for the rest there was aversion, assertiveness, aggression, command. This inner circle of friends included at some time a few senior Cabinet colleagues (especially Whitelaw), her PPS (Ian Gow), and senior officials (Powell, Whitmore, Ingham), and outside advisers and aides (e.g. Sherman, Hoskyns).

Mrs Thatcher's inner circle was comparable with the kitchen Cabinets, confidants and friends of other prime ministers. The characteristic qualities are loyalty, unfailing support in good and bad times, and no more criticism than is necessary to avoid disaster. Even the magnetism/aversion pattern can be discerned in other prime ministers, since it is in part a product of the Prime Minister's situation (powerful in an adversarial world of friends, enemies and opponents). But Mrs Thatcher was unusual in attracting to her inner circle senior civil servants below the highest ranks.

Mrs Thatcher's inner circle was unusual and significant in another way. Other prime ministers have used an inner circle to retreat into relative isolation from colleagues, but without cutting themselves off from the Government which they headed. By contrast, Mrs Thatcher at times seemed to distance herself from her Government. Prime ministers have often cried, 'Why wasn't I told?' – as Mrs Thatcher did at the end of the Westland affair. Mrs Thatcher sometimes, in effect, also cried, 'Don't blame me, blame the Government!' She once described herself as 'the rebel head of an established government' (Young 1989, p. 242). Such a view proceeded from her being initially in a minority in her

Cabinet, from her strong aversion to some departments, notably the Foreign Office, and from her concept of the office of prime minister as very far from 'primus inter pares'. Indeed, she saw her position as undoubtedly 'primus' and even (for the few remaining students of Latin) 'in partibus infidelium' (in the lands of the infidel).

In her relations with colleagues, ministers, advisers, officials, Mrs Thatcher acted characteristically as a commander. This was evident in the stream of minutes she issued; reading almost every document, commenting sharply, 'Nonsense!', 'Do this again!' (Young 1989, p. 158) and issuing prime ministerial minutes more often than was comfortable. She failed to understand (or perhaps she understood quite well) 'that ministers and officials must regard a prime ministerial minute as a mandatory instruction rather than merely helpful advice. Similarly, she neither noticed nor cared that, as Geoffrey Howe complained in his resignation speech (13 November 1990), 'some casual comment or impulsive answer' undermined the collectivity of her Government.

Mrs Thatcher's relations with the Cabinet were determined by her general approach to her office, and to the awkward fact that her own ideas and policy agenda initially lacked majority support in Cabinet. She was, as a dissident backbencher said, a Roundhead in a Cabinet of Cavaliers. She favoured argument rather than discussion, but not competitive argument in which she might be the loser. In consequence she hastened and hardened the shift away from full Cabinet to committees and informal meetings. The change is evident in the statistics of meetings – Cabinets halved compared with Attlee, Churchill and Macmillan, *ad hoc* committees down from 50 to 60 in the 1970s to 20 a year in the 1980s (see Hennessy 1989, p. 311).

Jim Prior recorded the change after his exit from the Government. His rather self-pitying complaint curiously and significantly reveals the impotence of The Colleagues:

> In the early days I think Margaret was worried that we would not accept her authority and would not do what she wanted. I dare say she was right since most of the powerful voices were ranged against her.
> In her early years as prime minister, Margaret adhered closely to the traditional principles and practice of Cabinet government. She operated very strictly through the Cabinet committee system, with

the Cabinet office taking the Minutes. . . . Unfortunately, after a couple of years, the formal Cabinet committees were very much down-graded and she began to operate much more in small groups dominated by her cronies. . . . Even before 1981 she had one small group which met her for breakfast and which was kept very hush-hush. It included Nigel Lawson, Norman Tebbitt – neither of whom was then in the Cabinet. . . . This cosy arrangement was later superseded by her close relationship with Cecil Parkinson.

(Prior 1986, p. 119)

The operation of a small 'War Cabinet' during the Falklands crisis in 1982 also convinced her that it was far easier to settle issues with just five or six people. In the years since she adopted *ad hoc* groups as one of her main methods of government. 'Margaret would give as her reason for working increasingly in small groups that she couldn't rely on her colleagues to respect her authority. I regret to say that this was true' (Prior 1986, pp. 133–4).

In meetings of full Cabinet, committees and bilaterals, Mrs Thatcher's style of argument did not encourage a collective approach to an agreed decision. Argument was a waste of time, and in any case was conducted as a battle of forceful assertions, of will rather than minds. Reasonable colleagues who believed, reasonably enough, that they might be wrong, went down to defeat, since Mrs Thatcher was very well-informed, a skilled forensic speaker and, above all, absolutely confident she was right. Cabinet was at best a sounding board, occasionally indicating to her that restraint was necessary. It was not a progressive discussion, moving through the weighing of various points of view, towards a collective agreement (cf. David Howell, quoted in Hennessy 1986, p. 96; see also pp. 97–8).

More business was transacted by correspondence, by informal meetings, *ad hoc* groups, and by 'judge and jury' sessions (see above p. 84 and Hennessy 1986, p. 102). In particular, economic policy was decided in a small group, a 'self-confident economic Cabinet, the secretive cabal at the heart of the government' (Young 1989, p. 151). The 1981 Budget, including the doubling of VAT, was widely regarded as profoundly damaging to British industry (as it proved to be, at least in the short term). Some senior ministers with economic responsibilities first heard of the main proposals from outsiders. Similar illustrations of

Mrs Thatcher's neglect of Cabinet could be drawn from foreign policy, for example the decision to allow US bombers to fly from Britain to attack Libya; or the immediate support offered to President Bush in the Gulf crisis, August 1990.

A significant difference?

The critical point here is not that Mrs Thatcher appeared to take significant decisions either on her own or in the company of at most one or two colleagues. Similar examples can be found in the record of all post-war prime ministers, and especially in the fields of high economic and foreign policy (Attlee and the manufacture of atomic weapons; Eden and the Suez intervention; Macmillan's nuclear deal with President Kennedy; Wilson's decision in 1964 not to devalue; Wilson, Callaghan and the Chevaline project). The critical difference to be established in Mrs Thatcher's case lies in the following considerations:

1. Locating the decision in the context of Cabinet discussion; the timing and significance of the referral of the decision to Cabinet (just reporting, or still open to consideration and comment).
2. The general approach to Cabinet discussion as an open, undirected seminar, building agreement; or a short, closed deliberation, leading to acceptance of a previously-stated position.
3. The extent of extra-Cabinet decision making (frequency, significance of subjects, whether they extend beyond the areas of high finance, national security and summitry which fall naturally extra-Cabinet).
4. The tendency to policy initiation outside the Cabinet system.

In the light of these considerations there is a strong case that Mrs Thatcher's prime ministership was significantly different from her predecessors, characterised by personal dominance rather than collectivity. But the evidence is uneven, and inevitably lacking the support of detailed and documented studies of the Thatcher administrations. The case as it stands rests on: the statistics of meetings; the testimony of colleagues (mainly ex-colleagues) about Mrs Thatcher's personal style and mode of argument; the evidence of particular decisions known to have been taken personally rather than collectively; and the occasional evidence of the initiation of policy, or of policy commitment by Mrs Thatcher 'on the hoof', in a conference speech or a television interview (the Community Charge is one such).

Mrs Thatcher's approach to Cabinet was reinforced by her sharp and occasionally even brutal handling of individual colleagues; and by the weakness, even supineness, of many of her colleagues. Pym, Soames and Prior, among others, were subject to private undermining, partly through the press, and public humiliation (Prior 1986, passim; Young 1989, p. 196). The response of most of her colleagues was loyalty or at least acquiescence. A few, in the end, fought back, notably Heseltine, Lawson and Howe, but their resignations indicated their lack of success in maintaining their own line. Pym and Prior threatened resignation, the former with some effect (Young 1989, p. 210).

Whitelaw 'bound himself completely to her' (Young 1989, p. 235) like the gentleman he was and, on the same model, once memorably rebuked her for the disloyalty of applauding his barrackers at the Party Conference (Young 1989, p. 236). Carrington supported her but had the standing and self-confidence to retain his personal independence. The critics Mrs Thatcher despised as wets for lacking backbone in their political outlook gave some substance to the insult by failing completely to stand their ground against her individually, or to organise coherently as a group (Prior 1986, pp. 204, 216, 241–2).

For all the weakness of her colleagues under her withering gaze, Mrs Thatcher did not always have her own way without a struggle. There were arguments in the Cabinet, sometimes fierce, notably over the 1981 Budget and the Civil Service strike in 1981, and over policy towards local government; though arguments diminished, and Mrs Thatcher won them more easily as her authority grew after 1982–3. Some ministers still managed to build small islands of independence outside the central areas of policy. There were a few examples of her conceding defeat (Ireland, Rhodesia, Hong Kong, NHS); though these are more than balanced by her many victories against substantial opposition (for example, the 1981 Budget, the Community Charge).

Mrs Thatcher's conduct of the office of prime minister was different from that of her predecessors, and is likely to remain unique. This is not to say that some of her predecessors have not been very powerful. The centre of policy making had long ago shifted away from the Cabinet itself; but Mrs Thatcher's exclusion of the full Cabinet was sharper than under Wilson or Heath, and her Cabinet rarely stood its ground. But Mrs Thatcher stands out because she was not much concerned with building agreement and maintaining collegiality and collectivity; and in the service of her personal political objectives, she was ready to exploit the full potential of her office.

The approach to, and manipulation of, her office, were much assisted by three factors:

1. The weakness of her colleagues, taken by surprise and emasculated by the Prime Minister's style and success. It is significant that of the three colleagues mentioned by Hennessy in his book on the Cabinet published in 1986 as 'positive forces' 'pressing reservations', one was later dismissed, one resigned in protest, and the third was exiled to Wales and later resigned quietly.
2. Political success aided by great good fortune, above all the suicide of her opponents, the Centre and Left, the miners, and General Galtieri. Once she had won a second election, she was irreplaceable – until it became clear that she might lose a fourth election.
3. The potency of her extraordinary personal style, the conviction and drive, the readiness to challenge, and – most unusually – not to be liked. Cabinet ministers and world leaders often wanted to say, 'You can't talk to me like that!' but she did and, if challenged, would back up her governessy reprimands with well-informed criticism. Mrs Thatcher had the manner of a governess, but the mind of an able lawyer-politician.

Mrs Thatcher's achievements as prime minister were more substantial and more visible than Wilson's. In economic policy, industrial relations and in foreign policy her work made a marked difference: some things would never be quite the same again. Nevertheless her prime ministership ended in apparent defeat and failure. Partly this was because of the humiliating manner of her fall; partly, and more seriously for her reputation, it was because her dismissal signalled the limits of the acceptability of her radical crusade.

The lesson of Mrs Thatcher's prime ministership is curiously parallel to Wilson's. It is never enough just to please your friends. Both Thatcher and Wilson were victims of the partisan adversarial nature of British politics in their time (a partisanship to which they had both contributed). Deluded by partisan triumphs, they came to believe that government was about pleasing your friends. For a prime minister there is no substitute for effective political leadership outside the Central Executive Territory among indifferents and opponents as well as friends.

Cases

Mrs Thatcher and the Civil Service

Generally, Mrs Thatcher was uneasy with most institutions, except Parliament and the Monarchy, and particularly critical of the Civil Service. Sir Frank Cooper, when Permanent Secretary in the Ministry of Defence, said it was not that she disliked civil servants 'in their own right', but 'she instinctively dislikes anybody who is not helping in the wealth creation process' (Young and Sloman 1986, p. 49). Her approach, her mind and temperament, were quite different. She showed impatience with 'the mandarin world of Whitehall, in which scepticism and rumination were more highly rated habits of mind than zeal or blind conviction' (Young 1989, p. 155). Mrs Thatcher was strengthened in this view by her adviser Sir John Hoskyns, who was influential in her early years in office, as previously in Opposition. Hoskyns was deeply hostile to the civil service approach which he regarded as too moderate and negative, failing to espouse, still less to pursue, radical solutions.

Mrs Thatcher added to this general scepticism her energetic disposition to command and drive. She had demonstrated this to officials on her first day as Secretary of State for Education. When her Permanent Secretary, Sir William Pile, introduced himself, he was presented with 'a page from an exercise book with eighteen things she wanted done that day'. Sir William said, 'We didn't stop to argue' (Young 1989, p. 71). Nevertheless Pile still assumed that the job of the Civil Service was to offer advice, 'speaking up for what the Department has done or what the Department should do' (Young 1989, p. 72). Mrs Thatcher regarded this approach as obstructive: she did not want advice in this sense, and refused to recognise contrary arguments.

In consequence, civil servants most frequently received instructions, not requests for advice. Prior commented on the sharpness of her many minutes to departments: 'I was quite amazed at the rudeness of the letters that came round as compared to the earlier time' (quoted in Young and Sloman 1986, p. 478). In an early attempt to come to terms with Mrs Thatcher, the head of the Civil Service arranged a dinner for all the Permanent Secretaries and Mrs Thatcher. The occasion was a disaster. In due course the head of the Civil Service retired (prematurely) and the Civil Service Department was abolished (Young 1989, pp. 230–2).

Alongside Mrs Thatcher's general dislike of civil servants, she came to like some sharp bright officials; indeed, a handful became quite close to her, and she depended on them. In this sense she 'politicised' some of her 10 Downing Street officials. Some of these favoured officials went on to rapid high promotion; others stayed, becoming almost too close for further movement within the service.

Charles Powell, an official in her Private Office, seconded from the Foreign Office, was one of her close official friends and supporters. Young wrote: 'No politician enjoyed such status. Some civil servants did. They were the replacement for what previous leaders might have called a Kitchen Cabinet' (1989, p. 446). Powell is known to have worked closely with the Prime Minister on foreign and in particular European matters (including her 1988 Bruges speech, expressing some scepticism about closer unity in the EC; and the development of her views on German reunification, which turned out not to matter very much, since the Germans did what they wanted anyway). Powell dealt at the Downing Street end with the question of the leaking of a confidential document in the Westland affair.

It was generally assumed that Powell was too closely associated with the Prime Minister to be able (or even to want) to return to the Foreign Office, or work for another prime minister. It is not possible to assess Powell's influence on Mrs Thatcher. It seems likely that there was a substantial element of mutuality in the relationship, Powell helping the Prime Minister to move in a direction she positively favoured and with which he sympathised.

Mrs Thatcher also had close working relations with other civil servants, for example, Clive Whitmore, her PPS for most of her first term; and, like most prime ministers, with the Cabinet Secretary, then Sir John Hunt. The most notorious member of this kitchen group of officials was Bernard Ingham, her Press Secretary. Ingham was chosen quite casually and not on party political grounds for Ingham had previously worked for Labour ministers, and served as a Labour councillor in local government. Mrs Thatcher and Ingham proceeded to build 'one of the great enduring partnerships' – as consistently close as she had with any other man. The bond between them, Mrs Thatcher herself said, was that 'neither of us are smooth people' (Young 1989, p. 166).

The Thatcher–Ingham relationship was unusually close, too close perhaps for a traditional civil servant. It was thought to have seriously weakened the rule of impartiality, serving different masters with equal loyalty – though some critics believe that rule to be unrealistic and unhelpful. At the least, as for Powell, sustained devotion to one master made future civil service employment uncertain. Further, the relationship with Ingham was part of a vigorous approach to news management, which again critics judged to be excessive. Ingham himself became Head of Profession for the whole Government Information Service in 1989, as well as Prime Minister's Press Officer. These criticisms were serious and substantial, though in general it is not unreasonable for prime ministers to look to officials as well as political colleagues for close support and advice.

Mrs Thatcher is said to have 'politicised' the Civil Service. This is true of a few officials in 10 Downing Street but is not true in the full sense. Indeed, it is not possible while the Civil Service retains its monopoly of posts at the highest level, formally based on appointment by merit through the professional procedures. It is still true, however, that Mrs Thatcher has exercised significant if uneven influence on appointments to civil service posts in her immediate entourage, and in some senior posts of strategic importance. The apex of these service appointment procedures lies in the Cabinet Office, and Mrs Thatcher took a sharp interest in the opportunity to exercise patronage through the mechanism of formal approval of appointments. By 1990 over 300 senior appointments (Permanent and Deputy Secretary) had been made under her administration.

Mrs Thatcher made a point of getting to know senior civil servants. When eight retirements at the highest level occurred in 1982–3, she had some influence on the new appointments. Promotion came unexpectedly (that is, not on Buggins' Turn) to a number of candidates, distinguished by character – unstuffy, doers rather than talkers, unsmooth – rather than policy commitment. The new Permanent Secretary to the Treasury had 'a perceptibly unmandarin-like commitment to the monetarist policy (Young 1989, p. 337); but then monetarism in its less zealous form had been introduced under the Labour Government in the mid-1970s. It is probably significant that some of these unexpected promotions fell on people with a grammar-school background, like Mrs Thatcher's. Her use of her influence over senior appointments in the Civil Service was in accordance with current left-wing criticism of official obstructiveness, negative power and so on. She has followed the democratic and constitutional principle that officials serve elected political masters.

Mrs Thatcher used civil servants to achieve her ends in government – nothing wrong with that, but one or two, and notably Sir Robert Armstrong, may have felt, if not over-used, then over-exposed in public. Sir Robert, wrote Young, 'was propelled into the front line to do work which no previous prime minister had ever asked the Cabinet Secretary, or any other official, to perform' (1989, p. 462). This was certainly true in the 'Spycatcher' case, when Sir Robert had to defend the Government's shaky position in an Australian court; and in the Westland affair, when he appeared, in effect on behalf of the Government, to defend the Government's even shakier position. He was also called on to defend the Government's assault on his own profession at GCHQ. This diminution in civil service anonymity marks a radical change in the working of the Civil Service, and is itself a significant modification of the basic constitutional principle of ministerial responsibility.

Mrs Thatcher's less public but more lasting impact on the Civil Service lies in the changes brought about by managerial reform. This was initially led by Sir Derek Rayner (as he then was) from Marks and Spencer. Mrs Thatcher established Rayner and his small Efficiency Unit in the Cabinet Office, and treated Rayner as an alternative head of the Civil Service. Rayner replaced the old Programme Analysis and Review with a Financial Management Initiative, backed by a series of 'Scrutinies' of sections of work in the departments (sometimes carried out by 'Rayner's Raiders'). Rayner was critical (perhaps excessively) of the civil service attachment to paper and committees. He wanted the large areas of government which were equivalent to business or industry to behave as such, follow modern management practice – defining objectives and responsibilities, gathering and analysing information suitable for management, assessing performance. His approach was dynamic, and oriented towards action. Rayner worked out that it cost every person in the country £3 each week just to maintain the Civil Service. He demanded value for money, and insisted that civil servants should be managers, and that ministers must take responsibility for the good management of their departments.

Rayner's work was strongly backed by Mrs Thatcher, and soon achieved impressive savings – a billion pounds within its first few years. Rayner returned to Marks and Spencer but his successor, Sir Robin Ibbs, pursued the logic of managerial reform. In a report, 'The Next Steps' (1988), which is likely to be much more significant than the Fulton Report of 1968, he set out proposals for the 'hiving-off' of up to three-quarters of government work into 'agencies', which would cease to work (in practice, though not in theory) under ministerial responsibility to Parliament. No ministerial control means no departmental control. In effect, large tracts of civil service work would be removed from the control of departments. By 1990 over 30 agencies had been established and nearly 30 more were planned. Agencies already established include the Drivers and Vehicle Licensing Agency, the Employment Service and the Stationery Office.

The Rayner Efficiency Unit and 'Next Steps' mark a radical change in the Civil Service. This was pushed through by the determination and force of Mrs Thatcher, and it represents her major reform of British government.

The Westland affair, 1985–6

This complex affair is highly significant for the Central Executive Territory. Briefly, the Secretary of State for Defence, Michael Heseltine, urged on the Government a 'European' solution to the problems of the Westland Company, which manufactured helicopters. The Government preferred the amalgamation of Westland with the American Sikorsky firm. In the course of the affair two ministers, Heseltine and Leon Brittan, resigned. Heseltine protested both at the substance of policy and at what he saw as breaches of collectivity in Cabinet decision making. Brittan carried responsibility for the leaking of a letter from the Attorney General implicitly critical of Heseltine.

The major points of significance for the Cabinet and the Central Executive Territory are as follows:

1. Cabinet collectivity: Heseltine argued that the issue was not fully debated within the Cabinet system, and his case was not given a fair hearing. Hence he felt justified in campaigning openly against the government position. The convention of collective responsibility (solidarity and confidentiality) depended on genuinely collective decision making in the Cabinet system. The Prime Minister, reluctant to dismiss Heseltine, accepted this breach of 'collective responsibility' for some weeks, until Heseltine resigned (perhaps out of a mixture of impetuosity, principle and calculation).
2. Prime ministerial power was evident, but so was prime ministerial weakness. Mrs Thatcher had too little regard for the support of her colleagues, and emerged from the affair as a tarnished victor, but a victor nevertheless.
3. Ministerial responsibility: the leaking of the Attorney General's letter was carried out by civil servants, believing they had the authority of a minister; and the minister probably believed he had 'cover' from 10 Downing Street. As a consequence, the minister, Leon Brittan, belatedly accepting responsibility, resigned, the civil servants felt unfairly exposed, the Cabinet Secretary appeared to be shielding the Prime Minister from embarrassment. The capacity of the Downing Street complex to protect the

Prime Minister, and the weakness of the investigating Parliamentary Select Committee, were demonstrated.

There are many accounts of the Westland affair. See especially Jenkins (1987); Young (1989); and Madgwick and Woodhouse (1988–9).

The resignation of Nigel Lawson

Nigel Lawson resigned as Chancellor of the Exchequer in October 1989. The resignation was significant for the understanding of the relations of Prime Minister and Chancellor of the Exchequer, and the role of advisers.

Lawson had resigned because of the continuing influence with the Prime Minister of her Economic Adviser, Sir Alan Walters, who disagreed with the Chancellor about the desirability of Britain's joining the Exchange Rate Mechanism of the European Monetary System. The Prime Minister at that time accepted Walters's view on the specific issue, and was beginning to lose confidence in the Chancellor's policies which had plainly failed to suppress inflation. For both Lawson and Mrs Thatcher the Walters problem focused and embittered long-term policy disagreements and loss of mutual confidence.

In his public statements following the resignation Nigel Lawson was unusually candid. In his letter he had stated: 'The successful conduct of economic policy is possible only if there is, and is seen to be, full agreement between the Prime Minister and the Chancellor of the Exchequer. Recent events have confirmed that this essential requirement cannot be satisfied so long as Alan Walters remains your personal economic adviser.' The article by Sir Alan Walters which had precipitated the resignation was, Lawson said, 'of significance only in as much as it represented the tip of a singularly ill-concealed iceberg, with all the destructive potential that icebergs possess.'

Like Michael Heseltine in the Westland affair, Lawson had policy disagreements, but based his resignation firmly on the constitutional principle of collectivity: 'For our system of Cabinet government to work effectively, the prime minister of the day must appoint ministers that he or she trusts and then leave them to carry out the policy. When differences of view emerge, as they are bound to do from time to time, they shoud be resolved privately and, wherever appropriate, collectively' (HC Deb., 1 November 1989).

In a speech a year later (HC Deb, 23 October 1990) Lawson was more specific. The Government had just joined the ERM. Lawson said it should have done so five years ago, adding, 'This was not for want of trying, as a number of my then Cabinet colleagues can testify'. It seems that Lawson had nurtured his disagreements with the Prime Minister over five years before resigning.

The Prime Minister expressed incomprehension that the Chancellor should resign 'over a personality' and re-affirmed that 'advisers are there to advise, ministers are there to decide'. But Walters's position clearly raised problems: he was a personal adviser to the Prime Minister, working in Number 10, not in the Cabinet Office, nor in the Treasury. The relationships were not in principle different from any arrangement by which the Prime Minister is advised by an independent outsider and a responsible minister. But strong personalities and a serious policy division exposed and magnified the inherent contradictions.

In this situation Cabinet ministers rightly appeal to the principles of collective responsibility and Cabinet government against prime ministerial intervention and dominance (though at other times chancellors are not great collectivists). Prime ministers bluff it out, and find a new minister – and in this case eventually a new adviser. The precipitating issue was resolved within the year in Lawson's favour, though by then it was clear that the economy was failing, and the Prime Minister was not displeased to have a new chancellor. Nigel Lawson acquired lucrative employment in the City: his political career was possibly at an end, but he could 'cry all the way to the bank'.

The episode reveals difficult relationships at the top and the tendency for ministers to stand on collectivity in times of trouble, which are never far away. (The Government's economic policies were not going well at that time). The episode demonstrated that Mrs Thatcher's methods of government were personal but could not be regarded as 'dictatorial'. The Government's position on Exchange Rate Mechanism was not laid down by the Prime Minister: it was 'fudged', left ambivalent. The Prime Minister could not persistently overrule her Chancellor without some damage to the standing of the Government. After all, the Chancellor is the Prime Minister's chief economic adviser.

A year later a new chancellor pushed through membership of the Exchange Rate Mechanism. Thus, in the end, she lost chancellor, adviser, and her policy and her reputation, such as it was, for the management of her team. A few weeks later, following another resignation (Sir Geoffrey Howe's) and another candid and damaging resignation speech, the Prime Minister lost her job too.

The resignations of three senior ministers (Heseltine, Lawson, Howe) all drew attention to the constitutional issue, Mrs Thatcher's conduct of the prime ministership, sometimes misleadingly called her 'style'. At the same time the three resignations reflected a deep division over European policy within the Government and the Conservative party. Disquiet over policy ran alongside concern over procedures and institutions (as it usually does). The grounds of resignation are always confused, a mix of procedure, policy and personality.

13
Case Notes

The Central Policy Review Staff

The Central Policy Review Staff was established by Edward Heath in 1970 and abolished by Margaret Thatcher in 1983. The CPRS, or Think Tank, represented a deliberate approach to the problem of 'the hole in the centre of British government', that is, the apparent lack of support and advice to the Cabinet and more especially the Prime Minister, in particular the furnishing of independent appraisal of departmental proposals, and forward or strategic thinking.

The origins of the CPRS lay in the early attempts of Lloyd George to provide himself with policy advisers (the 'Garden Suburb'). Churchill did the same in 1940–45 (Professor Lindemann's statistical section). These wartime arrangements lapsed but interest was revived in the 1960s as governments moved unsteadily into economic planning. Harold Wilson was interested in such matters and was more thoughtfully concerned than his predecessors about the nature of his office. But it was Edward Heath, another 'permanent secretary manqué' according to Hennessy, who, as Leader of the Opposition, established a high-powered study group and produced a paper, 'The Re-organisation of Central Government' (1970). This paper is highly significant for Heath's approach to British Government, but it turned out in practice not to be as significant as Heath had hoped.

The paper on 'Re-organisation' was very firm about objectives and style:

> Government has been attempting to do too much . . . weakness has shown itself in the apparatus of policy formulation and in the quality of many government decisions. . . .
> The aims [are] to improve the quality of policy formulation and decision-taking in government by presenting Ministers . . . with well-defined options, costed where possible, and relating the choice between options to the contribution they can make to meeting national needs. . . .
> The product of this review will be less government and better government carried out by fewer people.
> The basis of improved policy formulation and decision-taking is rigorous analysis of existing and suggested government policies, actions and expenditure.
>
> (Cmnd 4506, HMSO 1970)

Heath's specific proposals included the establishment of what were known as giant departments, the 'hiving-off' of departmental work into executive agencies, and the introduction of programme analysis and review. It also proposed the establishment of 'a small multi-disciplinary staff in the Cabinet Office'. This became the CPRS.

The CPRS was a small group of bright young people, including civil servants, academics and businessmen. Its personality changed over the years under different heads – the first, Lord Rothschild, was liberal, independent, sceptical; almost the last, Sir Robin Ibbs, was more concerned to follow the lead of the Prime Minister. The location of CPRS was always difficult. The Central Executive Territory is highly organised and crowded. At its centre are people of high standing and substantial weight. There was little space for the CPRS to squeeze into, and that space was jealously guarded. In fact the CPRS could function and prosper only by the active protection and encouragement of the Prime Minister. If that were withdrawn, the CPRS would languish, marginalised or smothered by the Prime Minister's Office and the Cabinet Office. This appears to have happened in its middle period, when it put 'Cabinet Office' at the head of its notepaper and, according to Tony Benn, became the voice of the Cabinet Secretary (Benn 1990, p. 172, confirmed by Donoughue 1987, p. 77).

In its early years the CPRS gained positional advantage from the support of the Prime Minister – including access to Cabinet committees and other ministerial meetings. But the inventor of CPRS, Edward Heath, as prime minister was 'cocooned in his relationship with Trend and Armstrong' (Cabinet Secretary and Head of the Civil Service) according to Rothschild. Mrs Thatcher naturally avoided dependency on a body for which she had little enthusiasm, and preferred a selective use of her Policy Unit. Mrs Thatcher's abolition of the CPRS is understandable, given the difficulties of slotting the CPRS into the area of Prime Minister and Cabinet, and Mrs Thatcher's own independent style in these matters. Yet the record of CPRS was far from barren, and the 'hole-in-the centre' critique persists.

The CPRS produced reports of high quality, some of them influential too. It was an early and accurate prophet of oil scarcity, and its recommendations for energy policy had some impact. It also accurately predicted heavy unemployment by the early or mid-1980s, but this was a prediction not acceptable to the Government. Similarly, radical ideas for the reduction of public expenditure were rejected as politically damaging; and the leaking of that report during the 1983 election fatally damaged the CPRS. Again, the bleak but realistic analysis of prospects for the British car industry and a proposal for a coherent and equally realistic strategy were unwelcome. The Government, against CPRS advice, supported Chrysler-UK (thus financing a foreign-owned competitor for British Leyland). On the Anglo-French supersonic passenger aircraft, Concorde, CPRS argued that it was a disaster but nevertheless must be supported, thus tempering sharp economic analysis with political sensitivity.

In all these cases CPRS had a useful effect on thinking, if not on policy. It assisted the process of re-education of policy makers, and the adjustment to economic decline. It was less successful in areas where departments were heavily entrenched, in particular the Treasury and the Foreign Office. The Treasury could match the CPRS in intellectual power, surpass it in detailed knowledge of departmental affairs, and defeat it by its close links to the Prime Minister. The destruction of the CPRS report on overseas representation was brought about by the entrenched weight of the Foreign Office and its exploitation of its connections in the 'establishment'. Indeed, the rapid rubbishing of the report provided an illuminating demonstration of what might be meant by 'the establishment', and made a good case for just such a countervailing institution as CPRS.

The demise of the CPRS can easily be explained, and not simply in terms of Mrs Thatcher's prejudices (in any case, a prime minister's prejudices are perfectly legitimate). The CPRS was, in the words of its biographers and former members, 'In some ways . . . the ultimate manifestation of the notion of the gifted amateur' (Blackstone and Plowden 1988, p. 208). The CPRS was always likely by its nature to know too little of the detail of a departmental position, and to take too little account of political imperatives. The Prime Minister's Office, the Cabinet Office and the Treasury knew about these matters, and left little space for alternative advice. But then a main justification for the CPRS was precisely to furnish Prime Minister and Cabinet with a view which was independent of departments, Treasury, Civil Service and politicians.

This left the CPRS with few friends. Most departmental ministers suspected, correctly, that the CPRS in practice worked either for the Prime Minister or for the Cabinet Office against departments. Mrs Castle hardly noticed it; Benn was hostile (e.g. 1990, p. 265). Nor are ministers so enthusiastic about strategic goals, broad purposes, and distant horizons. Politicians, faced with radical options, are uneasy. At the least there is one more paper to read; but the paper's message may be disturbing. Barbara Castle once wrote of her dislike of 'either–or' analysis of a problem 'when ministers are yearning for a clear indication of what policies will do the trick' (1980, p. 223, 17 November 1974). But this was not Mrs Thatcher's problem: she already knew, or thought she knew, what policies would do the trick, and had no need of anyone else to tell her – or no need of anyone outside the enlarged Downing Street complex.

The IMF crisis, 1976

Britain suffered an economic crisis in the summer and autumn of 1976. This was the historic moment when the endemic weakness of the economy was fully recognised, and the Labour Government embarked on policies which amounted to a primitive form of monetarism. It was time to recognise, in Tony Crosland's words (applied to local government), that 'the party is over'.

The Government (under Callaghan) needed the support of the International Monetary Fund, and in return was compelled to make substantial cuts in public expenditure, thus to reduce the Public Sector Borrowing Requirement. There was room for difference about the scale of cuts required. The margin of error in the figures was high; it later appeared that the economic situation was not as bad as the IMF and the markets believed. There was no doubt that a Labour government had to work harder than a Conservative government to gain international confidence – unfair but true. But, leaving aside the detail, this was the moment of truth for the British economy, and the beginning of the sea change, the tide of what was later called Thatcherism.

The crisis was significant constitutionally because Callaghan conducted it as an exercise in open Cabinet government, backed by confidential negotiations with the IMF led by the Prime Minister, the Chancellor, and senior officials from the Treasury and the Bank of England. The Policy Unit was privy to these negotiations, and regularly briefed the Prime Minister.

The Cabinet was divided: there was a Treasury group, two opposition groups, the old Keynesians led by Tony Crosland, and the Left by Tony Benn, and the trusties of the 'King's party' (Donoughue 1987, p. 90), which would back the Prime Minister at the end of the day. A King's party exists in most Cabinets, changing a little with the issues. Callaghan took Cabinet through 26 meetings in the autumn, and also met some ministers privately. He worked as an independent, but on the Treasury side. In the end Tony Crosland accepted the Prime Minister's position. 'In Cabinet tomorrow', he told Callaghan, 'I shall say I think you're wrong, but I also think that the Cabinet must support you' (Crosland 1982, p. 381). Callaghan told the remaining dissident, Tony Benn, agonising over whether he should resign, that he must accept collective responsibility or be sacked. He stayed.

Thus Callaghan had steered the Cabinet by firmness and openness to acceptance of a package of cuts low enough for the Cabinet and high enough for the IMF. This constituted a major shift in policy without the recrimination and persisting tensions which accompanied similar decisions under Wilson and Thatcher. Callaghan had supported his Chancellor without fully accepting Treasury demands for more ferocious cuts. At the same time an inner group had conducted negotiations in secret. Callaghan later developed this group into the 'Economic Seminar' to deal with internationally sensitive economic policy. Altogether the IMF episode displays prime ministerial government for what it needs to be, individual leadership by the Prime Minister within the Central Executive Territory, and embracing both the Cabinet and an Inner Group.

The Falklands War, 1982

The handling by British governments of the Falklands problem illustrates some characteristic features of British government in general and Mrs Thatcher's government in particular.

The Falkland Islands in the South Atlantic had been acquired by Britain in the 1760s despite, or even because of, the protests of the Spanish Governor of Buenos Aires. Independent Argentina inherited Spanish resentment of the British and regarded the islands (the Malvinas) as rightly hers; the claim had some historical and legal validity, but mainly it made good geographical sense. By the 1940s the British government had come to accept that the Falklands had no economic or strategic value and were indefensible, so British possession might be regarded as an embarrassing anomaly in a post-colonial age. However, the 1,800 or so inhabitants were mainly of British descent, and held a strong British allegiance. The Foreign Office had been working since the 1960s (without much urgency, it must be said) towards an agreement with Argentina. A favoured arrangement was the transfer of sovereignty followed by 'lease-back'. The difficulty was that the islanders objected, and their objections were strongly represented by a group in London and articulated in Parliament.

In the period 1980–2 Lord Carrington, the Foreign Secretary, pursued as his main strategy the 'education' of the islanders towards a leaseback solution. The British Ambassador protested strongly that this was 'no strategy at all beyond a general Micawberism' (*Falkland Islands Review* 1983, para. 104). The matter was discussed in the Defence Committee from time to time, but Carrington did not take it to Cabinet, nor to Parliament, because it was not perceived as urgent, and debate in Parliament was certain to be dominated by the vociferous Falklands lobby. A decision was taken as part of defence economies to withdraw the survey ship HMS Endurance, and this was probably interpreted by Argentina as a sign of a British lack of determination to hold on to the Islands. The Prime Minister did not take note of the problem until the beginning of March 1982 and Cabinet was alerted only a few days before Argentina invaded the Islands.

There is no doubt at all that serious errors of judgement were made: the Foreign Office did not appreciate the emerging situation, despite much evidence that it was critical. The evidence for this view is strong, and the committee later set up under the chair of Lord Franks concluded that this was so:

> 290. We conclude that the Government were in a position of weakness, and that the effect of Lord Carrington's decision [simply to keep some sort of negotiation going] was to pass the initiative to the Argentine Government.

> 291. Lord Carrington also decided on 7 September not to present a paper for collective Ministerial discussion in the Defence Committee. Instead he circulated a minute to his Defence Committee colleagues on 14 September. This was one of a series of minutes . . . by which he kept the Prime Minister and Defence Committee colleagues informed of progress in the dispute up to the time of the invasion. We recognise that Cabinet Committees, such as the Defence Committee, usually meet to take decisions at the invitation of the Minister with proposals to put forward: and we have noted that, in September 1981, the prospect of further negotiations still existed on the basis of agreed Government policy. Nevertheless, it was also evident at the time that the policy road ahead, last endorsed by Ministers in January 1981, could well be blocked, with serious political repercussions. Officials in both the Foreign and Commonwealth Office and the Ministry of Defence were looking to Ministers to review the outcome of the contingency planning they had done in view of a potentially more aggressive posture by Argentina. In the event, Government policy towards Argentina and the Falkland Islands was never formally discussed outside the Foreign and Commonwealth Office after January 1981. Thereafter, the time was never judged to be ripe. . . . There was no meeting of the Defence Committee to discuss the Falklands until 1 April 1982:

and there was no reference to the Falklands in Cabinet, even after the New York talks of 26 and 27 February, until Lord Carrington reported on events in South Georgia on 25 March 1982.

292. We cannot say what the outcome of a meeting of the Defence Committee might have been, or whether the course of events would have been altered if it had met in September 1981: but, in our view, it could have been advantageous, and fully in line with Whitehall practice, for Ministers to have reviewed collectively at that time, or in the months immediately ahead, the current negotiating position: the implications of the conflict between the attitudes of the Islanders and the aims of the Junta: and the longer-term policy options in relation to the dispute.

(*Falkland Islands Review*, 1983, p. 79)

On the basis of these paragraphs it does seem undeniable that serious mistakes were made; but there is room for alternative views about whether and how the mistakes can be explained and justified. The Franks Committee, having established and set out a record of error, concluded in its final paragraphs:

[W]e have pointed out . . . where different decisions might have been taken, where fuller consideration of alternative courses of action might, in our opinion, have been advantageous, and where the machinery of Government could have been better used. . . . But . . . there is no reasonable basis for any suggestion . . . that the invasion would have been prevented if the Government had acted in the ways indicated.

The Prime Minister seized eagerly on these paragraphs and read them to the House of Commons. But in the context of the whole report this was a curious kind of exoneration; for the imputation of error could only be based on the assumption that actions by Britain might affect the outcome. This after all was the justification for maintaining a Diplomatic Service, not to mention a Foreign Secretary. So exoneration on the fatalistic ground that Argentina would have invaded anyway undermines the whole basis of foreign policy.

The alternative view is the opposite of Franks's final position. Politicians and diplomats have to make judgements and act in difficult situations. The Callaghan Government certainly claimed to have acted more effectively in 1977–8. Further, it may be argued that Carrington's conduct of the matter, by neglecting

Cabinet and Parliament, lost the possibility of signalling the urgency and difficulty of the problem, and of seeking support for the Foreign Office strategy. Thus the conduct of the Falklands policy up to the invasion is revealing of policy making in British government, particularly about the role of Cabinet and Parliament – a very limited role on this occasion.

Lord Carrington shortly resigned as Foreign Secretary. Though this was regarded as a sacrifice on Carrington's part, taking the blame on his shoulders at the outset of a war, there is a good case for regarding it as a genuine case of resignation under the convention of ministerial responsibility for clearly demonstrable ministerial and departmental fault.

Events after the invasion also proved illuminating for the nature of British government in several ways, mostly now well-known. In a Saturday morning debate in the House of Commons just after the invasion the House displayed its capacity for high patriotic emotion, while Mrs Thatcher, who had by then considered the risks, spoke by comparison with moderation. The sinking of the Argentina warship, the Belgrano, demonstrated how the impetus of military preparedness and military operations leads and determines decisions on the brink of war. The Belgrano had been steaming away from the 'exclusion' zone at the time of the attack, and later, not totally convincing, attempts by the Government to explain the sinking demonstrated the readiness of governments to cover up embarrassment.

The eventual decision to send a naval task force to the South Atlantic was taken by the full Cabinet, with each member being asked by the Prime Minister individually to indicate his view. (Similarly, the Cabinet in the Suez crisis of 1956 voted on the question of an immediate airborne landing: a prudent prime minister seeks Cabinet support for the final commitment of armed forces). Thereafter the conduct of the war by a small 'War Cabinet' closely in touch with the military confirmed Mrs Thatcher in her preference for a particular style of decision making.

Victory in the Falklands did much to reinvigorate Mrs Thatcher's failing political reputation, and contributed to her election triumph in 1983 (though the divisions of the Opposition parties had already assured her a majority). The Falklands War had a powerful effect on Mrs Thatcher's subsequent performance and style as prime minister. She knowingly took horrendous but justified risks (justified by Parliament anyway) and learned then to play the Iron Lady role on a world stage. After the Falklands War the navy was able to resist threatened cuts, on the traditional grounds that the armed forces must be ready to fight the last war.

Sovereignty, an elusive term in political science, was adopted in political rhetoric to assert a claim to independent national power – in Europe as well as in the South Atlantic. The Anglo-American special relationship was reinforced in its post-1950s form as a relationship of British dependency, and a sharp constraint on all British governments.

The costs of victory in the Falklands were heavy – loss of life, the cost of the military operation and the continuing burden of defending the indefensible. The Falklands issue was not the only area of policy in which it was prudent before embarking on conflict first to define what would amount to victory, and assess its costs in comparison with defeat. There is scope for differing views about the costs of victory in Mrs Thatcher's battles in the Falklands, against the miners, against inflation, and against the public services.

Sources of policy ideas: commissions and specialist advice

Governments need policy ideas. There is rarely a shortage of ideas: the Government's problem is to select those which are appropriate to its concerns and dispositions, and which have a fair chance of success in the comparatively short time-scale of government planning (up to the next election). There are many appropriate and legitimate sources of policy ideas for a government, and rather less for a pre-government (that is, the Opposition). These include the departments, the Cabinet, the party and a range of official, party and independent 'think tanks' and specialist advisers, as well as an army of academics and writers (see Chapter 8).

Governments not knowing what to do, shopping around for policy ideas, sometimes resort to Royal Commissions and committees made up of persons of eminence, experience and weight, known as 'the Great and the Good'. This is a kind of extended 'Establishment', acknowledged and formalised at least in that a list of appropriate persons is maintained by a Public Appointments Unit. But of course the true inner 'Establishment' by definition does not need to be listed.

Harold Wilson was especially fond of the Royal Commission, the deluxe and weighty version, though it differs only in form of appointment and intimation of prestige from the simple Committee of Inquiry. (The Kilbrandon Report on the Constitution was prepared by a Royal Commission; the Fulton Report on the Civil Service by a departmental committee.) Wilson established Royal Commissions to 'report' on such matters as local government, industrial relations and the press. Mrs Thatcher abandoned Royal Commissions, and used departmental committees more sparingly than Wilson.

A commission or committee is a way of securing from outside the government extended 'advice', including information, research, and evidence submitted by interested groups and individuals. It may be that the busy and unpaid members of a commission can offer time, experience, reflection, wisdom; on the other hand, the report is likely to be drafted by civil servants, often along predictable lines. Hence, little is gained, except the deflection of criticism and deferment of decision. The government is still not bound in any way by the report, and the record of influence of reports is not impressive. There may be a gain in political information and education. Mrs Thatcher was criticised for not making available to her government the more extensive and public political advice to be derived from commissions and committees.

There remains for all governments the problem of making policy choices on technical matters. Most problems are 'technical' to some degree, that is, they involve information, concepts, vocabulary which are normally understood only by specialists, experts, professionals. This is true of civil service or local government reform, say; and more so of some other subjects of Royal Commissions, for example, on gambling, legal services, or common land. Beyond these lie matters of 'high technology', whether to build a supersonic passenger transport aircraft or a particular kind of nuclear reactor. There is here a scale of 'technicality' along which the politician moves warily, with a diminishing capacity for understanding (and so for independent decision) derived from his native intelligence and his education and experience. At some point the minister has to say 'I don't follow you, but I'll take your word for it'.

It is clear that most government decisions are in part technical, in part political. A Foreign Secretary may judge for himself the political consequences of an invasion or whether an arms limitation agreement is desirable; but he needs specialist, 'technical' advice from the military about the costs and practicalities of his decision. Herein lies the problem of modern government by non-specialist elected politicians in a complex, technology-dominated society. Commissions and committees work in more leisurely areas of government, where there is time for reflection and research. Amplitude of time is not characteristic of the Central Executive Territory.

Public expenditure

High public expenditure is characteristic of all modern governments. A substantial part of government policy is based on such expenditure. High expenditure requires high taxation, which is unpopular. This is the policy trap into which governments are locked.

In consequence, struggle over public expenditure is a significant part of the policy work of the Central Executive Territory. The process begins with the Cabinet agreeing on an overall figure for public expenditure. There follow negotiations between the spending departments and the Treasury, led by the Chief Secretary to the Treasury. At this point in the negotiations the responsibility of departments and the Treasury overlap, and the Treasury offers not only the general opinion that the total programme is too high, but views about particular parts of the programme. 'You really do not need that road programme, or building programme or weapons system.' Department ministers feel that is no business of the Treasury, but the Treasury officials will be well-informed about the relative merits of particular spending proposals. Encountering this process, Tony Benn wrote: 'I am not prepared to accept the Treasury's right to dart into individual Ministers' Departments and find savings to suit their particular policies' (1988, p. 2, 3 January 1968). But the most a minister can hope for by such protest is to be allowed to choose his own cuts. Department officials know the Treasury line; indeed, they probably helped to brief the Treasury officials.

Once the global total is set, individual spending decisions do not now normally go to full Cabinet. The Prime Minister and the Chancellor want to avoid an alliance of spending ministers against the Treasury – though accounts of Cabinet discussion of expenditure under Wilson indicate that such alliances fall apart, and the Prime Minister can divide and rule. However, Cabinet discussion of public expenditure was usually protracted and ill-tempered. Barbara Castle uses words such as 'a long agony', full of 'misery and tension', though she would not be one to shorten the proceedings by early graceful concession.

In the 1980s the process of normal settlement outside the Cabinet was confirmed. If agreement is not reached in the bilateral negotiations with the Chief Secretary, then the dispute is referred to a committee of ministers dubbed the 'Star Chamber'. In this the minister (who may be on his own) faces a board of senior Cabinet ministers, non-spending ministers, or ministers who have already settled. They are backed by Cabinet Office and Treasury officials. Appeal to the Cabinet is not permitted. In practice this means that only a minister on the brink of resignation could force an appeal.

It seems that the 'Star Chamber' procedure is itself a strong encouragement to settlement in bilateral negotiation; for the procedure is not regularly resorted to, and was not used in 1988, 1989 or 1990. (In earlier years the process was more troublesome.) In 1990 Mrs Thatcher made later personal interventions in response to political discontent over the funding of education and social security. This might be regarded as characteristic of Mrs Thatcher's interventionist tendencies, or a response to a particular situation, her lack of confidence in the Deputy Prime Minister, Sir Geoffrey Howe (soon to resign), who would have chaired the Star Chamber.

The power of the Chancellor, the Treasury and the Prime Minister is evident in decisions on public expenditure, hence over a large area of policy. Yet if Chancellor and Treasury are powerful in the process, their power is far from absolute and this is evident in the outcomes. Despite the best efforts of all chancellors since 1945, and some short-term success, the total of

lic expenditure has risen inexorably. Chancellors have
.epted (though under protest) the evasive device of assuming
optimistic rates of economic growth; and chancellors have
regularly threatened resignation.

In the public expenditure process the forces of politics come up
against the forces of good government. Since the 1960s the
Treasury has made vigorous efforts to rationalise public expenditure decisions through the PESC (Public Expenditure Survey
Committee) processes. These have brought more information
and more thought to bear on expenditure decisions. This helps to
trim expenditure at the margins; but there still remains one
reasonably good case competing with twenty others. Since the
mid-1970s the brute force of cash limits restricted the scope for
manoeuvre and for 'fudging' decisions. This leaves the Treasury
and the departments, the politicians and officials, to pick their
way each year to a less than satisfactory compromise. Barbara
Castle wrote that the final package is 'a sophisticated combination of principle and expediency and that is what politics is about'
(1984, p. 358, 15 January 1968). Put more bluntly, David
Howell, a former Cabinet minister, said: '. . . even in a more
refined system there is going to be a stage where issues cannot be
resolved by analysis or delicate agreement and can only be
resolved by crude political battering' (in an interview with Peter
Hennessy quoted in Hennessy 1986, p. 97).

Collective responsibility (and ministerial accountability)

The convention of collective responsibility offers an appearance
of collectivity and responsibility, two apparently desirable
features of democratic government. The appearance is also an
affirmation, an aspiration, and so affects understanding and
behaviour. The main practical significance of the convention is
that Prime Minister and Cabinet, and so the whole Government,
fall together when defeated in the House of Commons on a
specified vote of confidence. The fall of a government in this way
is rare: it has happened only three times in this century, twice in
1924 and again in 1979. What happens after such a defeat is
determined more by the condition of the parties than by any
convention. It would normally be expected that a party majority

is available or will be produced by a general election. The convention of collective responsibility in this 'confidence' form simply triggers the resignation of the Government. Under a normal two-party system this is a rare event, though the convention might be regarded also as a mild statement about the need for a government to be answerable to the House of Commons.

Apart from that, the practical effect of the convention is to support the solidarity of the Government behind the Prime Minister: it is in fact a support of prime ministerial power. So, in addition to the literal, 'confidence' meaning of the convention, it prescribes: (a) that all ministers support in public the policies and actions of the Government, at the least by silence (the unity or solidarity effect); (b) that all proceedings of government remain confidential (the secrecy effect).

The convention of collective responsibility is plainly in the interests of the Prime Minister – and arguably in the interests of good government. Prime ministers fight for it: prime ministerial exhortations on collective responsibility were a regular feature of Wilson's cabinets. The convention survives, it is still appealed to and it affects behaviour; but it is messy and often breached. There are five principal ways in which the convention is breached, softened or evaded:

1. *Agreement to differ*
   Wilson arranged in 1975 that the EC issue should be excepted from the normal provisions of collective responsibility during the campaign preceding the referendum on the issue. (A similar short-lived exception had been made in relation to free trade in the 1931 Government). Both major parties were divided, and during the campaign politicians including Cabinet ministers worked publicly in strange alliances. After the referendum the normal divisions of politics were reinstated. Ministers who opposed a major feature of government policy continued to serve in the Cabinet. It could be argued that this was hypocritical and made for weak government; alternatively it could be argued that disagreement was a normal feature of cabinets, the amount of hypocrisy was only a little higher than usual, and sceptics around the Cabinet table invigorated government.

The episode did indeed suggest that the convention, unknown elsewhere in its specific British form, was not essential to good government in Britain. However, the experiment has not been repeated.

2. *Non-resignation*

In its fullest form the convention is regarded as compelling the resignation of a minister seriously dissenting on a substantial issue. But this does not happen frequently – perhaps in 25 cases since 1945. Dissent is normal but judged to be either not serious enough, or best managed by 'staying to fight'. As Randolph Churchill said: 'I can hardly recall a single measure of first-class importance on which all members of the Cabinet had precisely the same views. . . . if I had resigned every time my wise and advantageous advice was rejected I should seldom, indeed . . . have been in office' (House of Lords, 22 May 1928, Report, cols 252–3).

In any case, resignation arises from more than one cause – other disagreements, difficult relations with colleagues and above all with the Prime Minister. (Most resignations are triggered in some part by tensions in that relationship.) Resignations are also obscured by reshuffles and dismissals. Resignation is of course temporarily damaging to a political career, but seems to do no harm in the long run. It is not at all damaging financially for Conservative ex-ministers, who are able to earn much more from directorships in commerce.

It is of course impossible to say whether there are enough resignations of an appropriate quality to reaffirm the convention. Usually it is possible to say, 'about time there was another resignation under collective responsibility' – and one occurs. So watch this space, wait and see! (As it happened, shortly after the above was written, Sir Geoffrey Howe, Deputy Prime Minister, resigned in November 1990, the third resignation of a senior minister on policy grounds in five years. The rate was not much above the average, but the seniority of the ministers was.)

3. *Leaks and memoirs*

The confidentiality part of the convention has been overridden by the publication of memoirs based on diaries kept by Cabinet ministers (Crossman, Castle, Benn) and including detailed accounts of Cabinet meetings. Crossman was the first, and his right to publish was upheld in the courts, though the confidentiality of Cabinet proceedings was also upheld. In any case, former prime ministers had already exploited their privileged position to publish accounts of their governments. Apart from the major volumes of memoirs, ministers, including (or even, above all) prime ministers, leaked confidential information 'unattributably'. The source may be described as, say, a senior minister, or Downing Street sources, or not indicated at all. In this way detailed accounts of Cabinet meetings have been published in the press, and presented on television. The quality, in particular the perceptiveness, of the best journalism quoted in this book, is due in part to the blessed non-operation of the confidentiality aspect of the convention of collective responsibility.

4. *Withdrawal of cover*
   The convention provides support for the Prime Minister, but it also offers cover for the minister. This is often quite good, but cannot be consistently relied on. A minister is most of the time out on his own with his departmental policy, sometimes wishing for a word of public support from his senior colleagues and especially from the Prime Minister, and not at all confident that the Prime Minister will furnish collective cover to an exposed minister. A policy which the minister would like to believe rates as an accepted part of the whole government's programme, will, if it begins to go wrong, become the minister's own policy. The rule is success belongs to the Government, failure to the Minister.

5. *Persistent successful challenge to the convention*
   There is a long and continuing record of defiance of the convention without serious retribution. This is true for all senior and heavyweight ministers, though it would not be true to say that the convention is almost optional for them. The convention was frequently flouted in the Wilson Cabinets. The party's divisions were reflected in the Cabinet, and the party's constitution reinforced such divisions; in particular, the National Executive Committee of the party served as an institutional focus for dissident

cabinet ministers. Some members of the Cabinet had the political standing, including support in the party, and the temperament, to challenge the Prime Minister. Tony Benn breached the convention persistently and as a matter of principle: 'collective responsibility is breaking down again, which is a good thing', he wrote cheerfully on 22 December 1974 (1989, p. 90). Other ministers were less open and vociferous in their complaints, despite major disagreements, and did not offer resignation (strictly, that was a breach of the convention too). Wilson for his part lacked the confidence and the stomach for confrontation: he was simply too 'nice' a person to discipline the dissenters, which in the end meant dismissing them.

Prime ministers love the convention. Some ministers (notably Tony Benn, but he is not alone) dislike it. Constitutionalists are uncertain of its operation and its value. It is effective and valuable in its literal form: governments depend on the confidence of the House. If beyond that it does no more than reinforce solidarity and secrecy then it may be harmful to public political perceptions, education and debate. Most other governments maintain what they find as acceptable levels of unity and confidentiality without brandishing a clause of the constitution. If the convention is to be strictly maintained, then the frequent incidence of resignations would indicate a heart-warming assertion of political principle against the majority.

Part VI
Conclusion

14

The Prime Minister in the Central Executive Territory: Modes of Influence

Prime ministerial power, roles and modes of influence, capability, force

Prime ministerial power has been a favourite topic for authors and examination candidates ever since Richard Crossman wrote his celebrated essay advancing the thesis (Crossman 1963). It was, and remains, an interesting idea in an area of politics previously either devoid of theories or dominated by self-congratulatory ideas of responsible parliamentary democracy (e.g. Jennings, Amery). Crossman's thesis had the attraction of all single-cause explanations: it enabled multiple and complex phenomena to be organised in one simple pattern – a gift for authors and for examination candidates. Real life was not as simple as that, but we should all be grateful to Crossman for stimulating reflection and in the end research about the very centre of British government.

In order to test the Crossman thesis it is first necessary to establish its precise meaning. This is not easy. Crossman dealt with the Prime Minister's power over Cabinet and party colleagues; and adduced the Prime Minister's evident power to force through particular decisions (e.g. manufacture of atomic weapons, the Suez invasion). Within these limits a plausible case for prime ministerial power could be made. But in practice a prime minister is involved in many more relationships, at the centre, in Parliament, and in the country, and these may be essential to the exercise of prime ministerial power. These relationships needed to be tested too.

There was a further necessary test of prime ministerial power – the Prime Minister's capacity to master events as well as colleagues, and to deliver his or her government's policy objectives. The examples offered by Crossman were neither numerous nor representative enough to sustain the thesis of continuous, as distinct from sporadic, political power.

As the terms of political power are defined, so problems of evidence arise. As it happened, Crossman was to lead the way in providing massive evidence of his own observation of Cabinet meetings, and two of his colleagues (Castle, Benn) also kept and published diaries. Other ministers have written memoirs. The new parliamentary select committees (another Crossman invention) have also provided some information about policy making at the centre. The evidence is comparatively abundant, but it does not easily yield simple demonstrations and tests of comparative power. There is great difficulty in establishing the precise influence of one person in a complex policy-making scenario. By its nature the prime ministerial power thesis was plausible but virtually untestable.

There remains the problem that the full understanding of British government at the centre requires more than a simple assessment of prime ministerial power. This was understandably an attractive topic and thesis for Crossman, since the culture – and the gossip – of Cabinet ministers is sensitive to, even obsessed by, gradations of power and pecking orders. But the student of politics requires a more detailed account of what goes on before making even a simple assessment of power. A more appropriate concern is with prime ministerial roles, and modes and areas of influence, and policy capability.

The term 'power' is complemented here by 'force', as explained in Chapter 1. 'Power' has come to mean effective force – force plus effect. 'Force' is used here as an equivalent of potential. There is a more limited assumption about effect; force is like, say, a jet of water, which may move heavy objects, or flow into a drain, with or without making everyone wet on the way. The term 'power' is still appropriate to connote force which moves others or, in a constitutional context, authority, that is, legitimate force, intended to move others.

Factors in prime ministerial force

The main factors in prime ministerial force can be summarised as follows:

Party: The Prime Minister is leader of the party, holds power and is expected to hold power and exercise leadership in policy, organisation and elections. But the party in Parliament and in the country expects to be listened to (with different procedures and influence in different parties).

Colleagues: The Prime Minister has the authority to appoint and dismiss. But senior ministers still have their own political standing and bases of support.

Central executive territory: The Prime Minister chairs the Cabinet, controls its agenda, manages the committee sy.tem, and has the major influence on how issues will be dealt with at the centre. The Prime Minister has the support of the Cabinet Office and the Prime Minister's Office. But there is both a constitutional tradition and a political necessity for an element of collectivity; the territory is not simply a prime ministerial domain.

Civil Service: The Prime Minister is not formally the head of the Civil Service, but he is the head's boss, and has the authority to manage and change the Civil Service, as Mrs Thatcher demonstrated. The Civil Service still has a formidable potential for resistance, and most government activity is located in the departments.

Public figure: The Prime Minister is the most prominent figure by far in the government, and has the potential to achieve high personal standing and popularity, notably through summit conferences and diplomacy. But prominence brings vulnerability, and prime ministers can also achieve great unpopularity.

The prime ministership is plainly an office carrying usable and effective force, that is, substantial power. At its simplest, the Prime Minister is a superstar, operating in a winner-takes-all constitution, and reigning supreme during Good Times. But, as the song almost goes, Bad Times are Just Around the Corner, and simple personal power is always under stress in bad times. This was a rule Mrs Thatcher neglected, and her brazen self-confidence overcame her normal prudence and brought about her downfall in November 1990.

In fact, prime ministerial force is not unconstrained. Some of the factors listed – Cabinet, party – form a system into which the Prime Minister is locked. The grant of force is limited: there is a contractual element (force is subject to good behaviour) and a constitutional element (force is subject to checks and balances). The debate about prime ministerial power demonstrates a concern about excessive power, and so becomes a factor restraining power. Mrs Thatcher's fall from office showed the ultimate force of collective interest sorely tried, and striking back at arrogant prime ministerial power.

Other factors in prime ministerial force – patronage, publicity – are for the Prime Minister alone. This is the pot of gold – effective force, power without restraint – or so it seems. Yet even here power is not absolute. Most Cabinets include members the Prime Minister would rather do without. The high publicity enriches prime ministerial capability, yet it carries with it a destabilising vulnerability. In the eye of the camera prime ministers can pay for their frequent triumphs with occasional disaster. Most prime ministers experience disasters, and can easily be destabilised, 'thrown' off their secure peak of power by evident failure – Eden in 1956, Macmillan in 1963, Wilson in 1967, Heath in 1974, Callaghan in 1979. Mrs Thatcher was tougher than the men, but she 'wobbled' on camera during the Westland crisis, and (happily for her, off camera) during the 1987 election campaign. Her fall came near to being a public humiliation; a hostile press would have made it so. It is not surprising that prime ministers should sometimes show signs of a breakdown in morale. Having been raised high, they have a long way to fall.

The 'factors' in prime ministerial force are the same for each prime minister, but they work in varying ways on different individuals in different situations. The prime ministership is a very personal office, and its modes differ with the holder as well as with circumstance. Individual prime ministers themselves vary during their periods of office, such as Churchill very plainly between his wartime and peacetime administrations; Wilson, both within 1964–70 and in 1974–6; Thatcher, roughly divided by the Falklands War 1982, the election of 1987 and the beginning of the Fall, 1990). These variations in prime ministerial behaviour lie within a broad spectrum. Most prime ministers play both president and chairman, strong and weak, at some time or in some area. There is an irreducible minimum of power (the capacity at least to hold up action) and significant force to create a 'plus potential'.

The Prime Minister at work: some general characteristics

A supportive system

The Downing Street system (Prime Minister's Office, Cabinet Office) provides substantial support and protection to the Prime Minister. The Office of Prime Minister functions if necessary without a prime minister, as it did during Churchill's disabling illness in 1953. In the short term the public will not know the difference.

The Prime Minister is the director of that system. He or she carries immense authority – hence references by a senior civil servant to the 'grovel count', high for Mrs Thatcher, but substantial for all prime ministers. The Prime Minister exercises the legitimating authority of the system, the Cabinet – controlling its composition, agenda, discussions, and conclusions. The Downing Street news machine manages the news on behalf of the Government, but directly on behalf of, and strongly featuring, the Prime Minister. The stage management of the drama of government is an instrument of prime ministerial promotion and influence. Overall, there can be little doubt that the development of the 10 Downing Street offices has enhanced the capability of the Prime Minister to influence government. This was the intention.

The indispensability of the Prime Minister in the conduct of business

The Prime Minister is an indispensable player in the game, in the transaction of the day-to-day business of government. But the Prime Minister is more than indispensable to the playing of the game: he or she is an essential element in a winning combination. Mrs Castle conceded that Wilson was difficult to beat, though he might often be in pursuit of a compromise. ('He is implacable when he has made up his mind to a compromise', 1984, p. 194, 29 November 1966.) Heclo and Wildavsky also argue that the Prime Minister's support is a minister's trump card:

> . . . the importance of having the Prime Minister on your side can hardly be exaggerated. He might persuade the Chancellor when a minister could not. He can argue the political merits more authoritatively than anyone else: if he says the party requires a programme it will be difficult to resist him. His summation of a Cabinet discussion can turn the tide of opinion. Except on the most vital issues, other ministers will think twice before opposing him. Persuading the Prime Minister, if it can be done, is a trump card.
> (Heclo and Wildavsky 1974, pp. 149–50)

The power to persuade

Prime ministers have 'the power to persuade'. This is the neat formula Richard Neustadt first used to sum up the power of the President of the USA – or, rather, as he intended, the limits on that power (Neustadt 1960). Lord Rosebery, Prime Minister 1894–5, and a biographer of Sir Robert Peel, would agree with this formula for the prime ministership, and his statements are quoted with warm approval by Harold Wilson. 'A First Minister has only the influence with the Cabinet which is given him by his personal argument, his personal qualities and his personal weight. All his colleagues he must convince, some he may have to humour, some even to cajole; a harassing, laborious and ungracious task. . . . His power is mainly personal, the power of individual influence' (Rosebery, *Sir Robert Peel*, 1899, pp. 34–5, quoted in Wilson 1976, pp. vi and 42).

We have, then, two considerable authorities declaring that the power of the Prime Minister is the power to persuade, no more and no less; the power to command is absent. The formula is attractive, but the American comparison raises doubts because of the very different relationships prescribed by the US Constitution and especially the weakness of the President's hold on the legislature. Moreover, the power to persuade comes in several modes. At one end persuasion connotes rational argument among equals; at the other, persuasion backed by physical force ('if you don't agree, you will be taken out and shot') is not persuasion at all. In between there are many gradations of persuasion from gentle to vigorous and quasi-coercive, depending on inequalities in force ('I do hope you will agree, and at this point I forbear to mention that I could make life uncomfortable for you'). The inequalities are evident enough in the case of the Prime Minister, notably the capacity to hire and fire, to damage (such as by press briefing) and to obstruct (through officials). The Prime Minister, like the US President, has many advantages in the persuasion game, amounting to a greater power to persuade.

Colleagues as countervailing power

Colleagues may be supportive, but are also potentially a source of competitive and countervailing power. The diaries of Wilson's Cabinet confirm this view. Indeed, there would be far less material worthy of the diarist's recording if Wilson had experienced no difficulty in getting his own way. But there were clearly three or four heavyweights in Wilson's Cabinets who required more persuasion than others, and whose concurrence was essential. They were, so to speak, swing voters, whose decision determined contentious issues. Wilson was himself the heaviest of the heavyweights. He was not often totally defeated, as on trade union legislation in 1969, and on some other matters (e.g. 'East of Suez' policy) he was himself the swing voter.

Mrs Thatcher's Cabinets seem not to have included any ministerial heavyweights, at least compared to the Prime Minister, and fewer matters were submitted in Wilson's way to full Cabinet discussion. Most governments include both 'trusties' and 'heavies'; a prime minister is fortunate if the two qualities combine (as Bevin to Attlee, Whitelaw to Thatcher). Mrs Thatcher was fortunate in that her few really forceful ministers admired her; it was not so for Mr Wilson. In these rough terms Mrs Thatcher's typical Cabinet minister was a middle-weight trusty, Wilson's was a heavyweight troublemaker.

The relationship of Prime Minister to Chancellor of the Exchequer is crucial: it is indicative, though not wholly representative, of prime minister–minister relationships. One of Mrs Thatcher's ex-ministers said: '. . . the nexus between No 10 and the Treasury is decisive, it overrules, it's everything. The Treasury always knows they can win' (David Howell, quoted in Hennessy 1989, p. 315). Some chancellors are very powerful in their own right, political heavyweights occupying the most important office after the prime ministership, and backed by the bureaucratic expertise of the Treasury.

R. A. (Lord) Butler, a former chancellor, expressed his own unquestioning approval of this position, emphasising the Budget but going beyond it. 'I am personally a great believer in the Chancellor of the Exchequer having the right to introduce his own Budget. . . . [It] is a striking feature of Cabinet government that the Budget and the economic situation are very much under the control of the Chancellor' (interview with Norman Hunt, September 1965, in Herman and Alt 1975, pp. 198–9). Butler adds that the Governor of the Bank of England knew more of what was in the Chancellor's mind than some ministers. He describes this – in a rather lordly way, irritating to colleagues and constitutionalists – as 'one of the freaks of the workings in the British constitution'.

Butler's record as Chancellor does not wholly support his complacent view of chancellor power. He was overruled on a proposal to float the pound in 1952, and again, like his predecessor Macmillan, he was not allowed to reduce the bread subsidy (1956). In both cases the Prime Minister's political judgement vanquished the Chancellor's financial plans. Similarly, the Chancellor and the Treasury team were pushed into resignation in 1958 by the Prime Minister's refusal to accept the political consequences of the Chancellor's stern financial proposals.

The Prime Minister–Chancellor relationship is crucial but often uneasy, notably between Wilson and Callaghan, Thatcher and Lawson. Two chancellors have been dismissed and three chancellors have resigned in unhappy circumstances since 1945, and at least one other came very near to resignation. The evident unease of the relationship indicates the weight of the Chancellor's countervailing power; but the resignations show that, 'when the chips are down', the Prime Minister wins much more often than not.

Controlling the momentum of events

A prime minister may dominate colleagues, but it is more difficult to dominate events. Roy Jenkins, a distinguished biographer and senior minister, contrasted the activities of writing and being a minister. Writing, he said, was like walking up a mountain, hard work but at your own pace. Being a minister was like skiing down a slalom course. 'The momentum is all on one's side, provided it can be controlled.' But there were major disadvantages – falling at speed in public, preserving perspective and a sense of direction (*The Observer*, 20 June 1971, quoted in Campbell 1983, p. 118).

A prime minister is clearly subject to the exhilaration and the perils of the slalom course. Riding the slalom, a prime minister is unstoppable – but he or she can also be swept to disaster. Moreover, a prime minister must judge and try to control the pace of events. Some matters are naturally dealt with more slowly, gradually, incrementally and patiently. There are mountains to climb, with tired legs, and sagging morale, as well as the invigorating downhill slalom. A wise and durable prime minister learns to judge the timing and pace of uphill slog and downhill slalom, and to choose when, and when not, to plunge downhill.

Success, as perceived by colleagues, party and people, is the supercharger of prime ministerial force. A successful prime minister gets his or her way easily with colleagues, party, people. 'When prime ministers are up, they are very, very up . . .' (Jenkins 1987, p. 184), but '. . . when they are down they can be virtually powerless.' The exhilaration of the downhill slalom turns into the humiliation of a tumble in the snow, and a broken limb.

The mastery of events requires the domination of major areas of policy. This is the fundamental test of the prime ministerial power thesis. If prime ministers are powerful, what are the achievements and failures for which they are personally responsible?

The Prime Minister and major areas of policy

The records of both Wilson and Thatcher show clearly their close involvement in, and impact on, both economic and foreign policy – for example, Wilson on devaluation, the Anglo-American relationship, and accession to the EEC; Thatcher on the monetarist policies of her first administration and, again, the Anglo-American relationship and the EC.

It is not surprising that the Prime Minister should be heavily involved in these areas. These are policies which are naturally decided at the highest level of government because of their national importance, their international aspect, their political sensitivity, the need for a degree of confidentiality, and their tendency to high momentum (the slalom) and crisis. However, these are also policy areas of immense difficulty, in which the potential of national action to solve problems is severely limited. Thus the policy areas to which prime ministerial power has easy access are also the areas where the power of the state is most circumscribed (see Rose 1980, p. 49). This is bad news for prime ministers, but not really surprising. It is the normal expectation of chief executives; they get the really difficult jobs, and outside politics they are much respected and well-rewarded for doing them.

Of the two major policy areas, foreign policy is the most rewarding and the most fun for prime ministers. They may hope to draw prestige and strength from foreign affairs and summit conferences. No modern prime minister, except perhaps Asquith, has resisted the attraction. Prime ministers are seen in carefully stage-managed appearances, arranging the destiny of nations in the company of world leaders. International affairs do not carry, or rather do not appear to carry, the directly painful consequences of domestic matters such as taxation, inflation, public expenditure; and they may be presented to give a spurious picture of wise and authoritative statesmanship. Foreign policy has an immediate, superficial appeal to the voters, and generally will not get the Prime Minister into much trouble. It is the general impression, not the detail, which counts, and if negotiation and diplomacy fail, the Prime Minister can play the patriotic card.

However, there are major disadvantages to the overseas role. First, playing on the international stage can become almost too attractive. Prime ministers return from their foreign trips suffering a combination of jet lag and spontaneous levitation. Wilson enthused over his Moscow trip in February 1975: 'They laid themselves out in an unparalleled way by all the standard tests' (including column inches in *Pravda*) (Castle 1980, p. 313, 20 February 1975). Callaghan was notoriously caught off guard in January 1979 when, returning to a cold, strike-bound Britain from a conference in the Caribbean, he failed to understand how critical the domestic situation had become, or was perceived to be.

The second disadvantage of the prime ministerial pursuit of foreign affairs is that the timetable and the extent of the commitment cannot be controlled, and the big problems turn out to be as intractable as domestic problems. A prime minister looking for quick success may find himself drawn into a costly and long drawn-out failure (Wilson over Vietnam, for example). Finally, the by-passing of the Cabinet, easily justified by the requirements of summitry and secrecy, isolates the Prime Minister, leaving him or her exposed and vulnerable when matters go wrong (e.g. Wilson over Vietnam and South Africa, Thatcher over Europe and Libya – and many more).

Economic policy is less inviting for prime ministers, though no recent prime minister has refrained from close involvement. A succession of governments has wrestled in vain with the problems of the post-war British economy, so far with little lasting effect. The main difference between Conservative and Labour governments is that in the case of the Conservatives economic failure is accompanied by electoral success.

Public expenditure offers little but worry and woe for prime ministers. They are all the prisoners of the high-spending, all-providing welfare state, whether they love it or not. If foreign policy is the balloon which raises a prime minister aloft, public expenditure is the millstone which weighs him or her down.

Mrs Thatcher more than most prime ministers ventured boldly into areas of domestic policy making, including local government, education and the Health Service. In local government the introduction of the Community Charge demonstrated the capacity of a prime minister to force through a personal, unpopular and probably unwise policy. In education, too, reform was pushed through, but with a notable retreat on a voucher system in education and on the funding of students in higher education. In this case, government and prime ministerial power were defeated by a revolt among middle-class Conservative voters. In the case of the National Health Service, reform turned out to be a long, hard road, and a prudent Prime Minister distanced herself from the effort and the political cost.

The Prime Minister cannot avoid being involved in foreign policy and the economy. He or she is not an outsider intervening, but rather in close consultation at least, and on some issues partner, competitor or leader to Foreign Secretary and Chancellor. In other policy areas a prime minister has more choice about participation, but must negotiate the disadvantages to the outsider of inadequate information, no time for follow-through, undermining the responsible minister, exposing his or her own authority. A prudent prime minister might more often make a suggestion, rather than a proposal or an instruction. He or she can, of course, in the last resort, replace the minister.

A prime minister is virtually irremoveable

Prime ministers win most of their arguments in the end (and hence, because of anticipation, before the end) since it is almost impossible to oust them. Mrs Thatcher was the first Prime Minister since 1940 to be ejected from office by her colleagues and her party. In normal circumstances pushing or persuading a prime minister out of office is so difficult as to be unthinkable. For the last fifty years prime ministers have easily survived periods of serious discontent among colleagues and frequent conspiracies. Barbara Castle claimed ministers had no time to carry through a conspiracy. But the problems are formidable – fear of the consequences of failure, and the difficulties of assembling support in Cabinet, Parliament and party; avoiding adverse electoral consequences (with headlines such as 'Party split', 'Knives are out'); above all, finding and agreeing on a candidate for the succession. The dissidents in Wilson's Cabinets were divided about the succession; the dissidents in Mrs Thatcher's Cabinets (and later outside them) could not agree on succession or policies. In Mrs Thatcher's phrase, there seemed to be 'no alternative'. But in extreme circumstances, with a general election threatening, this was not so.

Mrs Thatcher's fall from office in November 1990 was as unconventional as her tenure of office. Mrs Thatcher demonstrated by her eleven years in office that an electorally successful prime minister can make many enemies and still be unassailable. But, like Chamberlain in 1940, she demonstrated by her fall that a sitting prime minister with a large majority does not have an absolute hold on office. However, the circumstances in both cases were quite abnormal, so for once the exceptions really do confirm the rule.

Chamberlain resigned in 1940, making way for Churchill as prime minister of a Coalition Government. This was the immediate consequence of a substantial loss of support in Parliament following the disastrous Norway campaign. Britain seemed to be, in fact was, on the brink of catastrophe in the war against Germany. This was a situation of such abnormality that it hardly affects the rule of prime ministerial invulnerability.

The circumstances of 1990 were less critical for the nation, but dangerous enough for the Conservative Party. There were serious policy differences (especially over European policy and the Community Charge) between Mrs Thatcher and some members, and more certainly ex-members, of the Cabinet, and members of Parliament. There was some resentment of her style of governing, and a growing awareness of the possibility of defeat under Mrs Thatcher in the general election (regularly proclaimed in the polls). This situation would not have been fatal to the Prime Minister if Sir Geoffrey Howe's resignation, just before a leadership election was due, had not provoked Michael Heseltine to stand against Mrs Thatcher in that election. That again would not have been fatal if Mrs Thatcher had won, as she almost did, on the first ballot – and she might still have won on the second ballot if she had stayed in the contest, though that is not certain.

At this point finally the forces of opposition to Mrs Thatcher seized the opportunity, and a group of ministers, including members of the Cabinet, were bold enough to tell the Prime Minister her time was up. At the same time members of Parliament from marginal constituencies were expressing their anxieties to the leaders of the Parliamentary party. This was a unique chain of events. The ousting of the Prime Minister was brought about in a quite unusual situation, when the party faced defeat, and a candidate of substance was available. But the dominant lesson of Mrs Thatcher's fifteen years as leader and eleven years as Prime Minister is that in all normal circumstances a successful leader cannot be deposed.

The role of the Prime Minister: Collegial Insider, Individual Outsider

Margaret Thatcher and Harold Wilson provide two models of prime ministerial relations within the Central Executive Territory – 'Insider' and 'Outsider'. The Insider is concerned with collegiality and works from the centre of the Cabinet system. The Outsider aims at individual leadership and works outside or at the margins of the system.

Preferred modes	
Insider	Outsider
Cabinet and formal committees	Informal groups, bilaterals
Cabinet Office, and official elements of Prime Minister's Office	Prime minister's Office, advisers, 'Kitchen Cabinet'
Departments left to take initiatives	Intervention in departments
Civil Service integrity and autonomy respected	Civil Service regarded as a service to elected masters

In this perspective Mrs Thatcher was something of an 'Outsider'. She regarded the Cabinet as a conspiracy against her and, as far as she could, sidestepped or separated herself, acting as an independent power. In relation to government as well as to the Conservative establishment, she was an outsider, bringing in outsiders. She treated the Cabinet with what sometimes seemed malign neglect, punctuated by confrontations. Ironically the confrontations led to more defeats for her than for other prime ministers, but these confirmed her initial conspiracy theory about her colleagues.

Mrs Thatcher intervened in departments and she put the Civil Service in what may reasonably be regarded as its proper place. She used advisers, and had a shifting and quite modest set of 'Friends'. But she used the Prime Minister's Office and the Cabinet Office in largely conventional ways and she refused to set up a prime minister's department, which would have marked the institutionalisation of an outsider prime ministership. Mrs Thatcher is the first modern outsider Prime Minister, marauding and raiding across the whole Central Executive Territory, rather than staying fenced into the Cabinet area.

By contrast, Wilson was an 'Insider', not only a member of the Labour establishment but a Cabinet man, full of benign concern but also evasive, pursuing enveloping tactics rather than Mrs Thatcher's direct assaults. Like Mrs Thatcher he sought advice and support outside the formal Cabinet system, but the Cabinet remained his home base. Wilson's Cabinet crises were crises of consent, not confrontation. He manoeuvred against his Cabinet but regarded himself as locked into it. Either way, insider or outsider, Cabinet government in the strict and full sense is quite rare. It is unlikely that a large democratic state can be governed in two hours or so on a Thursday morning.

Reviewing these modern examples of the prime ministership, it becomes clear that simple prime ministerial government and simple Cabinet government are evident only in infrequent deviations from the normal system, which is variable individual leadership in a varying collective context. Mrs Thatcher practised a form of prime ministerial government. Her long tenure of the office shows that this is possible and acceptable in some circumstances. Her forcible ejection from office shows that prime ministerial government as practised by Mrs Thatcher is a deviant extension of the British form of executive government, acceptable only if it delivers continuous political success. This is a condition which is unlikely to be met in the long term.

The proper role of the Prime Minister: political leadership in a collective context

There is no single proper role for a prime minister in Britain. Different roles suit different prime ministers and different periods of history. The choice plainly lies between the roles indicated above, insider or outsider, individual or collegial. But, of course, there is a middle way – the individual leader in the collective context. This is, after all, the accepted position for most modern managers, including the managers of football teams and the captains of cricket teams – and the conductors of orchestras. If everyone plays as an individual the orchestra will do best (they all have the music score to follow); cricketers will do quite well, since good performances by individual bowlers and batsmen help the team to win; the footballers will do badly (since football is inherently more of a team game). However, these analogies fail to capture an essential element in the political game in which the Cabinet team competes: disagreement on goals (in both senses) is a fundamental characteristic of the game. Most of the players want to win, but some wish to move the goal posts, redraw the boundaries, shift the stumps, change the rules, take the ball home.

Thus the middle way has to be reformulated as individual leadership in a collective context with agreement on the rules and objectives of the game. Hence there is a difficult central managing and captaincy function for the Prime Minister. Within that function there are passive and positive interpretations, emphasising on one hand collegiality, on the other intervention and command. Both are forms of leadership.

Collegial leadership

The collegial position has been well stated by Professor Jones in arguing against the establishment of a prime minister's department (Jones 1987, p. 64).

> In the British constitution, government is ministerial government. Powers and duties are laid on ministers, not on the prime minister. They come together in Cabinet to resolve disputes between themselves and to determine a common line. The prime minister's

task, among others, is to help colleagues reach agreement, to promote collegiality and a collective strategy. . . . Personal initiatives come up against the constraints of Cabinet government. The urgings of the prime minister's own policy may hinder the achievement of a united Cabinet. The logic of the British Constitution is that prime ministers do not intervene in the policy responsibilities of specific ministers in order to advance personal prime ministerial objectives. Their intervention makes constitutional sense only if it is to enhance collective Cabinet responsibility.

This statement reflects some earlier 'constitutionalist' views of the office of prime minister. For example, the distinguished constitutional historian, Sir Ivor Jennings, wrote fifty years ago that 'a prime minister in peacetime ought not to have a policy. If he has able ministers he ought to rely on them' (1941, p. 160). Ministers themselves, and more recent commentators (notably Professor John Mackintosh), did not all agree. The Jennings view seems to exaggerate the collegial element in the constitution (as far as that is knowable) and political practice. Professor Jones allows that the Prime Minister may need to check a colleague:

If a prime minister is sceptical of the policy direction proposed by a minister, he should not intervene and take over that policy area. The course of action appropriate to the British constitution is for the prime minister to confine and redirect the ministers through the cabinet and a cabinet committee, or else to replace the minister.

Professor Jones goes on to accept in practice that prime ministers have personal political objectives which go beyond the maintenance of collegiality: 'A prime minister in practice usually has a dual motivation: the primary one is to help engineer a consensus between colleagues; the secondary motivation is to promote a personal policy. Too much emphasis on the latter can frustrate the achievement of the former' – sowing distrust and not facilitating the achievement of a united front (Jones 1987, p. 64).

Individual strong leadership

The individual leadership version of the Prime Minister's role accepts the constraints (and supports) of collegiality, but emphasises the Prime Minister's personal responsibility for the setting of goals, the giving of direction, the motivating and driving. This raises the general question of the value of 'strong' leadership.

There is clearly a need for leadership in some situations. These can be recognised in other activities – work, sport, domestic life. There are times when it is necessary positively to make a choice, set a direction, reinforce sagging morale. The occasion and need for leadership are most evident when there is a threat of some kind, and no clear escape or advance. At that point the 'strong' leader points the way with courage and a decisiveness not justified by reason alone. Britain, like most other countries, faces grave problems, and effective government sometimes requires strong, even heroic, leadership of this kind. However, most of the time such strong but irrational leadership is not required, and it can be disastrous if the decisive choice proves to be mistaken. On the contrary, 'wait and see' or Micawberism (hoping something will turn up) is often wise.

Moreover, in political leadership popular education may be more important than government activity, offering the people social and moral values, persuading to hard tasks with no immediate reward. Such political education in a democracy is quite different from mobilisation for a crusade. A third fallacy about leadership is that it is best exercised by one person. It *is* more easily and effectively exercised by one person, but is then defective in the quality of consent achieved.

In the light of these considerations it is evident that the choice for the Prime Minister is not between leadership and non-leadership, but between styles of leadership lying between the extremes of strong or heroic leadership: characterised by decisiveness, hyperactivity, crusade and command on the one side, and on the other, 'moderate' leadership, characterised by reflection and prudent hesitation, encouragement and gentle persuasion, a concern for consent.

If the country is about to be invaded, or collapse into chaos, you may prefer the strong form of leadership; in less dangerous times, moderate leadership looks preferable. Assessed as leaders in this perspective, Mrs Thatcher was plainly 'strong', Wilson 'moderate'. If you think that one was plainly the more successful prime minister then you have an indication of the advantages of one kind of leadership. On the other hand, you may conclude that it would be unfair to base a preference for one type of leadership on these two exemplars. Judging by the presently accepted records of their periods of office, neither Wilson nor Thatcher score the highest marks for their practice of leadership in a collective context.

British government is neither prime ministerial nor cabinet government: it is rather 'cabinet shaped' government, in which cabinet is the necessary framework and context of prime ministerial leadership.

Measuring the prime ministership

It may be illuminating to construct a scale of prime ministerial force on the lines of the Beaufort wind scale:

0–1   Calm or light air   Smoke rises vertically or drifts

A passive, almost do-nothing prime minister.

2–3   Light, gentle breeze   Leaves rustle and move, wind felt on face

Ministers feel the wind on their face. Prime minister, as a gentle chairman, may speak to colleagues but they do not have to take much notice.

4–5   Moderate, fresh breeze   Loose paper blows about, small branches move

Ministers adjust their position to feel more comfortable in the breeze. Prime minister, as a more vigorous chairman, produces some interventions, which must be taken into account.

6   Strong breeze   Large branches sway, wires whistle

Ministers sway and policies are shaken. Prime minister, as a chairman/chief executive, has considerable impact over large areas of government.

7–8   Moderate to fresh gale   Whole trees sway, hard to walk into wind

Whole departments sway, radical movements in policy. Prime minister is a dynamic and aggressive chief executive.

9   Strong gale   Damage to trees and roofs

The country sways and bits fall off; radical change. Prime minister is constitutional monarch.

10   Whole gale   Uproots trees, damages buildings

Revolutionary change and transformation. Prime minister is authoritarian monarch.

11–12 Storm and hurricane are rare inland, but disastrous.

Placing prime ministers on the scale is, of course, a hazardous business. But it is clear enough that prime ministers cannot be assigned to the lowest or the highest points in the scale. No modern prime minister approximates to 'calm or light air'. At the other end of the scale, only the most extreme and hostile (and hardly credible) interpretations of Mrs Thatcher's prime ministership would assign her to more than a force 9 gale. The tendency of this account is to re-emphasise the durability of the collective elements of the system, with moderate prime ministerial force. In her day Mrs Thatcher has metaphorically uprooted trees and damaged buildings, but her average force is rather less – let us say, a moderate to fresh gale. Thus, in practice, the Beaufort scale of prime ministerial force runs from 2–3 to 7–8, from a light breeze to a moderate to fresh gale.

A Beaufort scale is attractive, but of course it does not do justice to the complexities of political power at the centre. The office of prime minister needs to be measured by several complex factors:

1. Continuity and change: policy objectives which are (a) oriented towards the departments and their problems, coping if necessary with crises; or (b) driving towards fundamental change, creating crises on the way.
2. Consent or mobilisation: this is (a) governing by consent, in the negative sense of not venturing beyond what was already part of the accepted consensus, with just a little persuasion to extend the area of the consensus; or (b) government as a crusade, a more positive drive towards policy objectives, vigorous preaching, the mobilising of opinion; or the driving through of policy beyond and against the consensus.
3. Source of political energy and drive: this stems from (a) depending on the institutions, Parliament, the Civil Service, the core of the party (mainly 'Inside'); or from (b) developing ideas, an independent programme, even an ideology, supported by think tanks, a wing of the party or by appeal to the nation or people (mainly 'Outside', and populist).
4. Institutional base: this uses (a) the Cabinet system and the Downing Street complex in a collective mode; or (b) the Cabinet system and the Downing Street offices for prime ministerial initiatives and command; in particular it uses the informal elements of the Cabinet system and the prime ministerial elements of the Downing Street complex.
5. Personal aspirations: to act as (a) chairman or permanent secretary, a humdrum manager of a collective enterprise; or (b) as president and chief executive, to aspire to greatness, to heroic leadership.

Factors 1 and 2 constitute a radical conservative dimension. Factors 3 and 4 and 5 constitute an insider/outsider dimension.

The Beaufort scale of prime ministerial force can now be applied to take account of these dimensions. If we allocate up to 2 points of force for the more positive element (b) in each factor, and zero for (a) there is a maximum score of 10 (= a gale on the Beaufort scale). Further, we may designate the radical/conservative and insider/outsider dimensions by direction: westerly, warm and soft, for insider; northerly for radical, southerly for conservative; easterly, cold and hard, for outsider (see Figure 14.1).

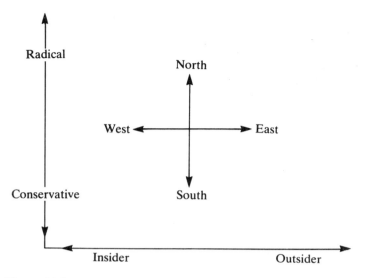

Figure 14.1

It might then be reasonable to locate prime ministers as follows: Mrs Thatcher, a radical outsider, as a north-easterly, gale force 8. Harold Wilson, a conservative insider, but not without some force – perhaps a moderate to strong south-westerly breeze, force 5. Edward Heath, a radical insider, would rate as a strong breeze from, say, west-north-west.

This meteorological concept of prime ministerial power could be further adapted to indicate areas of policy on which the wind blew. Finally, there should be some consideration of climatic change but, as the climatologists say, the evidence must accumulate over fifty years or so.

The sources of prime ministerial power

The sources of prime ministerial power have been set out above. They are institutional, political and personal. Institutionally it is clear now (especially after Mrs Thatcher's governments) that the prime ministership has a very high potential. The full exploitation of that potential depends on (a) the Prime Minister's personal qualities and application; (b) the political circumstances, including party and senior colleagues; (c) events and problems which may provide opportunities for leadership and success. Thus:

prime ministerial power = I (the institutions) × [(a) + (b) + (c)]

It should be understood that (a), (b) and (c) may be negative, and that (b) and (c) often are. They can be levellers of prime ministerial pretensions.

It is not of course possible to make a single laboratory test: rerun the 1980s without Mrs Thatcher. Did she make a difference? The answer surely is, yes – but there is room for doubt about how much difference she made – a great deal of difference to rhetoric, style, aspiration and direction, but perhaps not so much difference to actual policy achievements. It can certainly be argued that good Conservative policy in the 1980s would have followed broadly similar lines under another leader. It may even be argued that a Labour government would not have been so different.

Here it looks as if we are straining for simplicity. It may well be true that the impact of Mrs Thatcher has been exaggerated; but with a retreat to an opposite conclusion looks implausible. In most cases since 1945 a change of prime minister, even within the same party, has made a noticeable difference (Callaghan/Wilson; Heath/Home; Macmillan/Eden; Eden/Churchill); and the evident justification for the replacement of Thatcher by Major was precisely that it would make a difference.

15

The Central Executive Territory in British Government

In the mid-nineteenth century the Central Executive Territory was little more than the Cabinet, the Prime Minister and one or two Private Secretaries. Bagehot in the 1860s and Margot Asquith, forty years later, complained that cab drivers did not know where Downing Street was. Even Lloyd George's wartime introduction of advisers in the 'Garden Suburb' did not last, and their huts were dismantled after the war.

By the 1990s the Central Executive Territory had developed into the major arena of government. Within the Territory the basic activities of governing go on – making choices, taking decisions, developing policy, shaping programmes, managing crises, building consent and securing approval.

The British constitution is notoriously flexible or fluid, and continuously so. Fluidity is not necessarily virtuous; the bad may get better, but the good gets worse. The image of a Territory allows for flow and variability, and the inter-relationships of people rather than institutions. Within the flow of relationships in the Territory, the following points are characteristic:

- The dominance of the Executive over Parliament.
- The dominance of the Prime Minister within the Executive.

The Prime Minister has taken up a managing, co-ordinating, interventionist role, and exercises personalised executive power. This is not equivalent to prime ministerial government.

- The Cabinet has developed by fragmentation and multiplication as the source, but not the core, of a Cabinet system. The Cabinet itself retains a residual and irreducible solidity; it is not about to sink into merely 'dignified' status.
- The 'Downing Street complex', including the Cabinet Office and the Prime Minister's Office, has developed to support the Prime Minister in the fragmented Cabinet system.
- The contemporary prime minister, compared with forceful prime ministers of the past (for example, Gladstone, Lloyd George, Chamberlain), is powerful in a different way, has at his disposal much greater force, but meets more substantial resistance. Gladstone used pedal power on a level circuit; the contemporary prime minister uses an engine for a steep mountain track.
- The Civil Service does most of the governing, and the higher Civil Service 'manages policy', a function which falls short of determining policy.

A comparison

Most of the elements of the British Executive can be discerned in other systems – a chief executive, some kind of governing council, advisory and support groups, senior officials. But in detail there are major differences. For example, the office of prime minister is not similar to the US or the French presidency: the sources of power, support services and the status of officials are all different. The British Cabinet is unique, even if now a little elusive. The understandings and conventions, including those relating to responsibility to Parliament, are also peculiar to Britain. An essential part of the British system of government is to be discovered in the tacit understandings and the silences of the Constitution. The processes of British government are something of a mystery; other countries enjoy the illusion and the reality of open and well-understood procedures of government.

Hence use of the term 'presidential' to describe a powerful

prime minister is misleading, since a presidential system is so different from a cabinet/parliamentary system. A president is typically directly elected, not responsible to an assembly, free to choose his colleagues, and legitimately wielding personal power. For these reasons British government is here described as 'Cabinet-shaped'. This is not to deny that there are presidential elements and deformations in the Cabinet shape.

The triangle of forces

The Central Executive Territory is at the peak of the governing process, and contains within it a triangle of contending forces which is illustrated in Figure 15.1.

Political drives

It is evident that governments are properly concerned with the building of consent, and their actions are aimed at the very least to avoid the alienation of supporters, including the party, major interests and the electors. 'Presentation' weighs heavily against objective policy making. A prime concern of government is to

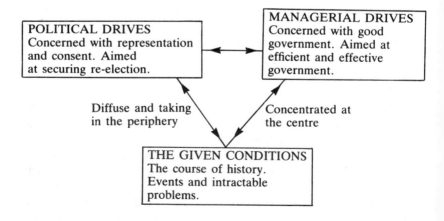

Figure 15.1

win the next election. A prime concern of members of the government is to gain personal credit, avoid personal blame, lead a satisfying and comfortable life (political life does seem to revolve around food and drink) – and to win the next election. The apparent obsession of government with 'presentation' and the new prominence of press officers are a consequence of this necessary concern.

Managerial drives

Elected politicians like to please people. In the Central Executive Territory they come up against the brute realities of infinite demand for finite resources, and face to face with non-elected officials, the guardians of the public purse, and the integrity of public management. These are the preachers and practitioners of 'good government' in the traditional American sense of honest and efficient administration, in contrast to the corrupt and partisan politics of the party 'boss' and 'machine'.

'Politicians often believe that their world is the real one: officials sometimes take a different view'. So wrote Lord Rothschild, first head of CPRS, to the Prime Minister in 1974 (quoted in Hennessy 1989, p. 247). This indicates the nature of the endless battle between officials and politicians. For the latter, now is never the time to confront reality, make hard choices, review priorities, choose death (losing the election) in preferance to dishonour. Such exhortations are the main component of 'good government'. The lessons of public administration form a second component. Governments need to escape from the limited short-term vision through the development of long-term strategy (which may be based on their political values). Policy making should be based on the best available information, analysed and focused towards clearly defined and evaluated options. Costs and consequences need to be calculated and set out, and so on.

Little of this is now unfamiliar to ministers, though to some it may be unpalatable; Gladstone might have used different words but would not have disagreed with the general principles. Ministers (including Gladstone) are experienced and often skilled in the language of forensic advocacy, making a case persuasively. Once in office they have now to move from the broad brush of political rhetoric to the detail and language of rational policy making.

Given conditions and events

Policy itself is more complex. In foreign policy there are continuing complex inter-relationships which make Chamberlain's visits to Hitler in 1938 look primitive (they were). Economic policy making is more fragmented nationally and internationally, and economic problems are harder to resolve.

In domestic policy the nineteenth-century reformist drive is done; the extension and sharing of middle-class privilege and quality of life turn out to be the easy part. For example, secondary education for all can be physically provided, but quality is in doubt; the National Health Service cannot meet unlimited demand at an affordable price; cars are no longer a luxury, but roads are overloaded . . . and so on.

There are new and influential interest groups – mortgagors, car owners, the old, the 'Greens' and the local NIMBY campaigners, as well as older and still very powerful groups – farmers, bankers and trade unions. Technological decisions, for example in energy policy, seem to governments like leaps in the dark. Most policy choices are expensive; there is often no alternative to throwing money at a problem.

Whatever governments try to do, the complex forces of history drive on, and the sovereign nation state ceases to exist, except perhaps on – and off – the football field. Thus many of the major changes of the century are not related to the coming and going of governments and the alternation of parties, but to the impact of war, the long sea changes in popular political culture, and the slow transformation of assumptions and notions of acceptability.

Bad government

Trapped in the triangle of forces (see Figure 15.1), government in Britain suffers many defects:

- Overload or inadequate capacity, both quantitative and qualitative (too much and too difficult).
- Ungovernability, not in the form of serious dissent, but the

prevalence of a conservative and protective self-interest, and the absence of well-informed, critical and tolerant consent to government-induced change.
- Inertia in the form either of a civil service-dominated directionless consensus or by way of concession to interest groups.
- Incoherence, lack of strategy and 'short termism'.
- A weak Parliament and some consequent remoteness and lack of participation.
- Excessive centralisation and metropolitan dominance, with no substantial centres of political force outside the two major national parties.
- Secrecy in detail, and in general a reluctance to engage in public argument.
- Partisan adversarial politics based on theatrical confrontations, weak rationality and no hint of partnership.
- The corruption of power inherent in a system which confers 'superstar' status in a 'winner-takes-all' competition.

The record of policy failure confirms the defects of British government. There has been an avoidance of hard decisions, an excessive concern for presentation and news management, and a persistent tendency to convert major strategic choices to short-term tactical decisions (for example, the slow retreat from 'East of Suez' measured out by troop withdrawals and weapons procurement decisions; or the whole business of Britain's reluctant backing into Europe). A case can be made that post-war governments, with one or two exceptions, have failed to achieve many of their policy objectives.

Some of the defects of British government are peculiarly British; others are the characteristic faults of government. Blackstone and Plowden sum them up:

> Governments, in all forms of regime in all parts of the world, are pluralistic, divided, under-informed, short-sighted, only partly in control of their own processes, and unable to guarantee the outcomes which they promise. There are enormous gaps, and sometimes no linkages at all, between realities, perceptions, decisions, actions and consequences. The collective interest is too often dominated and distorted by sectional interests; 'rational' decisions are distorted by political considerations; there is an

excessive focus on the short term. The responses to problems are incremental rather than radical. Individual decisions are often inconsistent with each other, with existing policies, and with any overall objectives that the government may have defined.

(Blackstone and Plowden 1988, p. 12)

Good government

Good government may be simply defined as government which maximises effectiveness and consent – leaving aside the difficulties of defining and applying these concepts. Thus governments may be divided into four types or, more accurately, may be measured under four heads and may be seen as tending towards four types. Figure 15.2 is a diagram which joins together effectiveness and consent as dimensions of government.

All democratic governments would like to occupy the NE quartile. In Britain, the NW is said to be a frequent destination. More savage critics may feel that the two southerly quartiles have had their occupants. How to move government toward the northeast, the quartile of good government? Much of the problem lies in the 'given conditions', the intractable problems faced by governments. However, there is scope for further reform within the Central Executive Territory to improve the managerial side of the system – notably the development of the Cabinet Office and the Prime Minister's Office, though much of the benefit of this kind of reform has already been achieved.

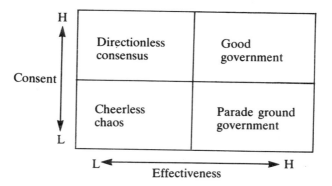

Figure 15.2

There is much greater scope for reform to rectify the 'deficit of consent', which appears to be much larger than the 'deficit of power' (the hole-in-the-centre). The deficit of consent arises, not because government in general lacks public confidence, but because the disagreements which underlie political activity are hidden. There is a basket of reforms on offer – proportional representation, devolution, a Bill of Rights, parliamentary reform (notably a new second chamber), the 'hiving-off' of much of the Civil Service.

In relation to the 'deficit of consent' the Central Executive Territory looks to be too closed, too managerial in purpose and style, too little concerned to argue out disagreements openly. Hence the operation of government within the Central Executive Territory will be improved less by further institutional adjustment than by fundamental change in the political education and culture of the British people. The British enjoy a remarkably stable democracy but (perhaps for that reason) they do not take politics seriously (otherwise they would surely not admire Prime Minister's Question Time, or tolerate the House of Lords). Political education requires political leadership of an educative kind. But the teaching function of leadership is easily neglected in the Central Executive Territory, which is designed for the management of policy, not for persuasion, public understanding and consent.

A select list of introductory reading

Burch, M. (1988) 'The United Kingdom', in J. Blondel and F. Muller-Rommel, (eds) *Cabinets in Western Europe*, Macmillan
Castle, Barbara (1980, 1984) *The Castle Diaries*, 1974–76 and 1964–70, Weidenfeld and Nicolson.
Constitutional Reform Centre (1988) Cabinet Government, Politics Briefings, No 4.
Donoughue, B. (1987) *Prime Minister*, Jonathan Cape.
Gordon Walker, P. (1972) *The Cabinet*, Fontana.
Hennessy, P. (1986) *Cabinet*, Basil Blackwell.
Hogwood, B. and Mackie, T. (eds) (1985) *Unlocking the Cabinet*, Sage.
King, A. (ed.) (1985) *The British Prime Minister*, Macmillan.
Rose, R. (1980) 'British Government: The Job at the Top', in R. Rose and E. Suleiman (eds) (1980) *Presidents and Prime Ministers*, American Enterprise Institute.
Willetts, D. (1987) 'The Role of the Prime Minister's Policy Unit', *Public Administration*, 65, Winter, pp. 443–54.
Wilson, H. (1976) *The Governance of Britain*, Weidenfeld and Nicolson.
Young, H. (1989) *One of Us*, Macmillan.

In addition the following journals are especially useful for this subject:

Contemporary Record
Parliamentary Affairs
Politics Review, formerly *Social Studies Review*

References

Books and articles referred to in the text or valuable as sources.

Barnett, J. *(1982) Inside the Treasury*, Andre Deutsch.
Benn, A. (1987, 1988, 1989, 1990) *Diaries, 1963–80*, Hutchinson.
Blake, R. (1975) *The Office of Prime Minister*, Oxford University Press.
Blackstone, T. and Plowden, W. (1988) *Inside the Think Tank*, Heinemann.
Boyle, Lord (1980) 'Ministers and the administrative process', *Public Administration*, 58, Spring, pp. 1–12.
Bray, J. (1970) *Decision in Government*, Gollancz.
Bruce-Gardyne, J. (1986) *Ministers and Mandarins: Inside the Whitehall Village*, Sidgwick and Jackson.
Burch, M. (1988) 'The UK' in J. Blondel and F. Muller-Rommel (eds) *Cabinets in Western Europe*, pp. 16–32, Macmillan.
Callaghan, J. (1987) *Time and Chance*, Collins.
Campbell, J. (1983) *Roy Jenkins: A Biography*, Weidenfeld and Nicolson.
Castle, Barbara (1980, 1984) *The Castle Diaries*, 1974–76 and 1964–70, Weidenfeld and Nicolson.
Cockerell, M. (1988) *Live from Number 10*, Macmillan.
Crosland, S. (1982) *Tony Crosland*, Jonathan Cape.
Crossman, R. H. S. (1963) *Introduction to W. Bagehot: The English Constitution*, Fontana.
Crossman, R. H. S. (1975, 1976, 1977) *The Diaries of a Cabinet Minister* (3 vols), Hamish Hamilton and Jonathan Cape.
Daalder, H. (1963) *Cabinet Reform in Britain 1914–63*, Oxford University Press.
Donoughue, B. (1987) *Prime Minister*, Jonathan Cape.
Dunleavy, P. and Rhodes, R. A. W. (1990) 'Core executive studies in Britain', *Public Administration*, 68, Spring, pp. 3–28.
Dunleavy, P., Jones, G. W. and O'Leary, B. (1990) 'Prime ministers

and the Commons: patterns of behaviour', *Public Administration*, 68, Spring, pp. 123–40.
Expenditure Committee, House of Commons (1977) 11th Report, 1976–7, *Minutes*.
Freedman, L. (1988) *Britain and the Falklands War*, Basil Blackwell.
Gordon Walker, P. (1972) *The Cabinet*, Fontana.
Griffith, J. A. G. (1987) 'Crichel Down: The most famous farm in British constitutional history', *Contemporary Record*, vol. 1, no. 1, pp. 35–40.
Haines, J. (1977) *The Politics of Power*, Jonathan Cape.
Harris, K. (1988) *Thatcher*, Weidenfeld and Nicolson.
Headey, B. (1974) *British Cabinet Ministers*, Allen and Unwin.
Healey, D. (1989) *The Time of my Life*, Michael Joseph.
Heclo, H. and Wildavsky, A. (1974) *The Private Government of Public Money*, Macmillan.
Hennessy, P. (1986) *Cabinet*, Basil Blackwell.
Hennessy, P. (1989) *Whitehall*, Secker and Warburg.
Hennessy, P. and Seldon, A. (eds) (1987) *Ruling Performance*, Basil Blackwell.
Herman, V. and Alt, J. (eds) (1975) *Cabinet Studies: A Reader*, Macmillan.
Hogwood, B. and Mackie, T. (eds) (1985) *Unlocking the Cabinet*, Sage.
Hunt, Lord (1987) 'The United Kingdom' in W. Plowden (ed.) *Advising the Rulers* (1987) pp. 66–70.
Hurd, D. (1979) *An End to Promises*, Collins.
Jenkins, P. (1970) *The Battle of Downing Street*, Charles Knight.
Jenkins, P. (1987) *Mrs Thatcher's Revolution*, Cape.
Jennings, I. (1941) *The British Constitution*, Cambridge University Press.
Jones, G. (1985) 'The Prime Minister's aides', in A. King (ed.) *The British Prime Minister*, Macmillan.
Jones, G. (1987) 'The United Kingdom' in W. Plowden (ed.) *Advising the Rulers*, Basil Blackwell.
Kaufman, G. (1980) *How to be a Minister*, Sidgwick and Jackson.
King, A. (ed.) (1985) *The British Prime Minister*, Macmillan.
Lee, M. (1990) 'The ethos of the Cabinet Office', *Public Administration*, 68, Summer, pp. 235–42.
Madgwick, P. (1988) 'The Westland Affair', *Social Studies Review*, vol. 4, No. 1.
Madgwick, P. and Woodhouse, D. (1989) 'The Westland Affair', *Social Studies Review*, vol. 4, No. 4.
Morgan, K. O. (1984) *Labour in Power*, Oxford University Press.
Morgan, K. O. (1990) *The People's Peace*, Oxford University Press.
Neustadt, R. (1960) *Presidential Power – the Politics of Leadership*, Wiley.
Pliatzky, L. (1982) *Getting and Spending*, Basil Blackwell.
Pliatzky, L. (1984) 'Mandarins, ministers and the management of Britain', *Political Quarterly*, 55, pp. 23–8.

Pliatzky, L. (1989) *The Treasury under Mrs Thatcher*, Basil Blackwell.
Plowden, W. (ed.) (1987) *Advising the Rulers*, Basil Blackwell.
Ponting, C. (1986) *Whitehall: Tragedy and Farce*, Sphere.
Ponting, C. (1989) *Breach of Promise: Labour in Power 1964–70*, Hamish Hamilton.
Prior, J. (1986) *A Balance of Power*, Hamish Hamilton.
Pym, F. (1985) *The Politics of Consent*, Hamish Hamilton.
Riddell, P. (1983) *The Thatcher Government*, Martin Robertson.
Rose, R. (1969) 'The variability of party government', *Political Studies*, XVII, 4, pp. 413–45.
Rose, R. (1980) 'British government: the job at the top', in R. Rose and E. Suleiman (eds) (1980) *Presidents and Prime Ministers*, American Enterprise Institute, pp. 1–49.
Rose, R. (1987) *Ministers and Ministries: A Functional Analysis*, Clarendon Press.
Seldon, A. (1990) 'The Cabinet Office and co-ordination, 1979–87', *Public Administration*, 68, Spring, pp. 103–21.
Wass, D. (1984) *Government and the Governed*, Routledge and Kegan Paul.
Willetts, D. (1987) 'The role of the Prime Minister's Policy Unit', *Public Administration*, 65, Winter, pp. 443–54.
Williams, F. (1961) *A Prime Minister Remembers*, Heinemann.
Williams, P. (1982) *Hugh Gaitskell*, Jonathan Cape.
Wilson, H. (1976) *The Governance of Britain*, Weidenfeld and Nicolson and Michael Joseph.
Woolton, Lord (1959) *Memoirs*, Cassell.
Young, H. (1989) *One of Us*, Macmillan.
Young, H. and Sloman, A. (1986) *The Thatcher Phenomenon*, BBC.

'The Re-organization of Central Government' (1970) Cmnd. 4506, HMSO.
Falkland Islands Review (1983) Cmnd 8787, HMSO.
Efficiency Unit, Report to the Prime Minister (1988) *Improving Management in Government: The Next Steps*, HMSO.

Index

adversarial government, 13, 14, 52
advice, 224–6
  advisers, 107, 117–19, 122–3, 125–7, 212–14
  see also Prime Minister, Policy Unit
agricultural policy, 55
Aquinas, 124
Armstrong, Sir Robert, 100, 101, 102–5, 209
Armstrong, Sir William, 102, 104, 127, 217
Attlee, Clement, 45, 64, 68, 72, 92, 116, 159–61, 163, 170, 171, 172, 176, 185, 203

Baldwin, Stanley, 161, 176
Bancroft, Lord
  on Civil Service, 29–30
Bank of England, 27, 55, 82, 157, 219
Barnett, Joel, 79–86
Beethoven, Ludwig van, 177
Belgrano, 223
Benn, Tony, 47, 48, 54, 82, 149, 153, 167, 189, 190, 192, 219, 226, 231–2
Bevan, Aneurin
  split with Gaitskell, 40, 184, 185
Biffen, John, 197
Brahms, Johannes, 177
BBC (British Broadcasting Corporation), 12

Brittan, Leon, 211
Brown, George, 39, 47, 184, 185, 188, 189
budget, 27, 68, 153, 202, 204
Butler, R. A., 156–7, 242

Cabinet
  agenda, 55–6, 58–9, 67, 154–8
  atmosphere, 65–5
  chairing, 59, 158–64
  collectivity, 211
  committees, 14, 70–85, 156–8, 194–5, 201, 221–2
    ad hoc, 72–3
    formal and informal, 71
    informal, 80–2
    official, 73
    standing, 72–3
  composition, 41, 54
  Conservative, 46
  conventions, 46
  exclusivity, 42–3
  Falklands War, 72, 223
  inner, 77–8, 80–2, 85
  Labour, 46
  leaks, 46–7, 65
  Minutes (Conclusions), 2, 61–2
  nature, 249, 259
  'partial', 77–8
  policy-making, 187–95
  prime ministers and, 164–6
  room, 57
  solidarity, 47–8

INDEX 271

Cabinet (*continued*)
  splits, 46
  Thatcher, Margaret, 200–6
  voting, 61, 163
  War Cabinet, 202, 223
  Westland Affair, 211–12
  Wilson, Harold, 184–7
  other references, 4, 5, 11, 19, 20, 21, 37
Cabinet Office, 21, 26, 62, 82, 84, 89, 91–3, 95–106
  ambiguities, 100–2, 129
  Central Policy Review Staff, 215–18
  development, 96–7
  influence on policy, 104–5
  origin, 72
  Prime Minister's Department, 127–9
  Prime Minister's Private Office, 126
  structure, 97
  work, 98–100
Cabinet Secretary, 14, 57, 62, 95, 97, 98, 100, 101, 102–5, 113, 127–9, 196, 215–18
Callaghan, James, 26, 28, 39, 44, 58, 63, 65, 73, 82, 110–11, 148, 156, 161, 165–6, 168, 172, 179, 184, 188, 189, 191, 203, 219–20, 222
Carrington, Lord, 45, 58, 199, 220–4
Castle, Barbara, 12, 49, 51–2, 54, 55, 63–5, 73, 74, 76, 77, 79, 83, 147–9, 164–5, 185–7, 189–193, 218, 227–8, 236
  quoted: 27, 44, 101, 155, 161, 240, 246
Central Executive Territory, 3, 5, 9–17, 29–30, 33, 89–95, 102, 108, 116, 126, 146, 170, 178, 191, 195, 211, 216, 220, 226, 258–9, 260–2, 264–5
centralisation, 10
Central Policy Review Staff (CPRS), 26, 82, 92, 102, 112, 114, 116, 155, 196, 215–18
Centre for Policy Studies, 114, 123
Chamberlain, Neville, 121, 176, 247
Chancellor of the Exchequer, 25–8, 42, 43, 49, 55, 66, 77, 93, 118–19, 128, 157, 188, 192, 193–5, 212–14, 219–20, 227–8, 242–3
Chief Secretary (of Treasury), 227
Chief Whip, 93, 174
Churchill, Winston, 25, 73, 91, 117, 121, 160–3, 170, 172, 176, 177, 199, 239, 247
Civil Service, 14, 16, 23, 28–30, 31–2, 57, 89, 93, 102, 120, 137, 206–10, 237, 259
Civil Service Department, 26, 92, 93, 112
Colleagues, The, (ministerial), 37–52
collective responsibility, 4, 11, 26, 28, 37, 38, 137, 191, 228–32
collegiality, 37
Commissions, Royal, 123
Concorde, 54, 217
confidentiality, 37
Conservative Party, 39, 114, 214
Constitution, British, 10–11, 32, 37, 100, 136–7, 157, 258–9
Crichel Down case, 3, 4
Crosland, Tony, 44, 48, 49, 54, 55, 61, 66, 185, 186, 189, 191, 219
Crossman, Richard, 24, 40, 54, 56, 95, 140, 185, 189, 192, 235–6
Crown, 10–11, 136–7, 142
culture, political, 11–12

Defence policy, 55, 165
  Committee, 221–2
Department of Economic Affairs, 14, 23, 26
Departments, 19–25
devolution, 58, 82
diarists, 2

Donoughue, Bernard, 120, 127, 194 *quoted*: 125, 158–9, 167, 168
Downing Street, 17, 91–3, 95

economic policy, 68, 168
economic seminar, 82–3, 220
Eden, Anthony, 172, 203
education, 188–90
Education, Department of, 21, 24, 25, 168
Efficiency Unit, 92, 107, 112, 118
elections, 134, 137
elites, political, 11–12, 16
Environment, Department of, 20
'Establishment', 12, 225
European (Economic) Community, (EEC, EC), 17, 33, 48, 56, 67, 158, 185, 242
Exchange Rate Mechanism (ERM), 17, 48, 56, 212–14
executive, 10–11
executive centre, 89–90
expenditure, public, 20, 42

Falklands War, 12–13, 198, 202, 205, 220–4, 239
Financial Management Initiative, 210
Foot, M., 149
force, 5–6
 prime ministerial, 5–6, 235–9
foreign affairs, 21, 23, 33, 55, 58, 67, 110, 114, 168, 184–5, 187–8, 207, 217
Foreign Office, 118, 201, 220–4
Foreign Secretary, 226
Franks, Lord, 12–13
freedom of information, 14 *see also* open government
Friends *see* Kitchen Cabinet
Fulton Report on the Civil Service, 93, 225

Gaitskell, Hugh, 40–1, 185, 186
'Garden Suburb', 91
Gladstone, W. E., 41, 57, 171, 176, 261
Goodman, Lord, 193
Gordon Walker, Patrick, 77–8, 81–2, 156–8, 189
Government
 bad, 262–4
 good, 264–5
Government, British
 evidence, 1–2
 federation of departments, 19
 gigantism, 13
 interpretation, 3–5
 nature, 9–10
GCHQ (Government Communications Headquarters), 103–4, 155, 209
Gow, Ian, 121

Hailsham, Lord, 45, 49
Haines, Joe, 116, 120, 125
Healey, Denis, 15, 27, 32, 43, 49, 54, 56, 60, 66, 82–3, 140, 153, 188, 189, 190, 192, 193
Heath, Edward, 28, 68, 73, 92–3, 102, 103, 120, 125, 127, 140, 141–2, 145–6, 154–5, 162–3, 170, 172, 173, 180, 186, 215–18
Hennessy, Peter *quoted*: 12–13, 37, 62, 72, 73, 74–5, 82–3, 84, 102
Heseltine, Michael, 47, 59, 63, 65, 71, 84, 147, 148, 149, 204, 211, 247
Home Office, 21, 27
Home, Sir Alec, 172, 180
Hoskyns, Sir John, 206
House of Commons Select Committees, 104, 223 *see also* Parliament
Howe, Sir Geoffrey, 41, 47, 48, 54, 65–6, 141, 147, 149, 150, 155, 165, 201, 204, 214, 227, 230, 247
Howell, David, 83, 228
Hunt, Sir John, (Lord), 62, 127–9, 140

INDEX

Hurd, Douglas, 120, 125

ideology, 16
incomes policy (pay policy), 68, 191–2, 193–5
Ingham, Bernard, 107, 116, 121, 153, 208
'In Place of Strife', 65, 83, 190–1
interest groups, 16
IMF (International Monetary Fund), 17
   crisis (1976), 58, 218–20, 161
IRA (Irish Republican Army), 199

Jenkins, Roy, 27, 47–8, 49, 65, 150, 189, 190, 191, 192, 243
Jennings, Sir Ivor, 251
Jones, George, Professor, 129, 250–1
Joseph, Sir Keith, 123

Kilbrandon Report on the Constitution, 225
Kinnock, Neil, 177, 180
Kitchen Cabinet, 85, 108, 109, 119–22

Labour Party, 39, 191
   NEC (National Executive Committee), 160, 173, 231
Lawson, Nigel, 28, 41, 43, 47, 48, 118–19, 125, 128, 150, 202, 204, 212–14
leadership, political, 133–4
leaks, 137, 186, 191
   and memoirs, 230–1
Lever, Harold, 26
Lloyd George, David, 40, 63, 72, 91, 101–2, 176, 215, 258
local government, 10, 19
Lords, House of, 11

Macmillan, Harold, 28, 42, 92, 102, 125, 143, 170, 172, 176, 203
Major, John, 46, 172, 257
media, 2, 16, 50–1, 146, 170–1, 176–80

Middle East, 187–8
Millar, Sir Ronald, 124
miners, 198, 205
ministerial responsibility, 31, 212, 223
Ministers, 15, 19, 22–3, 48–50, 54, 66
monarchy, 134 *see also* crown

NATO (North Atlantic Treaty Organisation), 17, 33
NHS (National Health Service), 193
'Next Steps', 210
Northern Ireland, 55, 68, 121

open government, 2, 14, 103, 153
Opposition, 13, 14, 38–9, 174
Overseas Development Minister, 39

Parkinson, Cecil, 202
Parliament, 13–14, 20, 30–2, 45, 134, 136–8, 174, 212
   sovereignty of Parliament, 10, 30
Parsons, Sir Anthony, 118
Party, parties, 16, 30–1, 122–3, 133, 138, 172–3, 180, 237
Permanent Secretary, 19, 24
PESC (Public Expenditure Survey Committee) *see* public expenditure
Pliatzky, Sir Leo, 101
Plowden Report, 92
Polaris submarine, 153
policy making, 22–3
polls, 242
Ponting, Clive, 103
Powell, Charles, 121, 207–8
power, 5–6, 17–18
Press Office, Prime Minister's, 46, 178
Prime Minister
   advice, 125–7, 239
   appointing power, 39, 136–7
   Cabinet, 53, 57, 137–8, 164–6
   agenda, 154–8

Prime Minister (*continued*)
  chairing, 159–64
  committee system, 72, 75–9, 80–2, 156–8
  minutes, 62
  Cabinet Office, 105
  Cabinet Secretary, 101
  chairman or chief executive, 139–41
  Chancellor of the Exchequer, 242
  Colleagues, The, 146–51, 241–2
  departments, 134, 166–9
  economic policy, 245–6
  expenditure, 42–3, 245
  factors in leadership, 255–6
  fall, 246–8
  foreign policy, 244–6
  indispensability, 240
  'Insider', 248–9
  kitchen cabinet, 119–22, 207–8
  leadership, 133–4, 250–6
  locating decisions, 152
  management of information, 153, 139, 146
  media, 139, 146, 170–1, 176–80
  methods of work, 142–3
  momentum of events, 243
  officials and advisers, 145–6
  'Outsider', 248–9
  Parliament, 173–6
  party, 172–3
  Policy Unit, 82, 84, 92–3, 101, 107, 109, 112–15, 193–5, 217, 219
  Political Office, 107, 117
  power, 235–9, 240–1, 257
  President of USA, compared with, 259–60
  Press Office, 107, 115–17
  Prime Minister's Department, 127–9
  Prime Minister's Office, 21, 89, 91, 101, 107–29, 153, 207–8, 218
  Principal Private Secretary (PPS), 101, 102, 107–9
  Private Office (Secretariat), 82, 84, 101–2, 107, 109–12, 126–7
  quasi-regal power, 138
  resignations, 47
  structure and style, 136–51
  'summitry', 146
Prior, James, 121, 162, 165, 197, 201, 204, 207
public expenditure, 68, 226–8
Pym, Francis, 141, 197, 204

quangos, 20, 23
Questions of Procedure for Ministers, 37
Questions, Parliamentary, 174–5

Radcliffe Declaration on ministerial memoirs, 63
Rayner, Sir Derek (Lord), 210
resignations, 28, 43, 137, 147, 152, 204, 212–14, 223, 243
  threat of, 47–8
responsibility
  collective, 37, 38, 46–7
  ministers to Parliament, 25, 72
  see also ministerial responsibility
  to Parliament, 10–11
Rhodesia, 17, 55, 68
Rosebery, Lord, 240–1
Rothschild, Lord, 216–17, 261
Royal Commissions, 224–6

secrecy, 14, 15, 72 *see also* confidentiality
Secretary of State *see* Ministers
Selective Employment Tax, 63
semi-detached organisations (SDOs), 20, 23
Shadow Cabinet, 39
solidarity of government, 72
speeches, speech writing, 124–5
'Spycatcher' affair, 104, 209
'Star Chamber', 157, 227–8
Suez Intervention 1956, 17, 223
Suffolk, 177
Sun, The 179

Tebbitt, Norman, 202
Thatcher, Margaret
  achievements, 205–6
  advisers, 118–19
  Cabinet, 53, 65, 68, 75–6, 84, 161–5, 197, 200–6
    agenda, 58
    committees, 74
    kitchen, 119–22, 196, 200, 207–8
    speeches, 63
  Cabinet Secretary, 101, 196, 208
  Central Policy Review Staff, 215–18
  Civil Service, 206–10
  colleagues, 40–1, 48, 241–2
  compared with Wilson, 159
  departments, 169
  dismissal of colleagues, 147–8
  domestic policy, 246
  dress, 51
  economic seminar, 82–3
  Falklands War, 171, 198, 220–4
  fall, 178, 238, 246–8
  foreign policy, 245
  interpretation of, 4, 6, 16, 28, 45
  Lawson, Nigel, resignation of, 212–14
  leadership, 252–3, 254–7
  leaks, 153
  media, 177–80
  miners, 198
  Minister of Education, 25, 52, 66, 208–9
  ministers, 198–9, 206–7
  officials and advisers, 145–6
  Parliament, 174–6
  party, 172–3
  personality, 199
  Policy Unit, 112–13, 196
  popularity, 180
  Press Office, 116, 196, 208
  Prime Minister, 195–214
  Prime Minister's Department, 127
  Prime Minister's Office, 126, 196
  public expenditure, 227
  resignation, threats of, 150–1
  Royal Commissions, 225
  speeches, 124
  style (approach, methods), 72, 140–5, 197–9
  Thatcherism, 195, 197–8
  'Think Tanks', 123
  Westland Affair, 147–8, 211–12
Think Tanks, 123
Thorneycroft, Peter, (Lord), 47
Trade Union Congress, 195
trade unions, 68
Treasury, 17, 21, 22, 23, 25–8, 47, 82, 102, 110, 114, 127, 137, 154, 168, 193–5, 209, 217–18, 219–20, 226–8
Trend, Sir Burke, 62, 101, 212

USA, 5, 17, 89, 137–9, 141, 155, 184, 203, 224, 240–1, 242, 259

Vietnam, 17, 68

Walters, Sir Alan, 26, 118–19, 212–14
Westland Affair, 59, 63, 71, 103, 104, 147–9, 165, 211–12, 238
Whitelaw, William (Lord), 45, 54, 199, 204
Wigg, George, 9, 120
Williams, Marcia (Lady Falkender), 81, 120
Wilson, Harold
  achievements, 187, 205–6
  advisers, specialist, 118
  'agreement to differ', 229
  appeals to Cabinet, 76
  Cabinet, 53, 65, 68, 75, 154, 164–5, 184, 185–6, 203
    agenda, 58
    chairing, 59–60, 161, 163
    committees, 74
    inner, 81
    kitchen, 81–2, 120–1, 184
    speeches in, 64
    summing-up in, 62

Wilson, Harold (*continued*)
   Cabinet Office, 99–101
   Callaghan, James, 188
   colleagues, 147, 241–2
   collective responsibility, 229–32
   crisis of 1975, 158–9
   departments, 167–8
   foreign policy, 184, 185, 245
   'In Place of Strife', 83, 190–1
   'insider', 249
   leadership, 252–3, 254–7
   leaks, 153, 186
   media, 171, 179
   Parliamentary Questions, 174
   party, 172–3, 186
   pay policy, 191–2, 193–5
   Policy Unit, 112
   Political Secretary, 81
   popularity, 180
   Press Office, 116
   Prime Minister, 183–95
   prime ministerial power, 78
   prime ministerial support
     reform of, 92, 183, 187
   Prime Minister's Department, 127
   Private Office, 127, 145–6
   resignations, 149–50, 152
   Royal Commissions, 225
   speeches, 124–5
   style (approach, methods), 140–5
   other references, 6, 16, 17, 28, 39, 40, 44, 45, 54, 93, 103, 159, 239, 241